Ovid

Greek and Latin Studies
Classical Literature and its Influence

Editors

C. D. N. Costa and J. W. Binns
School of Hellenic and Roman Studies
University of Birmingham

Greek and Latin Studies
Classical Literature and its Influence

Ovid

Edited by
J. W. BINNS

Routledge & Kegan Paul: LONDON AND BOSTON

First published in 1973
by Routledge & Kegan Paul Ltd
Broadway House, 68–74 Carter Lane,
London EC4V 5EL and
9 Park Street,
Boston, Mass. 02108, U.S.A.
Printed in Great Britain by
Butler & Tanner Ltd, Frome and London
© Routledge & Kegan Paul Ltd 1973
No part of this book may be reproduced in
any form without permission from the
publisher, except for the quotation of brief
passages in criticism

ISBN 0 7100 7639 8

Library of Congress Catalog Card No. 73/83118

Contents

Introduction   vii
J. W. BINNS, *University of Birmingham*

I. The *Amores*   1
    I. M. Le M. Du QUESNAY, *University of Birmingham*

II. The *Heroides*   49
    W. S. ANDERSON, *University of California, Berkeley*

III. The *Ars Amatoria* and *Remedia Amoris*   84
    A. S. HOLLIS, *Keble College, Oxford*

IV. The Style of the *Metamorphoses*   116
    E. J. KENNEY, *Peterhouse, Cambridge*

V. The *Tristia*: Poetry in Exile   154
    R. J. DICKINSON, *University of Durham*

VI. Ovid in the Middle Ages   191
    DOROTHY M. ROBATHAN

VII. Ovid in the Sixteenth Century   210
    CAROLINE JAMESON, *University of Birmingham*

Subject Index   243

Name Index   247

Introduction

The last twenty years have seen important changes in the attitudes
to Roman poetry of scholars and students, who are now, on the
whole, more aware of techniques of literary criticism forged in
other disciplines, particularly in the study of English literature.
These techniques, although they cannot usefully be brought to
bear upon the study of Roman poetry in a merely mechanical
way have, none the less, had their influence upon the manner in
which Roman poetry is now approached, so that studies of, say,
its imagery, formal structure, ambiguity, subtlety, careful use of
words, and poetic diction have done much in recent years to
enhance a reader's awareness of the range and complexity of
many Roman poets. The old Romantic attitude to Roman poetry,
which valued the poem chiefly as a document illustrative of the
author's life, which placed a high premium upon poetry which it
was easy to regard as 'sincere', which was interested in the personality of the poet rather than in the poem, lavished the greatest
praise upon Catullus and Propertius, whom it was easy to regard
as poets of spontaneous emotion, whilst Ovid was discounted as
shallow and insincere – heartless albeit artful.

Conversely, Ovid is more likely to appeal to us today, as a
poet for the study of whom the biographical approach is so obviously unfruitful, yet whose mocking wit and verbal dexterity
fit in with a conception of a poet as a brilliant and imaginative
user of words. Perhaps too, readers of the 1970s, which some
would say are more coldly sensual, more 'unromantic' in affairs
of the heart than any decade for the last 200 years, are ideally
suited to see in Ovid a kindred spirit.

Ovid is, at any rate, a poet whose reputation has only recently begun to recover from the disesteem of over a century and a half. The essays in this volume will, I hope, contribute still further to the re-establishment of Ovid's claims to our attention. The five discussions of Ovid's original writings presented here reflect the changing approaches to Roman poetry of the last few years. Thus Mr I. M. Le M. Du Quesnay in his essay on the *Amores* shows how Ovid developed the elegiac tradition handed down to him by Propertius, Tibullus and Catullus, and demonstrates the importance of the arrangement of individual poems. Mr R. J. Dickinson is also concerned to show the importance of the structural principles which underlie the much-neglected *Tristia*; Mr E. J. Kenney investigates Ovid's poetic diction in the *Metamorphoses*; Professor W. S. Anderson demonstrates the essential individuality of Ovid's treatment of his heroines and Mr A. S. Hollis writes on the humour and the blending of the didactic and elegiac traditions in the *Ars Amatoria* and *Remedia Amoris*.

Ovid was one of the Roman poets who enjoyed the greatest popularity and influence in the centuries following the fall of the Roman Empire. The essays by Professor Dorothy Robathan and Caroline Jameson explain and discuss the effects of this in the Middle Ages and Renaissance.

I

The Amores

I. M. Le M. Du Quesnay

In the *Amores*[1] Ovid takes over and develops the genre of personal love elegy which had already received its essential character from his predecessors, Cornelius Gallus, Tibullus and Propertius,[2] and his originality lies in the new twist that he gave to this well-defined tradition. Like the poems of his predecessors, his elegies are written in the first person and purport to tell of his amorous escapades as a young man about town and especially of his adventures with the lady whom he calls Corinna. Moreover he puts himself into similar situations, expresses the same range of emotions, borrows their imagery, and imitates and echoes their work throughout his poems. But he is not concerned simply with repeating their achievement: one of the great pleasures of reading the *Amores* is to see how Ovid turns the deeply emotional, almost tragic *persona* of the elegiac lover into the robust and amusing character that is the hero of his poems. Before turning to a more detailed examination of the poems there are two preliminary matters to be mentioned: the questions raised by Ovid's heroine, Corinna, and the problem of the relationship of the second, extant, edition of the poems to the first.

Ovid's Corinna poses the reader with two quite distinct, if related, problems. First, in the *Amores*, the main action is centred on the poet's various successes and disappointments in his relationship with Corinna, and so she occupies a similar position in his poems to that of Cynthia in the poems of Propertius or Delia and Nemesis in Tibullus. However, because Ovid is relying on the analogy with his predecessors and on the fact that his poems are to be read together as a collection, he names his heroine only in a handful of poems.[3] This is what causes the problem. In some poems it is quite obvious that the lady is not Corinna, even though she remains unidentified: this is clearly the case, for example, with the adulterous wife of II. 19, for she is compared unfavourably with Corinna.[4] At other times such certainty is not possible. In I. 4 Ovid instructs the unnamed lady how to flirt with him in the presence of her husband: in I. 8 Ovid overhears a *lena* trying to corrupt his mistress (again unnamed) and yet in the course of her lengthy advice she never suggests that the girl is married. But the difficulty is not insuperable if we accept that this would have been the last thing the *lena* would wish to remind her of while attempting to persuade her to be free with her favours and so to make herself rich. In short, as long as we do not press these 'inconsistencies' too closely there seems no objection against allowing the lady in any poem to be identified as Corinna, except in those instances where Ovid makes it quite clear that this is not the case.[5] Closely connected with this problem is the question of Corinna's social status. If, as suggested, we do identify the unnamed lady in I. 4 as Corinna, then she is obviously married and Ovid's affair is an adulterous one. He is blatantly flouting both traditional Roman morality and the clear desires of Augustus himself. But since he never suggests that Corinna belongs to a noble family[6] the effect of this is somewhat diminished: adultery was less exceptionable if committed with one of the *demi-mondaines* of Roman society. In view of Augustus' attempts to curb adultery by legislation this vagueness may even be deliberate: he would be able to shock (and so amuse) his readers with his *nequitia* but no specific charge could be levelled at him.

The second problem connected with Corinna is that we cannot be sure whether she ever existed or whether she merely represents an amalgam of all the women Ovid had ever known from both life and literature. The question is in the end insoluble: but it is important that we accept her existence in the course of reading the poems in the same way that we accept the existence of a character in a play or a novel, for without this they lose their impact. Of course that the poems are autobiographical in form does not mean that they are accurate descriptions of events that really took place. They are permeated with literary reminiscence and it is almost impossible to be sure that any detail was drawn from life rather than from Ovid's reading. But it is perhaps equally important to recognize that the fact that an idea may be described as a literary *topos* does not necessarily mean that it does not coincide with life. Thus Ovid, like his predecessors, rejects a life in the army or in the service of the state;[7] but we know that he did turn down the opportunity of a career in the senate and avoided holding the military tribunate.[8] Again Ovid claims to have attempted to write tragedy and that he was prevented from continuing by the intervention of Cupid. Clearly this is a witty adaptation of the so-called *recusatio*;[9] but in this instance it appears to be true. Ovid did indeed write a tragedy, the lost *Medea*, which Quintilian, at least, considered to show Ovid at his best.[10] With Corinna the situation is different only because we have no independent information about her and so speculation on the relationship of the *Amores* to life is pointless. If she did exist then Ovid succeeded in keeping the secret of her identity to himself, for no ancient authority tells us her name.[11] Moreover even if the poems were written with a real woman in mind, Ovid is obviously not concerned with expressing his love for her or with immortalizing their relationship.[12] The Cypassis poem, at least, would be incompatible with such an intention. But the poems may be taken as a compliment to the wit and the artistic taste of our hypothetical Corinna, in much the same way as the witty poem on Tibullus' death is a delightful tribute to the memory of a poet whom Ovid genuinely respected and admired,[13] but clearly is not an emotional outpouring of grief at the death of a friend.

Prefixed to the extant collection is a four-line epigram which tells us that the *Amores* had previously circulated in five books, and that Ovid himself has pruned the work to three. More than this he does not say and the nature of the relationship of the second edition to the first has been among the most discussed problems of Ovidian studies.[14]

In his autobiographical elegy in the *Tristia* Ovid tells us that he gave his first public reading of the poems soon after he had started to shave, that is when he was about eighteen years old (i.e. 25 B.C.).[15] The last datable event referred to in the *Amores* is the victory over the Germanic Sygambri in 16 B.C.[16] These dates indicate that the original *Amores* were composed at intervals throughout the decade 25–15 B.C., and in all probability the five books were first published separately. Whether at the end of this decade Ovid collected them together and published them as a single collection is unknown. However, some time before the composition of the third book of the *Ars Amatoria* he had reduced the number of books of the *Amores* to three.[17] It may be that this second edition was issued after the completion of the first two books of the *Ars*; this would give an approximate date of 1 B.C. But it seems more likely that it was in the course of revising the *Amores* that he conceived the idea of writing the *Ars*; that is to say that we should perhaps place the revision earlier in the last decade B.C.

Neither in the introductory epigram nor anywhere else does Ovid suggest that he had any reason for the revision other than that he had become dissatisfied with the artistic standards of some of his earlier writing.[18] He may have rejected as much as two-fifths of his earlier work. Whether he rewrote any of the earlier poems either in part or completely is unknown but is not impossible. It seems less likely that he should have included wholly new poems and there is no firm evidence to suggest that he did.[19] But such speculation is in the end futile and all that seems certain is that the *Amores* as we have them must have been recognizable as a second edition and not as a completely or even a substantially new work.

The arrangement of the poems is clearly that of the second edition. 1. 14, with the reference to the Sygambri, and 1. 8, which is modelled on a poem of Propertius' final book (IV. 5),[20] must have originally belonged to one of the later books, and this suggests that there was extensive revision of the order of the poems.

The *Amores* were clearly arranged as a single collection, and Ovid shows considerable skill in combining the needs for unity and variety in this arrangement.[21] The balance of the whole collection is assured by the formal similarities of Books I and III. Each of them contains fifteen poems and each has one of the two longest poems in the collection (1. 8; III. 6) and one diptych (1. 11 and 12; III. 11a and 11b). The central book is different in that it contains twenty poems; the poems are comparatively short and there is a heavy concentration of diptych poems.

Within this framework Ovid achieves an effect of unity by placing poems on related themes in different books. So 1. 10 and III. 8 are both attacks on Corinna's *auaritia*: in 1. 10 he attacks her for constantly demanding presents and not being content with the poems he writes in her honour. In III. 8 he attacks her more savagely, for now her greed has led her to prefer a soldier who has only recently been made an equestrian and she is quite indifferent to the fact that his social advancement has been achieved solely through the bloody spoils of war. Sometimes however the poems are more closely related by deliberate verbal echoes, and the effect of making the comparison is almost invariably to enhance the humour. In I. 3 he seeks to win Corinna by offering her his undying fidelity and fame through his poetry. This approach obviously meets with success. In II. 17 he expands and develops this theme round the new point that if Corinna does not cease to be so haughty with him he will no longer write poems in her honour.[22] A more pointed and elaborate use of this same technique can be seen in the much more closely related poems, I. 4 and II. 5, II. 19 and III. 4. Here the poems are connected by many more detailed echoes[23] than was the case in I. 3 and II. 17, and the fact that in II. 5 and III. 4 the advice Ovid gave in I. 4 and II. 19 respectively has rebounded on himself greatly enhances the comic effect of those poems. In I. 4 Ovid gives his mistress detailed instructions on how to flirt with him at a banquet at which her husband will be present. In II. 5 he finds that she has learned her lesson only too well and now it is he who is being duped. Similarly in III. 4 the husband has followed the advice Ovid gave in II. 19 that he should guard his wife more rigorously, with the result that Ovid can no longer rendezvous with her at all. The close inter-relationship of these poems makes a major contribution to the unity of the whole work. Yet each poem has sufficient point to be enjoyed for itself and the differences between the poems underline the quite different moods of the individual books. The fussiness and over-eager concern to secure the slightest contact with his mistress in I. 4 is suited to the beginnings of his love affair as described in Book I. In Book II he is unfaithful to Corinna in II. 19 and she to him in II. 5, while Ovid's complacency is illustrated by his ability to drop off to sleep at the party in II. 5 and his complaint in II. 19 that the husband is making life too easy for him. Finally, in III. 4 we see Ovid struggling with an apparently insuperable problem, and this well suits the disintegration of the love affair in this book.

The series of programmatic poems also lends unity to the collection, while the differences between them create an effect of movement, from the acceptance of elegy in I. 1 in its final rejection in III. 15.[24] So in Book I Ovid willingly submits to Cupid; he is happy to reject epic in favour of elegy and convinced that it will bring him immortality. In Book II his commitment to elegy and love begins to waver as he attempts first a *gigantomachia* and then a tragedy. And finally in Book III it is clear that he has decided to abandon elegy for the greater challenge of tragedy. In each of the books the attitude to elegy revealed in these programme poems helps to define the attitude to love.

Having thus effected the unity of the collection Ovid is concerned to impart variety to his work. This he does mainly by constantly changing the moods and situations he depicts. Here one of the chief devices used is juxtaposition. Sometimes the effect achieved is contrast, as when in Book I he places the short poem describing his noon-time rendezvous with Corinna (I. 5) next to the longer poem in which he spends the whole night outside her door (I. 6). This contrast may produce a comic piquancy, as when he juxtaposes III. 7, in which he has managed to seduce a girl but then finds that he is impotent, with III. 8, in which he is now eager to make love to Corinna, who is, however, already in the arms of her rich soldier. The most fully developed and effective use of this device occurs in the diptych poems such as the famous Cypassis poems (II. 7 and 8). Here the two poems are centred round a single dramatic incident, for example an exchange of letters with Corinna (I. 11 and 12), and their impact depends on the surprise of finding the mood or basic idea of the first poem completely reversed in the second.[25] Apart from this desire for *uariatio* it is occasionally possible to see other considerations which may have affected the arrangement, as when the poem on Tibullus' death is placed among others especially rich in echoes of that poet's work.[26] On the other hand there appears to be no simple schematic pattern underlying the collection, nor any concern with dramatic or narrative continuity.

Perhaps the most significant aspect of the *Amores* when viewed as a single collection is Ovid's obvious desire to recall to the reader the first three books of Propertius. Every poem in the collection contains echoes of Propertian imagery and phraseology: many of the poems clearly have a single model in Propertius; others are expansions and variations of themes which form only part of a single poem in his predecessor.[27] Each of the books has its own introduction and conclusion dealing with the choice of elegy as a genre on the pattern established by Propertius in Books II and III, and in the third book of the *Amores* Ovid includes poems which have only a tenuous connection with his personal love life or no connection at all, in the same way as Propertius does in Book III.[28] His whole affair with Corinna mirrors that of Propertius with Cynthia. He finds himself locked outside her door; he sees her off on a journey; he is elated when successful, wretched when separated from her; he has affairs with other women; he is deceived by her and attacks her for using cosmetics.[29]

The relationship between the two poets is not, however, a simple one, for Ovid is concerned neither with repeating what Propertius has achieved nor with deriding everything he has written. None the less the *persona* which Ovid adopts in the poems is clearly a parody of Propertius. But it is, at least primarily, the kind of parody in which the laughter is directed at the parody itself rather than at what is being parodied. For all that Ovid's *persona* is modelled on the character of Propertius it is a comic figure in a way that Propertius' is not. This is brought about partly by simplification and exaggeration of Propertian traits[30] and partly by magnifying the character of his predecessor by the addition of characteristics of lovers portrayed elsewhere in literature. For these he draws mainly on Tibullus; but Catullus, Hellenistic epigram and comedy all make their contributions.[31] Thus in the end Ovid's *persona* appears to be a caricature of the elegiac lover generally and not simply of the Propertian lover, and it has no more, but perhaps no less, reality than the character of Corinna.

This kind of parody or caricature depends for its main impact on the use of incongruity, and in the *Amores* this incongruity lies chiefly in the prevalent mood of gaiety and light-hearted frivolity which is quite at odds with Ovid's pose as a lover serious in his protestations of undying love and tormented by frustration and despair at the immorality of his mistress and at being continually kept from the fulfilment of his desires. It is not that Propertius and Tibullus are not themselves at times humorous and witty; far from it.[32] But one leaves those poets convinced of the sincerity and the seriousness of their love and their bitterness at finding that fulfilment of their ideal is impossible. This is not the case with Ovid. One leaves the *Amores* convinced that Ovid has enjoyed being in love, that he has relished his difficulties, chiefly because he remains always in control of his emotions, always aware of the impact he is having on his addressee and his audience.

This mood of irrepressible good humour is created in a number of ways. Ovid avoids the darker subjects of his predecessors, especially their concentration on death[33] and the tension between their private world of love and the public world of the Augustan state, which finds a focal point in their work in the figures of Maecenas and Messalla.[34] In a more positive vein Ovid's humour lies in his treatment of his difficulties. Thus in 1. 6 when Ovid finds himself locked out of his mistress' house the reader's attention is focused not on his despair and frustration but on his witty attempts to persuade the doorman to let him in. This aspect of the *Amores* is best illustrated in Book III. Here Ovid is confronted by a whole series of difficulties, but he never allows the reader to feel genuine concern. In III. 3 he expresses his indignation that the gods allow his mistress to deceive him with impunity. His amusing realization that the gods are just like him and helpless before the might of female charms prevents us from taking him seriously. In III. 4 the humour lies in the fact that the problem is of his own making; in III. 6 it lies, at least in part, in the absurdity and unreality of his attempts to flatter and cajole the flooding river to subside; in III. 10 in the impudent tone in which he addresses Ceres and the shocking proposal that she should make love-making and general festivity part of her worship instead of demanding sexual abstinence.

In the last resort Ovid's use of a comic lover does imply a criticism of Propertius, at least in so far as it ridicules excessive emotionality and the folly of demanding too much from love. But it is perhaps better to think of it as offering an alternative to Propertius rather than a criticism of him. Ovid's idea of love is less noble, less idealized than that of Propertius, but at least it is possible: it may be that he reduces love to a game, but the participants in it can at least be happy as long as they adhere to the rules. In the main this means accepting difficulties as just a part of love's warfare.[35] At the end of the *Amores* Ovid takes his leave of elegy with the same wit and panache that characterized his initial acceptance of it. Unlike Propertius he is able to accept the infidelities of his mistress as long as she co-operates and does not insist on bringing them to his attention.[36] On the other hand he rejects personal love elegy in III. 12 as being responsible for Corinna's unfaithfulness: by advertising her beauty and the poet's deep love for her it has brought her irresistible temptation. So finally his position is exactly the reverse of that of Propertius, who rejects a Cynthia whose immorality he can no longer endure but who makes no explicit rejection of elegy.[37]

However serious the situation in which he finds himself, however tortured the despair which he is expressing, Ovid never allows the reader to take him seriously for long. He undercuts himself directly either in parenthesis or by introducing some quite irrelevant argument;[38] or more subtly by over-reacting or indulging in some delightful but absurd hyperbole.[39] He distracts the reader's attention from what is being said to how it is being expressed by playing with words and form, and he comments obliquely on the antics of his *persona* by the use of imitation both of the earlier elegists and the older Augustans, especially Horace. In short the chief source of humour in Ovid's parody lies in the incongruity of the style with the situations and the moods it purports to describe. It is in his style that the reader will find Ovid's real originality and the real pleasure that reading the *Amores* can give.

The individual poems are usually confined to a single situation or proposition and, for all the variety of treatment, the poems unfold in a clearly defined and orderly fashion. The poem may consist of a series of arguments with each couplet or pair of couplets presenting a new point. Sometimes there is a simple accumulative process which determines the structure as in the famous *militat omnis amans* (I. 9) or the catalogue of all the women he finds attractive (II. 4). More frequently the shape of the poem depends on the shifting emotional reactions of the speaker. This may take the form of a simple *volte-face* as in II. 5: the poet begins with a hurt and indignant outcry against his flirtatious mistress but ends by forgiving her. Frequently, however, the shifts and changes in the attitude of the speaker are more complex. In II. 2 Ovid is attempting to persuade Bagoas to admit him to his mistress and he employs every technique from the cordial politeness of the opening lines to the scarcely concealed threats at the end. Even in a poem as subtle in its changes of mood as the *propempticon* to Corinna (II. 11) the reader is never in doubt in what direction the poem is moving.

This essential clarity and simplicity of structure is quite distinct from the manner both of Tibullus with his subtle digressions and of Propertius with his harsh transitions. It makes a major contribution to the speed of the action and thus sharpens the impact of the sudden twists and reversals which Ovid uses to make a humorous point. It is a necessary counterpart to his tendency to use the couplet as his main unit of composition. Finally it leaves the reader free to concentrate on the subtlety of the verbal texture, the imitations of earlier writers and the touches of irony with which Ovid undercuts the *persona* of lover that he assumes.

The devices which Ovid employs to make the reader aware that he is striking a pose are various. This awareness is brought about primarily by his constant play on the reader's expectations. So at the beginning of I. 2 (1–4):

> Esse quid hoc dicam, quod tam mihi dura uidentur
> strata, neque in lecto pallia nostra sedent,
> et uacuus somno noctem, quam longa, peregi,
> lassaque uersati corporis ossa dolent?

(What am I to say is the trouble? My couch seems so hard, my covers won't stay on the bed – I've spent the whole night long unable to sleep and my bones are weary and aching from my constant tossing and turning.)

The reader of course knows that these symptoms must mean that Ovid is in love.[40] But then Ovid deflates his confidence:

> nam, puto, sentirem, si quo temptarer amore –

(for I think I would know if I were being assailed by love –)

He obviously knows as well as the reader how to diagnose such symptoms but he has already dismissed the possibility that he is in love. But now, having temporarily confused his audience, he continues (6–8):

> an subit et tecta callidus arte nocet?
> sic erit: haeserunt tenues in corde sagittae,
> et possessa ferus pectora uersat Amor.

(Or does love creep in and with stealthy skill cunningly perform its mischief? That must be it: the tiny arrows are implanted in my heart and cruel Cupid causes turmoil in my conquered breast.)

Of course this new twist confirms the reader's original diagnosis. The deliberately misleading statement in line 5 now appears to have been included for comic effect. And having thus sharpened the reader's reactions by this surprise tactic he increases the impact of the witty conceit: the arrows of Cupid must indeed have been *tenues* for him not to have noticed them piercing his heart and, in view of his previous uncertainty, the final line is clearly an extravagant over-statement.

Ovid shows the same awareness of his audience and the same playful control of their reactions in poem I. 5, the description of the rendezvous with Corinna. The beginning of the poem is again deliberately misleading. The mid-day setting and the indication that he is quite alone and not expecting any visitors[41] combine to suggest that we are about to witness the poet indulging in erotic day-dreams while he takes his siesta. *Ecce, Corinna* (l. 9) introduces the sudden realization of his dreams as Corinna stands before him, enticing and willing. The suddenness of her appearance may quicken the reader's pulse but Ovid simply surveys her with his cool and professional eye. Finally, however, excitement overcomes him and he clutches her to him. *Cetera quis nescit*, who does not know the rest? With this remark he deliberately frustrates the curiosity of his audience which he has just as deliberately aroused in the increasingly excited and intimate description of Corinna's charms which precedes it.

However it is frequently the end of a poem which reveals that Ovid's pose is insincere. This revelation is sometimes brought about by his obvious awareness of the impact he is making on his audience. So at the end of III. 4 his final outrageous piece of advice to the kill-joy husband is evidently concerned less with persuading him to comply with Ovid's wishes than with shocking and amusing the audience (III. 4. 45–8):

> et cole quos dederit (multos dabit) uxor amicos:
>   gratia sic minimo magna labore uenit;
> sic poteris iuuenum conuiuia semper inire
>   et, quae non dederis, multa uidere domi.

(And cultivate those friends your wife brings you (she'll bring you plenty): then you'll enjoy great esteem for doing next to nothing; then you'll always be able to go to the young people's parties and see many things around the house which you have not provided.[42])

At other times the insincerity of the pose is revealed by a
final couplet which deflates the mood of the whole poem. In I. 7
he pours out his great remorse and expresses at length his self-
disgust at having struck his darling Corinna, but he ends the
poem (67–8):

> neue mei sceleris tam tristia signa supersint,
> pone recompositas in statione comas.

(And lest any of these hideous traces of my crime remain,
go and straighten your hair.[43])

This technique of undercutting the emotionality of his *persona*
occurs also within the body of the poems, though the effect here
is less complete; for if he did not allow us to retain some belief
in the character he is portraying the subtlety of the parody would
be lost. So in the same poem (I. 7) the highly emotional colouring
is intensified by his comparison of his crime with that of Diomedes
striking Venus (I. 7. 31–4):

> pessima Tydides scelerum monimenta reliquit:
> ille deam primus perculit; alter ego.
> et minus ille nocens: mihi quam profitebar amare
> laesa est; Tydides saeuus in hoste fuit.

(Diomedes left a hideous precedent for crimes: he was the
first to strike a goddess and I'm the second. In fact his crime
was less: I struck the girl I professed to love; Diomedes
displayed his brutality against an enemy.)

It is almost, but not quite, conceivable that the extension of the
mythological *exemplum* reflects his intense despair. In the end,
however, the fact that Ovid first pinpoints the inappropriateness
of the parallel and then makes the point explicit reveals that he is
scrutinizing closely everything he says for the effect it will have.
Similarly in II. 16, where the poet, although at home in his
beautiful native Sulmo, pours out his torments of despair at being
separated from Corinna: the emotional outburst is prefaced by
(11–12):

> at meus ignis abest – uerbo peccauimus uno:
> quae mouet ardores, est procul; ardor adest.

(But my flame is absent – I've chosen the wrong word:
she who fans the flames of my love, is far away; the fire is
present.)

This technique appears in a modified form in Ovid's frequent use of asides and parenthetical comments[44] and combines with more subtle means of distracting the reader from the seriousness of what he is saying. In II. 11 he first attempts to dissuade Corinna from going away on a sea voyage and suggests that she should stay on shore with him and learn of the horrors of the deep from others. She may believe even their most fantastic yarns and come to no grief (21–2):

> haec alii referant; at uos, quod quisque loquetur,
>   credite: credenti nulla procella nocet.

(Let others tell these yarns; but whatever anyone says, you believe them: no storm harms you just for believing.)

But his pleas are unsuccessful, so he wishes her well and looks forward to her return when she will tell him all the hardships she has endured. (53–4):

> omnia pro ueris credam, sint ficta licebit:
>   cur ego non uotis blandiar ipse meis?

(I shall treat it all as gospel truth, even if it is lies: why should I not flatter myself at the effectiveness of my prayers?)

In these lines he makes two witty points: the implicit comparison of his position here with his earlier advice to Corinna, and the amusing paradox in the thought: he is going to deceive himself deliberately into believing her so that he may feel proud that his prayers have saved her from harm.

The same delightful incongruity between playful stylistic effects and the pose of deep emotionality characterizes Ovid's use of lists and catalogues. As with the other devices it is just possible to regard them as being produced by the deep emotion felt by the *persona*. So the lists of mythological *exempla* at III. 6. 23–44 or III. 12. 19–40 are in a sense part of the (supposed) indignation that the lover feels. But this technique really distracts the reader's attention from what is being said (this is usually established at the beginning anyway) and makes him concentrate on the elegance and skill with which it is expressed. This device occurs frequently within poems, and sometimes, as in I. 9 (*militat omnis amans*), it takes up the whole poem. In III. 3 Ovid complains that the gods allow his mistress to perjure herself with impunity.[45] The opening of the poem states the theme (1–2):

> Esse deos, i, crede: fidem iurata fefellit,
> et facies illi quae fuit ante manet.

(Go on, believe that gods exist: she has sworn and gone back on her oath, yet her beauty remains what it was before.)

His 'indignation' causes him to expand this point by point: but there is no real development of the thought and the reader's attention is held by the magnificent display of Ovid's skill in handling language (3–10):

> quam longos habuit nondum periura capillos,
>   tam longos, postquam numina laesit, habet.
> candida, candorem roseo suffusa rubore,   5
>   ante fuit: niueo lucet in ore rubor.
> pes erat exiguus: pedis est artissima forma.
>   longa decensque fuit: longa decensque manet.
> argutos habuit: radiant ut sidus ocelli,
>   per quos mentita est perfida saepe mihi.   10

(Long hair she had before she perjured herself and hair just as long she has even now that she has misused the gods. Before then she was fair, her fairness tinged with the red of roses: on her snow-white cheeks the red still blushes. Her foot was tiny: it is still of a shape most slender. Long and lithe she was: long and lithe she remains. Sparkling eyes she had: the eyes by which she has often treacherously lied to me, still shine like stars.)

The parallelism of the first couplet is achieved by balancing *quam longos* and *tam longos*, *nondum periura* and *postquam numina laesit* and by shaping the two lines in a similar way: in both cases the sense of *longos* is not completed until the end of the line, in the hexameter by *capillos*, in the pentameter by *habet*.[46] The next couplet has a quite different shape, since the thought of the hexameter flows over into the pentameter. The participial phrase expands and qualifies *candida*. Exactly the same idea is expressed in *niueo lucet in ore rubor*,[47] but the elegant variation in the wording produces an effect of antithesis. The contrast of red and white has a long pedigree in Latin poetry[48] and the resulting 'poetic' effect is enhanced by a series of stylistic devices: the repetitions; the intricate pattern of assonance and alliteration; the Greek accusative construction, *candorem . . . suffusa*; and the antithesis of *roseo . . . niueo*.[49] The third couplet is different again, for now the balance is between the two halves of the individual line: *pes erat exiguus* is amplified into the ornate periphrasis *pedis est artissima forma*, while in the pentameter only *fuit* changes to become *manet*. A further contrast is achieved by balancing the smallness of her feet in the hexameter with her tallness in the pentameter. The hexameter of the final couplet is perhaps the most elaborate of all: there is the bold ellipse of *ocellos* in *argutos habuit*; the striking apposition of the singular *sidus* with the plural *ocelli* and finally the vivid use of *radiant* with *ocelli* rather than *sidera*. With the pentameter the thought returns to that of the opening line, thus closing the circle and defining the limits of the passage, while the new idea that this deception has happened frequently looks forward to the rest of the poem.

The general impression of playfulness and irrepressible gaiety which the poems create is due in no small measure to Ovid's obvious enjoyment and skill in manipulating the language and the elegiac couplet, the raw materials of his art. Some aspects of this element of his style have already been mentioned in the above analysis. But the question is important enough to justify further comment.

When Ovid began to write, the elegiac couplet had already received its essential character from the practice of his predecessors.[50] His realization that the couplet has a natural rising and falling rhythm, more suited to effects of balance and antithesis than to continuous narrative, led him to accentuate this tendency rather than to attempt to overcome it. Thus he took over from his predecessors and rigidly applied the 'rule' of ending the pentameter with a disyllabic word, and so ensured a firm sense of completion at the end of the couplet. To a greater extent than his predecessors Ovid isolates the couplet by avoiding both enjambment and anaphora, and treats it as his basic unit of composition. Within its strict confines, however, he uses every opportunity to vary the sense pauses and to exploit the separative possibilities of the language in order to achieve variety, as the analysis of III. 3. 1–10 clearly revealed. It is indicative of his mastery of the form that he can produce within the space of a single couplet such a brilliant thumb-nail sketch as (III. 11a. 25–6):

> dicta erat aegra mihi: praeceps amensque cucurri;
> ueni, et riuali non erat aegra meo.

(I was told she was ill: quite beside myself I ran along there at full speed; I arrived: and for my rival she was not ill.)

It is because Ovid generally uses the couplet as a separate entity that he shows a marked tendency to divide the pentameter from the hexameter. The effect thus achieved is one of balance: the pentameter may expand and restate the idea of the hexameter or it may contrast with it as in (III. 10. 21–2):

> illic sideream mundi qui temperat arcem
> exiguus tenero lac bibit ore puer.

(There, as a baby, he who rules the starry citadel of the heavens gently sucked his milk.)

This constant desire for balance within the couplet led Ovid finally to develop the so-called reciprocal couplet[51] in which the first half of the hexameter is repeated exactly in the last half of the pentameter as in (I. 9. 1–2):

> Militat omnis amans, et habet sua castra Cupido;
> Attice, crede mihi, militat omnis amans.

(Every lover is a soldier and Cupid has his own army; Atticus, believe me, every lover is a soldier.)

Ovid takes an obvious delight in words. His diction reveals his inventiveness and willingness to experiment with the language, and from this the verbal texture of his poems derives much of its freshness and individuality. His originality in this respect is apparent throughout the poems, but its effects are subtle and unobtrusive. His vocabulary includes many words like *credulitas* (III. 3. 24) or *moderatius* (III. 3. 47) which, though quite colourless in themselves, gain a certain novelty from finding a place in poetry for the first time.[52] But more significant is his creation of new words. Most, like *populifer* (II. 17. 32), are formed on well-established principles and in fact most frequently his method is to add a new prefix or suffix to an 'ordinary' word. Sometimes

this increases its expressiveness as when he coins *emodulanda*
(I. I. 30) to convey the undulating progress of the elegiac Muse.
Alternatively, it may increase the vividness and the precision of
the word: thus he coins *praetepuisset* (II. 3. 6) to describe the hot
excitement that comes with the anticipation of love, and *subrubet*
(II. 5. 36) for the red glow of sunrise starting at the horizon and
gradually filling the sky and for the blush of a young girl spread-
ing upwards from the neck. Other coinages have a less definable
quality, like the impressive and mysterious *incaedua* (III. I. I)
or the slightly extravagant *semiadaperta* (I. 6. 4). At other times
his inventiveness takes the form of using an established word in
a new way: thus he calls tablets with the letters cut into the wax
peraratas . . . tabellas (I. II. 7), 'ploughed' or perhaps 'furrowed'
tablets.

The lucid simplicity of Ovid's style, which is such a fitting
vehicle for the clarity of his thought and the naïvety of his lover
persona, is due, at least in part, to his sparing use of any metaphors
except those which form a natural part of the lover's diction. They
are rarely sustained or complex but used to enhance the force-
fulness of his language. So at I. 3. 15 he employs the word
desultor, literally a switchback-rider in a circus, in the phrase
desultor amoris to describe a fickle lover. But the effects of his
metaphors are various. They may underline the intense emotion
of the lover as when he refers to Corinna's new lover as *sanguine*
pastus eques (III. 8. 10), an equestrian gorged with blood. Here the
bestiality of the man is brought out by the use of *pastus*, a word
normally used of animals. At other times they are used for comic
effect as in Dipsas' witty deflation of prudish hypocrisy in (I. 8.
45-6):

> has quoque, quae frontis rugas in uertice portant,
>   excute, de rugis crimina multa cadent.

(Also search those women who wear wrinkles on their brows
and much incriminating evidence will fall from the folds.)

The humour lies in the play on the two meanings of *ruga*,
'wrinkle' or 'fold of a garment' (in which things could be hidden),
and of *excute*, 'shake out' or 'scrutinize'.[53]

However, in accordance with his desire for simplicity he prefers
to broaden the perspectives of his poems by the more direct

devices such as similes and series of *exempla* taken from mythology, city life or nature.[54] These may achieve an almost lyrical
beauty as in (I. 14. 11–12):

> qualem [sc. colorem] cliuosae madidis in uallibus Idae
> ardua derepto cortice cedrus habet.

(Like the colour of the lofty cedar in the lush valleys of steep
Ida when stripped of its bark.)

A further source of humour in the *Amores* lies in the incongruity of the cynically realistic outlook of the hero and his
naïvety, his flights of sheer fantasy. Ovid can accept the blatant
infidelities of his mistress (II. 5; III. 14); he can coolly lie his way
out of a corner as in the Cypassis incident (II. 7 and 8); or say to
Corinna when she has lost her hair after excessive use of dyes
(I. 14. 55–6):

> collige cum uultu mentem: reparabile damnum est:
> postmodo natiua conspiciere coma.

(Recover your complexion and your composure: the loss is
not final and you will soon attract attention again with your
very own hair.[55])

And at I. 10. 53–4 he even has this comment:

> nec tamen indignum est a diuite praemia posci:
> munera poscenti quod dare possit habet.

(But it is not shameful to demand rewards from a rich man:
he has the wherewithal to be able to give the presents you
demand.)

His naïvety appears often as an over-literal interpretation of
the clichés of elegiac *topoi* as in the *reductio ad absurdum* of the
idea that an emaciated appearance is characteristic of lovers at
(I. 6. 3–6):[56]

> quod precor exiguum est: aditu fac ianua paruo
> obliquum capiat semiadaperta latus.
> longus amor tales corpus tenuauit in usus
> aptaque subducto corpore membra dedit;

(It is a tiny favour I am asking: open the door – just a little:
even if it is only half-ajar I can slip through sideways. Being

so long in love has trimmed down my figure for just such
feats as this: my body has been wasted away and I'm now in
splendid shape.)

At other times the (supposed) strength of his emotions blinds
him to the limits of physical possibility as when at II. 16. 51–2
he cries:

> at uos, qua ueniet, tumidi subsidite montes,
> et faciles curuis uallibus este uiae.

(But you, you swelling hills, shrink down where she passes
and you roads in the winding valleys make her journey easy.)

Alternatively it may cause him to misinterpret reality as when
in III. 2 he assumes that the fact that the citizens' call for the race
to be re-run is due to his demand (73–5):

> fauimus ignauo. sed enim reuocate, Quirites,
> et date iactatis undique signa togis.
> en reuocant;

(The fellow we are backing has no spirit. Come now, citizens,
call them back, throw up your togas altogether and give the
signal. Look they are calling them back.[57])

This effect, achieved by the constant contrast of these two
incompatible characteristics, his realism and his naïvety, can be
seen in miniature when he says of the goddess Aurora, the rising
sun (I. 13. 47–8):

> iurgia finieram. scires audisse: rubebat,
> nec tamen adsueto tardius orta dies.

(I finished my complaints. You might know she had heard
me: she blushed. And yet the day broke no more slowly than
usual.)

The most complex aspect of Ovid's art in the *Amores* is his
imitation of earlier writers. This does not, of course, mean that
he slavishly copied his predecessors because he lacked imagination
and originality. On the contrary his is a creative imitation: out
of the raw materials of the genre, its language, metaphors and
themes Ovid created something quite new. In fact he exploits
the traditional nature of his material for his own advantage: it

creates in the reader certain expectations which Ovid can then manipulate.

In a series of poems Propertius attacks Cynthia for her use of cosmetics.[58] His complaints are not without sarcastic humour and even irony, but we take him seriously. That she uses these artificial aids to beauty shows how much she is tainted by the base values of her age, how far removed she is from being Propertius' ideal lover. To see her so made up reminds him that she is not content with his love but anxious to attract other men.[59] Ovid's use of the theme in 1. 14 is very different. He is too urbane to be really shocked or offended by Corinna's use of hair dyes, though as an elegiac lover he has to say that he is. But since the poem opens with the information that Corinna is now bald from her excessive use of these dyes, the lengthy moralizing serves only to ridicule the folly of her actions, and not to attack them for their immorality. Of course this means that Ovid does not have to fear her attracting any suitors. And yet he does not omit the idea completely but gives it a brilliant twist to fit his context (47–50):

> o quam saepe comas aliquo mirante rubebis
> et dices 'empta nunc ego merce probor:
> nescioquam pro me laudat nunc iste Sygambram;
> fama tamen memini cum fuit ista mea.'

(O how often will you blush when some gentleman admires your hair and say: 'So now I'm found attractive for my wig, this piece of merchandise I've bought. Now it's not me he's praising but some Sygambrian woman. Yet I remember the time when I really deserved these compliments.')

The reader's natural expectation that he will find this motif in the context of an attack on the use of cosmetics is more than satisfied. He can hardly fail to be amazed at the ingenuity with which Ovid has found it a place, given the initial fact that Corinna has gone bald, and delighted by the new use to which it is put. Ovid shows no jealousy nor even triumphant joy that he will no longer have to fear any rivals. Instead he makes the motif blend in perfectly with the mocking sympathy he uses in this poem to suggest that Corinna is really making a fuss about nothing.

Here Ovid is not following Propertius at all closely but combining a number of elements from a whole series of his poems on this and related themes, and he is able to capitalize on the reader's knowledge of the tradition with which he is working. At the other extreme he may base a poem on a single elegy of Propertius.[60]

In II. 22a Propertius tells his friend Demophoon that he is now in love with many women; they are all so beautiful and owing to a flaw in his character he cannot resist them. There is no need to worry, he continues, that his frail physique will not stand up to the exertions of such a life: love does not drain one's strength as the examples of Achilles and Hector show, who rose from their beds to wreak havoc on the enemy. In fact, it is safer to have two lovers than one: if one refuses you, you can turn to the other. With this last remark Propertius makes it clear that his promiscuity is part of an attempt to escape from the love of Cynthia,[61] and this emotional context colours our reading of the poem.

Ovid makes use of this poem both in II. 4 where he claims to find all women irresistible and again in II. 10. The latter opens with Ovid telling his friend Graecinus that he has fallen in love with two girls at the same time. This establishes a similarity with Propertius. At first, however, it seems that Ovid is going to reverse the attitude of his predecessor. Love for two women brings, not relief or security, but twice as much pain and anguish. But after a brief complaint against the cruelty of Venus for so punishing him he suddenly performs a complete *volte-face* (15):

> sed tamen hoc melius, quam si sine amore iacerem:

(but this is still better than if I had to lie alone and without love.)

The comic effect of this sudden switch in direction is greatly enhanced for the reader who has caught the allusion to the Propertian poem, by his awareness that Ovid has given a new twist to Propertius' suggestion that two lovers are better than one: in Ovid the comparison is between two lovers and none at all. Then, like Propertius, he goes on to claim that the effort will not prove too great for his slender physique and that love does not drain away the lover's strength. But unlike Propertius he draws his example not from the heroes of old but from his own personal experience, and so Ovid's bold impudence is heightened by the implicit suggestion that he is to be compared with Achilles or Hector. This mood of exuberant self-confidence is continued to the end of the poem. In complete contrast to the Propertian model Ovid breaks off with the shocking wish (35–8):

> at mihi contingat Veneris languescere motu,
>   cum moriar, medium soluar et inter opus;
> atque aliquis nostro lacrimans in funere dicat
>   'conueniens uitae mors fuit ista tuae'.

(But let me pass away in the act of love; when I die let me
go in the midst of my performance; and let someone shed
a tear at my funeral and say, 'your death made a beautiful end
to your life'.)

Frequently Ovid takes a short passage in one of the poems of his predecessors and with wit and ingenuity expands it into a whole poem of his own.[62] Such poems make a major contribution to the general impression that his character is a caricature of the elegiac lover: sentiments the earlier elegists utter in passing or situations to which they allude appear in Ovid fully developed and their minor and unobtrusive traits are exaggerated.[63]

When Tibullus found it impossible to realize his dream of idyllic happiness with Delia, he turned for relief to drink and other women (I. 5. 39–42):

> Saepe aliam tenui, sed iam cum gaudia adirem,
>   admonuit dominae deseruitque Venus.
> Tunc me discedens deuotum femina dixit
>   et pudet et narrat scire nefanda meam.

(I have often held another woman in my arms but just as I
was approaching the sweet climax Venus would bring my
mistress to my mind and desert me. Then as the woman
left she said I was bewitched. Smarting at her treatment,
she put it about that my darling knows the black arts.)

These few lines of Tibullus provide the framework for *Amores*, III. 7. Ovid has seduced a girl but found himself impotent. The girl is obviously not Corinna, whom he mentions specifically[64] by way of illustrating his normal prowess in love-making and to highlight the unprecedented nature of his present predicament. But she is not part of an attempt to alleviate the misery Corinna has brought him. Free from any such sombre overtones the poem becomes more amusing and ironic than the Tibullan passage. The mood of mock indignation and the tone of withering irony is sustained throughout. But Ovid does not forget, nor allow the reader to forget, his model. At the end of his poem the unfortunate girl suggests that he must be *deuotum* – or that he has at least spent his energies elsewhere – and leaves. But unlike Tibullus' friend Ovid's girl is eager to keep her secret (III. 7. 83–4):

> neue suae possent intactam scire ministrae,
> dedecus hoc sumpta dissimulauit aqua.

(and so that her maids would not know that I had not touched her, she camouflaged her dishonour with a little water.)

The irreverent reversal of normal morality, enhanced by the use of the words *intactam* and *dedecus*, makes a witty ending to the poem. But the comic effect is sharpened by comparison with the different, but still ironic tone in the Tibullan passage.

The effects of Ovid's creative imitation may be felt not only in whole poems but within short passages and even occasional lines and phrases. This is not to suggest that all echoes of the earlier elegists contribute positively to the enjoyment of the poems. Many serve only to lend general colour to the poems, to keep the reader aware that the poems are following an established tradition. Many are perhaps unconscious or merely arise from the fact that Ovid is talking of similar topics and expressing similar emotions in the same language and in the same metre. The only criterion can be the effectiveness of the echo: if it adds to the impact of a phrase or a passage we can treat it as imitation. Obviously on such matters it is impossible not to be, at least to some extent, subjective: the author's intentions can never be ascertained. Thus when Ovid says (III. 11a. 5):

> uicimus et domitum pedibus calcamus amorem:

(I am victorious and trample conquered love beneath my feet:)

we cannot be sure that he is intending us to catch the echo of Propertius, I. 1. 4:

> et caput impositis pressit Amor pedibus.

(and love has bowed down my neck beneath his feet.[65])

But in this instance it does seem probable: the impact of the Ovidian line is intensified when it is seen as an exact reversal of Propertius' situation. And there is further pleasure in noticing how Ovid has substituted the vivid *calcamus* for Propertius' rather vague *pressit*.

At other times, however, virtual certainty is possible. In his elegy on Tibullus' death Ovid depicts the meeting of Delia and Nemesis at their lover's funeral (III. 9. 55-8):

> Delia discedens 'felicius' inquit 'amata
> sum tibi: uixisti, dum tuus ignis eram.'
> cui Nemesis 'quid' ait 'tibi sunt mea damna dolori?
> me tenuit moriens deficiente manu.'

(As she was leaving Delia said 'Those were happier days when it was I that you loved. While I fanned your passions you still lived.' Nemesis answered her 'And why does my loss cause you grief? It was I he held with weakening grasp as he lay dying.')

Here the point of Nemesis' retort to Delia's sly innuendo is lost if we do not remember Tibullus' own wish addressed to the latter (I. 1. 59-60):

> Te spectem, suprema mihi cum uenerit hora,
> te teneam moriens deficiente manu.

(Delia, may I gaze on you when my final hour comes, may I hold you in my weakening grasp as I lie dying.)

More often, however, the wit is less sharp and the effect of the allusion to a model less definable. In III. 10[66] Ovid is complaining to Ceres that her requirement of sexual abstinence to honour her festival is interfering with his love-life: her demands are also hypocritical since she has herself enjoyed the love of Iasion. Before making this last point he suggests that her demand is not in keeping with her reputation as a benefactor of mankind (III. 10. 11-14):

> prima Ceres docuit turgescere semen in agris,
> falce coloratas subsecuitque comas.
> prima iugis tauros subponere colla coegit
> et ueterem curuo dente reuellit humum.

(Ceres was the first to teach the seed to swell in the fields
and to harvest with the sickle the ripened crop. She was
the first to force the oxen to submit their necks to the
yoke and to tear up the ancient earth with the curved
plough-share.)

This is clearly an adaptation of Tibullus, I. 7. 29–34:

> primus aratra manu sollerti fecit Osiris
>   et teneram ferro sollicitauit humum,
> primus inexpertae commisit semina terrae
>   pomaque non notis legit ab arboribus.
> hic docuit teneram palis adiungere uitem,
>   hic uiridem dura caedere falce comam;

(Osiris was the first to fashion a plough with his skilful
hands and to turn over the tender earth with the iron share;
he was the first to entrust seed to the virgin soil and to
pick fruit from previously unknown trees. It was he who
taught men to fasten the young vines to stakes and to cut
away the green foliage with the hard sickle.)

But even here the pleasure is not simply that of recognition.
It is satisfying to our aesthetic sense to note how Ovid has
transformed Tibullus' praise of Osiris to fit in with his complaints
against Ceres. This he does by changing the tender pathos of
Tibullus[67] into a sharper irony through emphasizing the violence
of Ceres' innovations by his use of the word *turgescere* and the
ideas in *coegit* and above all in *ueterem . . . reuellit humum*. Here,
despite the fact that the imitation is put to a purpose which is
almost the reverse of the model's, the effect is not humorous. Even
the irony is barely enhanced by the comparison. None the less the
allusion is pleasing and effective for all that it is unobtrusive.

In I. 7 Propertius contrasts his choice of elegy as his genre
with epic, the choice of his friend Ponticus. The theme was a
favourite one with Propertius, but here he treats it less seriously
than later, after he had been subjected to the ideas and sug-
gestions of Maecenas. He begins (I. 7. 1–12):

> Dum tibi Cadmeae dicuntur, Pontice, Thebae
>   armaque fraternae tristia militiae,
> atque, ita sim felix, primo contendis Homero,
>   (sint modo fata tuis mollia carminibus:)

nos, ut consuemus, nostros agitamus amores,   5
    atque aliquid duram quaerimus in dominam;
nec tantum ingenio quantum seruire dolori
    cogor et aetatis tempora dura queri.
hic mihi conteritur uitae modus, haec mea fama est,
    hinc cupio nomen carminis ire mei.   10
me laudent doctae solum placuisse puellae,
    Pontice, et iniustas saepe tulisse minas;

(While you, Ponticus, tell the tale of Cadmean Thebes and
the tragic battles of fraternal strife – and, I vow, you rival
even Homer, prince of poets, if only the Fates are kind to
your poems – I, as usual, am occupied with my love and
with finding something to soften the hard heart of my
mistress; I am forced to serve my passion rather than my
talent and to lament the unhappiness of my life. Thus
I waste away my life's span, this is my glory, from this I
hope my poetry will win a reputation. Ponticus, let them
say in praise of me that this cultured girl loved me alone
and that I often bore her angry outbursts, though they
were undeserved.)

Pretending to adopt the traditional scale of values according
to which elegy was intrinsically inferior to epic, Propertius
attributes his 'failure' as a poet to his overruling passion. But
his praise of Ponticus and his self-depreciation are ironic: he is
clearly confident that he will win fame as a poet and as an exem-
plary lover. This passage serves as a model for Ovid's very different treatment of the same theme in *Amores*, II. 18 (1–12):

Carmen ad iratum dum tu perducis Achillem
    primaque iuratis induis arma uiris,
nos, Macer, ignaua Veneris cessamus in umbra,
    et tener ausuros grandia frangit Amor.
saepe meae 'tandem' dixi 'discede' puellae: 5
    in gremio sedit protinus illa meo;
saepe 'pudet' dixi: lacrimis uix illa retentis
    'me miseram, iam te' dixit 'amare pudet?'
implicuitque suos circum mea colla lacertos
    et, quae me perdunt, oscula mille dedit.   10
uincor, et ingenium sumptis reuocatur ab armis,
    resque domi gestas et mea bella cano.

(While you advance your poem down to the 'Wrath of
Achilles' and while you equip the heroes, who have now
taken their oath, with their first issue of weapons, I, Macer,
laze around in the enervating shade of Venus, and young
Cupid shatters my grandiose designs. 'Now' I said to my
girl on many an occasion, 'it really is time you were off':
she just continued to sit on my knee; often I said 'it's
shameful'. She was hardly able to keep back her tears and
said: 'I'm terribly hurt: so now even you are ashamed to
be a lover, are you?' Then she flung her arms round my
neck and gave me a thousand kisses. That did the trick.
I am beaten and my talent is called back from the campaign
it had started. Now I'm a poet of home affairs and sing of
private wars.)

Both poets are making the same point, that their inability to
write epic is due to the power of love. Propertius, however, is
unhappy and is forced to write elegy because only that kind of
poetry will secure his mistress' love. Ovid, on the contrary, has
already so well secured the devotion of his mistress that she
tries to prevent him from sending her away – and succeeds. He
is not held captive in a miserable and confining love, he is simply
unable to resist the pleasure it affords. Even more forcefully
than Propertius, Ovid concedes that his choice of genre is immoral:[68] but only so that he can highlight the impudence of his
choice. Unlike his model he makes full use of his *ingenium* in his
love poetry,[69] and as he goes on to mention the success of his
Medea and *Heroides* it is clear that although love may shape his
handling of epic material it does not preclude him from using it
successfully. In all this Ovid seems to imply a playful criticism
both of Propertius' view of love as something which may bring
fame but only at the cost of misery, and also of his pretence that
elegiac poetry is not only morally less worthwhile than epic but
also that the fame it can confer is less. In Ovid it is clear that he
remains within the power of love because he finds it irresistibly
delightful, and that his fame and his achievement have not
suffered at all because of this. This playful criticism of Propertius
characterizes many of Ovid's allusions to his work, though it is
frequently very difficult to define.

The *Amores* also contain allusions to the work of the older

Augustans, Virgil and Horace, though they are obviously less frequent. Ovid is usually concerned to contrast Virgil's ideals and morality with his own to shock and amuse his audience.[70] So in III. 13 he describes Halaesus, the founder of Falerii, as an anti-Aeneas: he is Greek, devoted to Iuno and the murderer of his father Agamemnon.

The allusions to the poetry of Horace are more numerous. Frequently it is the incongruity of Ovid's application of the allusion that adds to the comic effect. In *Epistles*, 1. 5 Horace invites Torquatus to a party to celebrate Caesar Augustus' birthday. To explain his burst of 'extravagance' he says (12–14):

> quo mihi fortunam, si non conceditur uti?
> parcus ob heredis curam nimiumque seuerus
> adsidet insano.

(What point is there in having a fortune if I'm not allowed to use it? The man who is miserly and too austere out of consideration for his heir comes close to being a madman.)

To this passage Ovid ironically alludes when he is remonstrating with himself over his wasted opportunity with the beautiful and willing girl he has seduced in III. 7 (49–50):

> quo mihi fortunae tantum? quo regna sine usu?
> quid nisi possedi diues auarus opes?

(What point is there in my having such a fortune? What point in a kingdom that you don't enjoy? What is it but to sit over my wealth like a rich miser?)

Here the effect of the allusion is to deflate Ovid's indignation by emphasizing his incongruous pomposity. A more sophisticated technique is employed when Ovid uses the Horatian echo to poke fun at himself by making his *persona* behave in a way which Horace has ridiculed. In II. 9a Ovid, tired at last of his suffering, has decided to give up love. But in II. 9b he changes his mind, having realized that such a celibate existence would be unbearable, and he begins (1–2):

> 'Viue' deus 'posito' si quis mihi dicat 'amore',
> deprecer: usque adeo dulce puella malum est.

(If some god were to say 'Put love aside and live', I should decline: a girl is always such sweet anguish.)

This constant wavering between acceptance and rejection of love is characteristic of the elegiac lover, but Ovid here levels implicit criticism at his behaviour *qua* lover by alluding to Horace *Satires*, I. I.[71] Horace points out that for all their constant grumbling and envy of the lot of others, people would not change their occupations even if they were able (15–19):

> si quis deus 'en ego' dicat,
> 'iam faciam, quod uoltis: eris tu, qui modo miles,
> mercator; tu consultus modo, rusticus; hinc uos,
> uos hinc mutatis discedere partibus: eia!
> quid statis?' – nolint. atqui licet esse beatis.

(If some god were to say 'Here I am: I shall make you whatever you like: you who are now a soldier, shall be a merchant; you who are at present a lawyer, shall be a farmer. Off you go – and you! Change roles and go your ways: Come on! Why are you just standing there?' – They would not want to. But it's their chance to be happy.)

Now it is possible to see that the lover's constant lack of resolve is ridiculous and, perhaps as important, that in it he is just like everyone else, no worse but certainly no better. The allusion is an important device in Ovid's attempt to guide our reactions to the antics of his *persona*: it enables him to deflate and ridicule the normal behaviour of the elegiac lover indirectly and without breaking through his *persona*.

Imitation and allusion, then, are among the most sophisticated aspects of Ovid's art. They make a considerable demand on the reader's memory and knowledge of earlier literature, and because they are techniques which Ovid uses creatively they are intellectually stimulating and aesthetically satisfying. Moreover because the intention of the allusions and the imitations is never made explicit Ovid is able to suggest and stimulate reactions both to his own *persona* as a lover and to the model without limiting and confining them. Indirectly they help to define the originality of his contribution to the elegiac genre and to reveal the implications that his parody has for the understanding of love as an element in human nature.

Such a piecemeal approach to poetry as that offered above must in the end prove inadequate; it is only within the poem as a whole that the interaction of the various elements of the poet's art can really be appreciated, and it therefore seems appropriate to conclude this survey of Ovid's style with an attempt to illustrate and justify this assertion.

The first diptych in the collection (1. 11 and 12) is centred round an incident in the lover's life that is frequently referred to by the elegists. Ovid has written a letter to Corinna to arrange a rendezvous; in the first poem we see him trying to persuade her coiffeuse, Nape, to act as messenger and we follow the steady escalation of his hopes; in the next we witness his dejection and despair at being refused.[72] The scene opens directly with his address to Nape (1. 11. 1-8):

> Colligere incertos et in ordine ponere crines
>   docta neque ancillas inter habenda Nape
> inque ministeriis furtiuae cognita noctio
>   utilis et dandis ingeniosa notis,
> saepe uenire ad me dubitantem hortata Corinnam,   5
>   saepe laboranti fida reperta mihi,
> accipe et ad dominam peraratas mane tabellas
>   perfer et obstantes sedula pelle moras.

(O Nape, you show such skill in gathering together the
straying locks and setting them in order, you are not to be
considered just another slave girl: at the nocturnal rites
of illicit love you have proved your worth and you have
shown yourself resourceful in delivering letters. Often you
have persuaded a hesitating Corinna to come to me, often
proved faithful to me at times of distress. Please Nape
take these tablets which I inscribed this morning and deliver
them to our mistress: diligent and dutiful thrust aside any
obstacle or cause for delay.)

The purpose of the whole of this opening sentence is to flatter Nape, and to ensure her services and her goodwill for the mission he wishes her to undertake.[73] To this end he flatters her vanity by praising her skill as a hairdresser and by encouraging her to feel superior to the other slave girls. Moreover to prevent her feeling that her services are taken for granted he expresses his deep gratitude for everything she has done for him; this also serves to prepare her for his new request and makes it doubly difficult for

her to refuse. The sentence unfolds inexorably and with great
dignity to its climax in the final couplet. The sense of expectation
aroused by the vocative, *Nape*, itself held back until the end of
the pentameter, is not satisfied until we reach the imperatives
accipe . . . perfer, and this tension binds the period together. The
impression of unhurried dignity is created by the use of parallelism in the structure of the first two couplets[74] and in the shape of
the hexameter and pentameter in the third.[75] Then the new feeling of urgency at the end of the sentence is created by structuring
the couplet round the three imperatives *accipe . . . perfer . . . pelle*.
The tone of this opening address is reinforced in every detail of
the style: the theme and variation of the opening line closely
linked by the interlocking word order; the grecizing infinitives
with *docta*; the anaphora *saepe . . . saepe*; the striking syntax of
dandis ingeniosa notis;[76] the solemnity of the archaic anastrophe
ancillas inter, and the sacral connotations of *ministeriis*: all these
play a part. The urgency of the final couplet is emphasized by the
vividness of *peraratas*[77] and *obstantes . . . pelle moras*.[78] Nape
could hardly fail to be flattered and impressed by such a display.
Yet it is obviously playfully ironic: it is only Nape's sense of
self-importance that prevents her realizing that to use such lofty
language for such a lowly creature is incongruous.

Now that Ovid has so eloquently conveyed the suitably high
esteem in which he holds her he can relax a little and adopt a
more conversational and comradely approach (9–12):

> nec silicum uenae nec durum in pectore ferrum
>   nec tibi simplicitas ordine maior adest;
> credibile est et te sensisse Cupidinis arcus:
>   in me militiae signa tuere tuae.

(Yours are not veins of flint nor is your heart of hard iron:
you are no more innocent than you ought to be; I can quite
believe that you too have known the arrows of Cupid: in
helping me, defend your legion's colours.)

The comparative brevity of the phrases and the commonplace
metaphors bring a lighter tone: but there is still a certain formality
in the repetitions *nec . . . nec . . . nec*, the impersonal *credibile est*,
and the antiquity of the formula[79] in the first hexameter. But the
playful hints that to refuse his request would reveal her to be

either insensitive (l. 9) or deplorably unsophisticated (l. 10), and
the new twist he gives to the commonplace idea of the warfare
of love finally make his persuasion irresistible. The control and
the expertise which Ovid shows in winning Nape over to his side
are highly amusing in themselves and reveal Ovid's great
dramatic skill: at the finish we have a clear impression both of
the character of Nape with all its weaknesses and of the meticu-
lous attention to detail that characterizes Ovid's approach to his
amorous adventures.

He turns at last to his real purpose and issues detailed orders.
Having overcome his problem of finding a means to deliver his
letter he can now concentrate on the consequences (13–24):

> si quaeret quid agam, spe noctis uiuere dices;
>   cetera fert blanda cera notata manu.
> dum loquor, hora fugit: uacuae bene redde tabellas,   15
>   uerum continuo fac tamen illa legat.
> aspicias oculos mando frontemque legentis:
>   et tacito uultu scire futura licet.
> nec mora, perlectis rescribat multa, iubeto:
>   odi cum late splendida cera uacat.   20
> comprimat ordinibus uersus, oculosque moretur
>   margine in extremo littera rasa meos.
> quid digitos opus est graphio lassare tenendo?
>   hoc habeat scriptum tota tabella 'ueni.'

(Should she ask what I'm doing, tell her I live only in hope
of tonight; the wax tablet bears a letter from my hand that
will touch her heart and tell her everything else. While
I speak, time flies: when she's not busy choose your moment
and give her the tablets: perhaps you had still better make
sure she reads them at once. Now I'm trusting you to
watch her eyes and her brow as she reads: even from a silent
face one can see what will happen. Do not delay, tell her
to write me a long letter as soon as she has read mine:
I hate it when the wax stares back at me all shiny and
unbroken. Tell her to write the lines close together, let a
letter erased on the outermost edge cause my eyes to linger.
But her fingers! What need to tire them with holding a pen?
Let the whole tablet contain just this one word: 'Come.'

His first instruction is simple and businesslike. But his mention of the letter and his realization that the time for his meeting with Corinna is growing ever closer begin to arouse his excitement. At first he is unsure of the outcome and his anxiety is expressed in the ebb and flow of the next three couplets (15–20), where each of the pentameters qualifies the instruction in the hexameter. Even here, however, his eagerness is beginning to affect his judgment: his plea that Nape should watch Corinna's expression as she reads will not help him to know her answer any sooner and that he should even suggest that Nape should order her mistress to do anything indicates how far he has lost contact with reality. In the next couplet (21–2) he no longer envisages anything but a favourable reply. His eager anticipation of a long and loving letter is reflected in the style: the separation of *oculos* and *meos* and the surprising change of subject from *comprimat* (Corinna) to *moretur* (*littera*). With this new confidence comes an upsurge of exaggerated sentimentality as he thinks of her fingers tired and aching from the effort of writing such a letter. The effect is conveyed by the emphatic placing of *digitos* and the choice of the grecism *graphio* to express his contempt for the instrument that can cause his darling so much pain. It is a brilliant and witty parody of the excitability and emotionality of the elegiac lover.

Twice in the course of this section Ovid uses allusions to the poems of Horace to suggest appropriate reactions to the antics of his *persona* and to anticipate the turn events will take in the next poem. *Dum loquor, hora fugit* is clearly modelled on Horace's words to Leuconoe (*Odes*, I. II. 7–8):

> dum loquimur, fugerit inuida
> aetas: carpe diem, quam minimum credula postero.

(Even while we converse, hateful time will already have fled past: grasp today and put as little trust as you can in tomorrow.)

At first it is merely amusing to see Ovid flying in the face of such sound advice as he looks forward with growing confidence to a night of pleasure with Corinna. Only in the next poem do we realize the full implications of the allusion: if Ovid had not so fondly convinced himself that the outcome would be favourable he would have been less vulnerable to being rejected.

33

The other allusion reinforces the effect and the implications of this one. *si quaeret quid agam, spe noctis uiuere dices* (13) is probably an echo of Horace *Epistles*, 1. 8. 3–4:

> si quaeret quid agam, dic multa et pulchra minantem
> uiuere nec recte nec suauiter.

(If he asks what I am doing, say that for all my fine talk I live neither wisely nor pleasantly.)

Horace admits that he is finding it difficult to live as a wise man should but that his ambitions to do so prevent him from giving himself up to pleasure. At first Ovid again seems to be mocking Horace's efforts: at this stage he feels that he is at least happy. Only when the consequences of his foolishness are made apparent in the next poem do we realize that Horace was correct in believing that wisdom, however difficult it may be to achieve, is an absolute prerequisite for real happiness.

Now Ovid ends the poem in complete confidence that his wishes will be fulfilled (25–8):

> non ego uictrices lauro redimere tabellas
> nec Veneris media ponere in aede morer.
> subscribam VENERI FIDAS SIBI NASO MINISTRAS
> DEDICAT. AT NVPER VILE FVISTIS ACER.

(I would not hesitate to bind my victorious dispatches with laurel nor to place them right in the middle of Venus' temple. I would write beneath them: To Venus Naso dedicates his faithful servants. But you were only recently nasty maple-wood.)

The excited confidence conveyed by the playful figurative language and the detailed prediction of the vow he will pay to Venus quite outweigh the hesitation implied by the subjunctives. But even here he arouses our doubts as he refers to the true nature of the tablets, *uile acer*, in unconscious anticipation of the following poem. These lines also allude to the end of Propertius, II. 14a (23–8):

> haec mihi deuictis potior uictoria Parthis,
> haec spolia, haec reges, haec mihi currus erunt.

34

> magna ego dona tua figam, Cytherea, columna,
> taleque sub nostro nomine carmen erit:
> HAS PONO ANTE TVAS TIBI, DIVA, PROPERTIVS AEDIS
> EXVVIAS, TOTA NOCTE RECEPTVS AMANS.

(This victory is dearer to me than the conquest of Parthia, these delights will count as my spoils, my captive kings, my triumphal chariot. Rich offerings shall I hang on your column, Cytherea, and beneath my name there will be some such epigram as this: these spoils, I, Propertius, place before your shrine in your honour, my goddess. For a whole night she took me as her lover.)

The allusion is again significant. It confirms that Ovid is utterly confident of success but it also suggests that the confidence may be premature. Propertius is expressing his triumphant happiness at having just spent a night with Cynthia, while Ovid's joy is only in the anticipation of the event. Secondly, the allusion reinforces the impression that the *persona* Ovid presents in the poem is that of a Propertian lover: hence the excitability and the sentimentality. But at the same time the difference in the situations of the two poets makes it clear that Ovid's *persona* is really a parody, not merely an imitation of his predecessor.

The poem is simply constructed. Ovid's intelligent self-control in the first half as he cleverly manipulates Nape is a perfect foil to the progression in the second half from anxiety to ill-founded confidence in the outcome. The poem as a whole provides an excellent counterpoint to the reactions in the next poem where Ovid has learned of his rejection. Sometime in the course of I. 11 we must presume that Nape has left on her errand.[80] Before I. 12 opens she has returned with the answer.

All this happens off-stage and the next poem opens with Ovid's woeful lament (I. 12. 1–2):

> Flete meos casus: tristes rediere tabellae;
> infelix hodie littera posse negat.

(Bewail my fate: my tablets have returned with gloomy news; the unhappy letter says that she cannot make it today.)

This opening couplet informs us directly that the situation has now completely changed. The information comes as a sharp contrast to the end of the preceding poem, though in fact it only fulfils the forebodings suggested by the allusions. The rest of the poem depicts Ovid's emotional reactions to this new situation, but their intensity would be unintelligible had we not seen his high hopes and confident happiness in the earlier poem.

These opening words are clearly a reminiscence of Propertius, III. 23. 1:

> Ergo tam doctae nobis periere tabellae.

(So my tablets, my eloquent tablets, are lost.)

At the same time as he focuses our attention on the writing tablets, the main subject of the poem, he also directs us to his Propertian model. The misery and wretchedness which Ovid expresses is however undercut by the awareness the allusion brings that Ovid is wittily reversing Propertius' situation: Propertius is depressed because his tablets have been lost; Ovid because his have been returned. There is further irony in the fact that Propertius is anxious because he does not know whether the reply that the tablets were carrying was favourable or not, while Ovid is even more distressed because he knows for certain that the answer is 'no'.

Once he has established the tone of the poem and its situation Ovid now tries to understand why his hopes and his plans have been frustrated (3–6):

> omina sunt aliquid: modo cum discedere uellet,
>   ad limen digitos restitit icta Nape.
> missa foras iterum limen transire memento
>   cautius atque alte sobria ferre pedem.

(So omens do mean something: when she was just about to leave Nape stubbed her toe on the threshold and stopped. Next time you are sent on an errand remember to cross it more carefully: act like a sober woman and pick your feet up properly.)

As he searches for a reason to help him in his present distress he remembers that Nape had stumbled as she turned to go: in his present state of mind he is willing to believe that this bad omen caused the failure of his plans. Having found her the cause of his unhappiness he seems ready to vent his spleen on Nape: the peremptory commands and the barely-veiled insults in the suggestion that she is slovenly and a drunkard make an amusing contrast with the excessive deference of the last poem. But she is not really a suitable target since she has already left and in any case it would obviously be foolish to alienate a slave whose services may be of use in the future.[81] In part the clarity of Ovid's motives in finding a new object on which to pour his wrath is responsible for the effect of bathos in what follows. Even more however it is due to the incongruity of expending his lofty eloquence on such trivial objects (7-14):

> ite hinc, difficiles, funebria ligna, tabellae,
>   tuque, negaturis cera referta notis,
> quam, puto, de longae collectam flore cicutae
>   melle sub infami Corsica misit apis.   10
> at tamquam minio penitus medicata rubebas:
>   ille color uere sanguinulentus erat.
> proiectae triuiis iaceatis, inutile lignum,
>   uosque rotae frangat praetereuntis onus.

(Away with you, cruel tablets, you coffin planks, and you, you wax crammed full with words of refusal. I see it now, you were gathered from the flower of the long-stalked hemlock and sent by the Corsican bee as the comb for its notorious honey. Yes you blushed nice and pink as though deeply dyed with cinnabar: but in fact that was the colour of blood. Lie there at the crossroads where I've tossed you, you useless block, and may a passing wheel grind you to splinters beneath its load.)

Ovid's indignant anger finds expression in this steady stream of withering contempt directed at the writing tablets. The whole passage gains its effectiveness from the carefully balanced structure. The first couplet introduces the tablets, their wooden casing and the wax surface. The next two couplets are devoted to the wax and the final one returns to the wooden casing. The tightness of structure is supported by the pervasive use of alliteration. Within this framework each of the first three couplets moves from elegance and formal beauty in the hexameter to harsh bitterness in the following line. This ironic effect of beauty is created by the elaborate and stylized word order of *difficiles, funebria ligna, tabellae* (7)[82] and especially *de longae collectam flore cicutae* (9)[83] and the choice of the words *minio* and *medicata* (11).[84] This is then undercut in the harshness of the sound and of the words *negaturis, referta* and *sanguinulentus*, all rare in poetry.

In the next section this control has broken and the emotional outburst reaches its climax (15–20):

> illum etiam, qui uos ex arbore uertit in usum,
>   conuincam puras non habuisse manus;
> praebuit illa arbor misero suspendia collo,
>   carnifici diras praebuit illa cruces;
> illa dedit turpes raucis bubonibus umbras,
>   uolturis in ramis et strigis oua tulit.

(I'll also wager that he who converted you from a tree into an object for use had unclean hands. That tree offered a branch for some wretch to hang himself; it provided hideous crosses for the executioner; it gave its foul shade to hooting horned owls and supported the eggs of the vulture and screech owl in its branches.)

The effect of rising emotionality is achieved by the gradual intensification of alliterative patterns and by constructing the whole passage round the repetitions *illum . . . praebuit illa . . . praebuit illa . . . illa.* The last two sections (7–20) together form an amusing contrast with the high honours which Ovid had promised to confer on the tablets at the end of the previous poem and this amusement undercuts the agonized misery he is expressing here. The contrast also serves to caricature the way a lover's outlook is totally dependent on the state of his relationship with his mistress, while the incongruity between the emotion and the object at which it is directed achieves an effect of parody.[85]

Ovid's denunciation of the wax tablets has been so persuasive and complete that he can no longer understand why he used them for his love letters in the first place (21–6):

> his ego commisi nostros insanus amores
>   molliaque ad dominam uerba ferenda dedi?
> aptius hae capiant uadimonia garrula cerae,
>   quas aliquis duro cognitor ore legat;
> inter ephemeridas melius tabulasque iacerent,
>   in quibus absumptas fleret auarus opes.

(Was I so crazy that I entrusted my love letters to these,
that I gave them my tender words to take to my mistress?
This wax should rather be used for the verbiage of legal
undertakings for some pinch-faced lawyer to read; better that
they should lie amid the account books and ledgers over
which the miser weeps for his squandered wealth.)

The change in the tone and the direction of the attack coupled
with the ironic comments on his own foolishness is in itself
amusing. The comic effect and the consequent undercutting of
the *persona* is strengthened by the allusion to Propertius, III. 23.
17–20:

> et quaecumque uolens reperit non stulta puella
>   garrula, cum blandis dicitur hora dolis.
> me miserum, his aliquis rationem scribit auarus
>   et ponit diras inter ephemeridas!

([My tablets carried this message] and whatever else a willing,
talkative and cultured girl can invent when an appointment
is being made for secret love. Alas! now some miser is
entering his accounts on them and placing them among his
odious ledgers.)

Ovid shows a delightful ingenuity in his adaptation of this
passage: his vignette of the weeping miser is much more vivid and
amusing than Propertius'; his introduction of the *cognitor* with the
implied contrast between him and the gentle lover intensifies the
contemptuous tone; and it was a brilliant stroke to transfer the
epithet *garrula* from the *puella* to the *uadimonia*. Even more
important is the fact that Ovid has completely reversed the
sentiments of Propertius. The latter is emotionally attached to his
writing tablets and fears that they are now being used for some
menial task. Ovid, on the contrary, wishes that his tablets were
used for such work so that they could not ruin his happiness.
Again the allusion is used to reveal that Ovid's *persona* is a
caricature, a parody of the Propertian lover.

Ovid finishes with a parting curse on the offensive tablets
(27–30):

> ergo ego uos rebus duplices pro nomine sensi:
>   auspicii numerus non erat ipse boni.

quid precer iratus, nisi uos cariosa senectus
rodat, et immundo cera sit alba situ?

(So now I realize that you are as two-faced in your dealings
as your name suggests: the number itself was a bad omen.
What should I pray for in my present rage except that
decaying old age gnaw at you, that your wax grow white
with filthy mould?)

The contemptuous tone is sustained by the word-play with
duplices,[86] the balanced malevolence of the final curse[87] and, above
all, the striking phrase *cariosa senectus rodat*.[88] But the emotion is
no longer credible. The attack on the tablets has been too
prolonged, the incongruity too great. Above all, however, it is
the constant awareness of the play with the Propertian model
that prevents us taking it seriously, and the effects of the preceding allusion are felt to the end of the poem. Propertius finally
sends his slave off to post a notice offering a reward for the
return of the tablets (III. 23. 21–4); Ovid ends by viciously cursing
his tablets.

Taken together the two poems form a satisfying unit. Their
effectiveness is due only in part to surprise and reversal; on a
closer reading it can be seen equally to lie in the fact that the second
poem properly fulfils all the expectations aroused by the use of
allusion to Horace and Propertius in the first. It is clear that the
insincerity and imitativeness is deliberate and subserves the
creation of an amusing and delightful parody.

Ovid's *persona* in the *Amores* displays amusing impudence in
his persistent flaunting of the values and the morality of the
establishment. Religion and the gods are mere butts for his
wit;[89] the life of the soldier and martial prowess are derided either
directly or by being compared to the life and virtues of a lover.[90]
The buildings and games of which Augustus was so proud are for
him only suitable places to pick up a girl.[91] His affairs are, on
occasion at least, adulterous and in all probability we are to think
of Corinna herself as married.[92] Ovid's vagueness on this issue
may be deliberate and reflect his awareness that such behaviour
would be disapproved of, even to the point of his poems being
used in evidence against him.[93] It hardly matters that Corinna
may never have existed or may not have belonged to a noble

family: in tone and spirit Ovid is defying the wishes of Augustus and his attempts to legislate against adultery.[94]

But the *Amores* are not a bitter attack on the Augustan régime nor a lament for the lost republic. Ovid's prime intention is to shock and amuse: he presents himself as the eloquent poet of the 'other Augustans', the rich and leisured young Romans too irresponsible or disillusioned to put their services at the disposal of the state. This was a period of peace and sophistication and it was irksome to confine pleasure by practising an old-fashioned morality (III. 4. 37–40):

> rusticus est nimium, quem laedit adultera coniunx,
> et notos mores non satis urbis habet,
> in qua Martigenae non sunt sine crimine nati
> Romulus Iliades Iliadesque Remus.

(The man who is offended by a wife's adultery is far too provincial and not well enough acquainted with the well-known ways of the capital, where even the offspring of Mars, Romulus, son of Ilia, and Remus, Ilia's other son, were born as a result of a misdemeanour.)

When Ovid does mention the *princeps* specifically the compliments are glib and the tone one of mocking admiration: he is held up as an example of leniency to his brother, Cupid; Ovid duly expresses his gratitude that Venus did not abort Aeneas and so deprive posterity of its beneficiaries, the family of Caesar. Such compliments would hardly satisfy the man who had let it be known that he wanted tributes to be made only in the serious work of the best poets.[95] This anti-establishment pose is, in part at least, a more pointed expression of the general opposition to the ideals of the new régime in Tibullus and Propertius,[96] and as such is only part of Ovid's caricature of the elegiac lover.

Ovid, however, was known to have rejected the opportunity of an excellent political career and the glory of becoming the first Paelignian senator.[97] But having withdrawn from public service he refused to fade into obscurity and instead paraded his 'life', his devotion to the trivial, in his poetry. He boasts of his equestrian status and pays homage to no patron: he is proud to be a Paelignian, one of that race which was spurred on by its love of *libertas* to attack Rome.[98]

The *Amores* are, however, only implicitly poems of protest against the Augustan Establishment. Ovid is eager to enjoy the fruits of the peace, not to brood over the cost of achieving and maintaining it. The existence he portrays in these poems is one devoted to the trivial, to love, *Amor*. Yet his attitude to love is quite original, distinct at once from the views of the philosophers and of the traditional Roman that it is morally evil and foolish,[99] and from the noble but impossible vision of the earlier elegists. From them, and perhaps from personal experience,[100] he knew that uncontrolled passion could bring anguished misery and worse. But through his wit and his parody Ovid shows how it is possible to remain unscathed by its ravages and also enjoy its pleasures.[101] Nor does his defiant refusal to serve the new republic mean loss of personal glory. Love has inspired his poetry and through his poetry he is confident of achieving a fame more lasting and more valuable than that gained by kings.[102] Thus, although the *Amores* are hardly profound, they do contain interesting and intelligent insights into the reactions of the individual to his society, and into the nature of love as a human phenomenon. But above all they deserve to be read because they contain some of the most witty and polished work of one of the most creative and thoroughly enjoyable Roman poets.[103]

Notes

1 All quotations in this paper are taken from the text of E. J. Kenney, *P. Ovidi Nasonis Amores etc.* (Oxford [corrected edition], 1965). I have followed him in considering II. 9a and II. 9b, III. 11a and 11b as separate elegies and III. 5 as spurious. On III. 5 see now E. J. Kenney, 'On the *Somnium* attributed to Ovid', *Agon: Journal of Classical Studies* (Berkeley), 3 (1969), 1–14. But these questions are still controversial.

2 Cf. *Tristia*, IV. 10. 53–4.

3 See G. Williams, *Tradition and Originality in Roman Poetry* (Oxford, 1968), pp. 513f. The heroine is named as Corinna in I. 5, 11; II. 6, (7), 8, 11, 12, 13, 17, 19; III. 1, 7, 12.

4 Cf. III. 7. The lady in III. 4 is probably the same as the lady of II. 19. For Ovid's infidelity to Corinna see II. 4, II. 10, and especially II. 8.

5 The identity of the girl in III. 2 is one of the most difficult to decide on but Williams (*op. cit.*, 515f.) has suggested that Ovid may here be depicting his first meeting with Corinna.

6 There is at present no general agreement as to the social status of the elegists' mistresses and each case must be judged independently, since we know that Catullus' Lesbia was married and a noble woman; Gallus' Lycoris a freedwoman and an actress.

7 See, e.g., I. 15. 1–8; II. 10. 29–38; cf. Tibullus, I. 1; Propertius, I. 6.
8 *Tristia*, IV. 10. 35–40: it is perhaps more probable that Ovid designed his career to avoid the military tribunate rather than that he withdrew from politics in order to avoid holding this position as suggested by L. R. Taylor, 'Republican and Augustan writers enrolled in the Equestrian centuries', *Transactions of the American Philological Association* (Cleveland, Ohio), 99 (1968), 480. See now T. P. Wiseman, *New Men in the Roman Senate* (Oxford, 1971), p. 151.
9 II. 18; cf. III. 1, 15. For the *recusatio* cf. W. Wimmel, *Kallimachos in Rom* (Wiesbaden, 1960).
10 Quintilian, *Inst.*, x. 1. 98.
11 Ovid seems to have enjoyed his secret; cf. *Am.*, II. 17. 29; *Ars Am.*, III. 538. For these lines to have point we must assume that Corinna did exist (cf. *Am.*, III. 12). Apuleius, *Apologia*, 10, fails to mention her. Sidonius Apollinaris (*Carm.*, 23. 159–60) seems to have guessed that she was none other than Julia, Augustus' daughter: an interesting but wild conjecture.
12 If *Tristia*, II. 339ff. refer to the *Amores* then Ovid tells us specifically that the love he professes is a pretence (for *falsus amor* cf. *Ars Am.*, I. 618). This has no bearing on the reality of Corinna, and the reference may be to the *Ars Amatoria*.
13 Cf. *Tristia*, IV. 10. 51–2.
14 Most recently A. Cameron, 'The first edition of Ovid's *Amores*', *Classical Quarterly* (Oxford), n.s. XVIII (1968), 320–33, with references to earlier discussions.
15 *Tristia*, IV. 10. 57–8, but the date 25 B.C. can only be approximate.
16 A vexed problem. The Sygambri had made war briefly against the Romans in 16 B.C. and Augustus secured a diplomatic victory and a few hostages. The peace did not last. In 11 B.C. Drusus campaigned against them and celebrated an *ouatio* in the following year. But the tribe was not really put down until after Tiberius' campaign and resettlement in 8 B.C. which was followed by a triumph in 7 B.C. It is sometimes maintained that *Amores*, I. 14. 45–50 must have been written, or at least rewritten, after the triumph of Tiberius or at least the *ouatio* of Drusus, i.e. for the second edition. But the phrase *triumphatae . . . gentis* (l. 46) may only be a daring hyperbole (cf. the strong language used by Horace, *Odes*, IV. 2. 36; 14. 51 and Propertius, IV. 6. 77) and refer, perhaps sarcastically, to Augustus' diplomatic success of 16 B.C. The objection that the Roman wig-makers would not be able to use the hair of captive women of the tribe until after a more substantial defeat has been countered by H. L. Levy (*Classical World* [Bethlehem, Pa.], 62 [1968], 135) who draws attention to a Germanic custom of shaving the head and sending the hair to the conqueror as a gesture of submission. (He cites Martial, XIV. 26; Claudian, *De Quarto Consulatu Honorii*, 446–7; *In Eutropium*, I. 383.) Such a witticism is at home in this poem.
17 *Ars Am.*, III. 343.
18 Cf. *Tristia*, IV. 10. 61–2; with *poena* of the epigram (l. 4) cf. *suppliciis* at Catullus, 14. 20.

19 *Am.*, I. 14, 15; II. 18; III. 9, 15 *inter alia* have been credited to the second edition. On I. 14 see above n. 16. *Am.*, II. 18. 19–20 may as easily apply to the *Amores* as the *Ars Amatoria*. For examples of *praecepta* in the *Amores* see II. 19 (with III. 4); I. 4 (with II. 5) etc. For the phrase and the idea cf. Tibullus, I. 6. 9–10. To believe with F. Munari (*P. Ovidi Nasonis Amores* [ed. 5. Florence, 1970], p. xv) that the first edition was published in 20 B.C. leads to the strange result of having to attribute all the datable elegies (I. 14, 15; III. 9, 15) to the second edition.

20 The latest date in Propertius, Book III is 23/22 B.C.; in Book IV, 16 B.C. H. Tränkle (*Die Sprachkunst des Properz* [Wiesbaden, 1960], p. 106, n. 2) is almost alone in believing that Propertius is here following Ovid.

21 *Amores*, I. 1 and 2 seem to be two separate accounts of how Ovid came to write love elegy and Cameron (*op. cit.*, 320ff.) suggests that they originally belonged to two separate books. But the inconsistency is slight and becomes less important when we recall that the poet's *Dichterweihe* (I. 1) is usually assumed to take place in a dream (cf. E. J. Kenney, '*Doctus* Lucretius', *Mnemosyne* [Leiden], Ser. 4. 23 [1970], esp 375ff.).

Another problem is the. ack of a formal conclusion to Book II. G. Luck (*Antike Lyrik*, ed. W. Eisenhut [Darmstadt, 1970], 464–5, n. 1) has recently suggested that an epilogue has fallen out in the transmission of the text but such a hypothesis seems unwarranted. The false sense of ending created by II. 18 leads to an amusing play on the reader's expectations and is perhaps intended to emphasize the continuity of the collection. In any case a formal conclusion is not obligatory, cf. Horace, *Odes*, I. In short neither of these points is adequate evidence of clumsy editing.

22 With II. 17. (5–6; 27; 33; 34) cf. I. 3. (1; 7–12; 25–6; 20 respectively).

23 With II. 5. (15; 16; 17–18; 21ff.; 29ff.) cf. I. 4. (19; 17; 20; 55ff.; 39ff. respectively) and with III. 4. (25–6; 21–2; 32; 31; 45ff.) cf. II. 19. (4; 27–28; 19ff.; 52; 59–60).

24 *Amores*, I. 1, 2, 15; II. 1, 18; III. 1, 15.

25 Cf. I. 11 and 12; II. 2. 3; II. 7. 8; II. 9a. 9b; II. 13. 14; III. 11a. 11b.

26 III. 7 develops the situation described at Tibullus, I. 5. 39–42; with III. 8. 35–44 cf. Tibullus, I. 3. 35ff.; with III. 10. 7–14 cf. Tibullus, II. 1. 37–48; and with III. 10. 11–14 cf. Tibullus, I. 7. 29ff. This is not to neglect the Propertian models for these poems: for *Am.*, III. 8 and III. 10, cf. Propertius, II. 16 and II. 33 respectively.

27 For full details see the edition of Munari, *op. cit.* (n. 19). The older work of A. Zingerle, *Ovidius und sein Verhältnis zu den Vorgängern und gleichzeitigen römischen Dichtern* (Hildesheim [repr.], 1967) and C. Ganzenmüller, 'Aus Ovids Werkstatt', *Philologus* (Berlin), 70 (1911), 274–311 is still useful. The basic treatment of this aspect of the *Amores* remains R. Neumann, *Qua ratione Ovidius in Amoribus scribendis Properti Elegiis usus sit* (Diss. Göttingen, 1919).

28 Ovid, *Am.*, III. 9 and 13; Propertius, III. 7; 14; 19 and 18 (the epicedion for Marcellus, the counterpart to Ovid's poem on the death of Tibullus

[III. 9]). For poems not primarily connected with the poet's love-life see *Am.*, III. 6, 10; cf. Propertius, III. 11, 17.

29 See Ovid, *Am.*, I. 6, II. 2, III. 8; II. 11; I. 5; II. 16; II. 4, 8, 10, 19; II. 5, III. 8, 12; I. 14; cf. Propertius, I. 16; I. 8; II. 14, 15; II. 19, 32; II. 22; II. 17; II. 18c.

30 Propertius' problems are almost invariably related to the infidelity of Cynthia; Ovid's are usually imposed from outside his relationship (cf. I. 6; II. 2; III. 6; III. 10) and are therefore less serious in themselves.

31 Nor should we forget the works of Cornelius Gallus and Valgius Rufus etc.

32 For Propertius see E. Lefèvre, *Propertius Ludibundus* (Heidelberg, 1966). But there is a more pervasive and subtle humour and irony in both these poets than has been generally recognized.

33 For Ovid's treatment of death see II. 10. 35–8; II. 6; III. 9; contrast Tibullus, I. 3; I. 10 or Propertius, I. 19; II. 8.

34 His attitude to Augustanism is always irreverent. None of the addressees in his poems is of any political consequence although C. Pomponius Graecinus was *cos. suff.* in A.D. 16 (see Wiseman, *op. cit.*, 253). Contrast Tibullus, I. 1, or Propertius, e.g., II. 1, 10.

35 See *Am.*, I. 9; II. 19, especially 5–26; III. 14.

36 *Am.*, III. 14.

37 Cf. W. Stroh, *Die römische Liebeselegie als werbende Dichtung* (Amsterdam, 1971), 157ff.

38 Cf. III. 7. 82; I. 8. 22; II. 5. 33–42.

39 Cf. I. 7; II. 16.

40 For sleeplessness as a sign of love see, e.g., Virgil, *Aeneid*, IV. 1ff.; cf. Ovid, *Am.*, II. 9b. 39–42, and often in the elegists.

41 For *medio . . . toro* cf. *Am.*, II. 10. 18. For the setting cf., however, *Ars Am.*, II. 617–24; III. 807–8.

42 For the full impact of these lines cf. Horace, *Odes*, III. 6. 17–32.

43 Despite the bathos of the thought in the pentameter the language is still striking: *statio* is used in a slightly unusual sense; *recompositas* occurs first here.

44 See n. 38.

45 The theme is of course a commonplace; cf. Horace, *Odes*, II. 8. But the reasons Ovid suggests are amusing and different, since proverbially lovers' vows did not reach the gods' ears.

46 But within the parallelism there is variation, which can be represented schematically as: A b C D1 B / A b D2 C.

47 The colour effect Ovid seems to be describing is that produced by sunrise on a snowscape.

48 Ennius, *Ann.*, 352 V.³: cf. Propertius, II. 3. 10–12.

49 Adjectives in -*eus* have a poetic colour.

50 For a full discussion of Ovid's treatment of the elegiac couplet see M. Platnauer, *Latin Elegiac Verse* (Cambridge, 1951).

51 Also *Am.*, III. 2. 27–8, 43–4; III. 6. 61–2; cf. I. 4. 13–14.

52 But the loss of so much earlier poetry makes it difficult to estimate the extent of this practice.

53 The point is made by A. G. Lee, *Ovid's Amores* (London, 1968), 183.

54 See, e.g., *Am.*, I. 2. 11–17; I. 7. 13–18, 51–6; I. 13. 11–24.

55 Again the style is vivid: note the zeugma in *collige cum uultu mentem*; *reparabile* makes its first appearance here.

56 For thinness as a symptom of love see, e.g., Theocritus, 2. 89–90; Virgil, *Ecl.*, 3. 100–1; Propertius, I. 5. 22; Ovid, *Am.*, II. 9a. 14.

57 The mock-solemnity of the tone is emphasized by the use of the formal *Quirites* and the archaism *sed enim*.

58 Propertius, I. 2; I. 15; II. 18c; cf. Tibullus, I. 8. 9–16.

59 Propertius, I. 2. 23–6; I. 15. 1–2; II. 18c. 35ff.

60 An outstanding example is *Am.*, I. 8, and Propertius, IV. 5.

61 For promiscuity as a cure for love cf. Cicero, *Tusc. Disp.*, IV. 75; Ovid, *Rem.*, 441ff.

62 Or he may take a passage from an earlier poem as a starting point, e.g., *Am.*, II. 4 and Propertius, II. 22a. 4–10; *Am.*, I. 10. 1–8 and Propertius, I. 3. 1–8; *Am.*, III. 11a and 11b and Catullus, 85.

63 Cf. especially *Am.*, I. 9, *militat omnis amans* with Tibullus, I. 1. 75 or Propertius, I. 6. 29–30; *Am.*, II. 12 and Propertius, II. 14.

64 III, 7, 25–6.

65 This is in turn based on Meleager, *A.P.*, 12. 101.

66 The whole poem is modelled on Propertius, II. 33a.

67 Note especially the juxtaposition *teneram ferro* (l. 30).

68 With Propertius, I. 7. 9, *hic mihi conteritur uitae modus*, cf. *Am.*, II. 18. 3, *ignaua Veneris cessamus in umbra*.

69 With *Am.*, II. 18. 11, contrast Propertius, I. 7. 7.

70 E.g. *Am.*, I. 1. 1., cf. Virgil, *Aeneid*, I. 1; *Am.*, I. 2. 31–6; cf. Virgil, *Aeneid*, I, 292–6.

71 This seems possible despite the appearance of the idea at Cicero, *De Sen.*, 83 etc.

72 With this diptych compare Propertius, III. 6.

73 For the importance of the mistress' slaves to a lover, especially her hairdresser, cf. *Ars Am.*, I. 351ff.

74 *docta* and *utilis* are both held over to the pentameter.

75 *saepe . . . hortata; saepe . . . reperta.*

76 This construction with *ingeniosus* is unique to Ovid; cf. *T.L.L.* s.v. For the phrase cf. *Ars Am.*, III. 470. For the ingenuity needed in passing lovers' letters cf. *Ars Am.*, III. 619–28, Tibullus, II. 6. 45–6.

77 Not used of writing letters before this passage.

78 Perhaps a deliberate variant for the Virgilian coinage *rumpe moras* (*Georgics*, III. 43).

79 Cf. Homer, *Od.*, XXIII. 103; *Iliad*, XXII. 357; Tibullus, I. 1. 64 etc.

80 It is just possible that we are to imagine her leaving after the brief command at l. 14. This would give the poem a symmetrical structure, with Ovid shouting the other commands after her or muttering them to himself. Others may prefer to have her present at least until l. 24 or even right to the end. In any case it is obvious that after l. 14 Ovid pays less and less attention to her.

81 See above, n. 73.

82 On this type of word-order see Williams, *op. cit.*, 317; 726–8.

83 This elaborate dislocation is paralleled only elsewhere in Ovid: see Platnauer, *op. cit.*, 102, who compares *Ibis*, 443; *Ex P.*, II. 10. 1; II. 2. 2.

84 *minio* is a Spanish loan word and *medicata* seems to be an archaism revived by the Augustan poets. For the concept of poetic diction in Latin poetry cf. Cicero, *De Or.*, III. 153; Horace, *Epistles*, II. 2. 111–21; *A.P.*, 46–72. But the question is a complex one; see now Williams, *op. cit.*, 736f.; 743–50.

85 The passage may be a conscious adaption of Horace, *Odes*, II. 13. 1ff.

86 *duplex* meaning deceitful is rare; cf. Catullus, 68. 51; Horace, *Odes*, I. 6. 7.

87 Note the interlacing word order: b A c a B.

88 *cariosa* is used as an epithet for age for the first time here: normally it is used of material things. *rodat* almost personifies *senectus*.

89 Cf. *Am.*, I. 13; III. 3, 6, 10.

90 See especially *Am.*, I. 9; II. 12, and cf. R. Syme, *The Roman Revolution* (Oxford, 1939), 467f.

91 *Am.*, II. 2. 3–4; the portico at the temple of Apollo on the Palatine: for more serious appreciation cf. Horace, *Odes*, I. 31; Propertius, II. 31. *Am.*, III. 2; for the games cf. Augustus, *Res Gestae*, 22.

92 At least in I. 4; II. 2; II. 19; III. 4. See above p. 1f. Of course he also reveals that he was married himself (III. 13. 1).

93 As indeed they were – although Augustus seems to have been concerned rather with the *Ars Amatoria* when he relegated Ovid to Tomi.

94 On Augustus' marriage laws and their importance for Roman elegy see Williams, *op. cit.*, 532ff.; cf. 58ff.; 631ff.

95 Suetonius, *Divus Augustus*, 89. 3; the allusion to Augustus in (III. 9. 63–4) *tu quoque, si falsum est temerati crimen amici, Sanguinis atque animae prodige Galle tuae* may contain a sarcastic reference to Augustus' own lament on hearing of the death of Gallus: *quod sibi soli non liceret amicis, quatenus uellet, irasci* (Suetonius, *op. cit.*, 66. 2). *temerare* is normally used of offences against the divine and the sacred; cf. Virgil, *Aeneid*, VI. 840; Ovid, *Met.*, VIII, 742. See also *Am.*, III. 8. 51–2: this would be the most outspoken criticism but the authenticity of these lines has been doubted.

96 See especially Propertius, II. 7; 15. 41–8.

97 See Wiseman, *op. cit.*, 152 and n. 3. For Q. Varius Geminus, the first Paelignian senator, see *ibid.*, 270.

98 Cf. *Am.*, I. 15; II. 1. 1–2; III. 15 etc.

99 See Cicero, *Tusc. Disp.*, IV. 68–76; Lucretius, *D.R.N.*, IV. 1037ff.; Horace, *Sat.*, I. 2.

100 At least he had two unsuccessful marriages (*Tristia*, IV. 10. 69–72).

101 Cf. *Ars Am.*, III. 41–2.

102 *Am.*, I. 15. 31–42. For a detailed analysis of this poem see now F. Stoessl, 'Ovids Lebensentscheidung' in: *Festschrift K. Vretska zum 70 Geburtstag* (Heidelberg, 1970), 250–75. But he goes too far in suggesting that *Livor* is a pseudonym for *Caesar* (267).

103 For reasons of space footnotes contain few bibliographical references. This is not intended to conceal my great debt to other writers on Ovid.

Full details can be found in the edition of Munari, *op. cit.* (n. 19). There are two excellent translations of the *Amores*: A. G. Lee, *Ovid's Amores* (London, 1968) and Christopher Marlowe, *The Elegies of Ovid* (c. 1597). The latter will be of special interest to those interested in Ovid's influence upon English literature – see chapter VII below.

II

The Heroides

W. S. Anderson

The Heroine as an Elegiac Figure

sic ubi fata vocant, udis abiectus in herbis
   ad vada Maeandri concinit albus olor.
nec quia te nostra sperem prece posse moveri,
   adloquor: adverso movimus ista deo.
sed merita et famam corpusque animumque pudicum
   cum male perdiderim, perdere verba leve est.
certus es ire tamen miseramque relinquere Didon,
   atque idem venti vela fidemque ferent?
certus es, Aenea, cum foedere solvere naves,
   quaeque ubi sint nescis, Itala regna sequi?
                              (*Heroides*, VII. 1–10)

(It is in this way, when death calls, that the white swan,
lying in the damp grass beside the Maeander River, sings its
last song. Not that I might hope that you could be moved
by my plea; the prayer I have set in motion goes to a
hostile deity. But after I have wasted so ignobly good
deeds, reputation, and chaste body and soul, wasting words
is a trivial matter. Are you determined to go, however,
and to abandon poor Dido; and will the same winds carry off
your ship and your sacred trust? Are you determined,
Aeneas, at the same time to free yourself from your oath and
your ships from Carthage, then to hunt out the Italian
kingdom about whose location you are totally ignorant?)

Ovid opens his seventh *Epistle* with six lines that establish the
mood of the speaker and prepare us, once we hear the name of
Dido in line 7, to define the dramatic situation. In the opening
couplet the speaker compares herself to the dying swan and

alludes to the familiar ancient belief in the 'swan song'. If the analogy has any precision, we may expect that the speaker regards herself either as dying or as ready for suicide, and the elegiac form of verse takes on the plaintive note appropriate to its age-old use in funereal situations. The second couplet opens up a gap between swan and speaker. Whereas the swan sings without reference to audience, with no expectation of changing its doom, this speaker is addressing someone and trying to move him, although she voices little hope. Her professed hopelessness acts in spite of her words, or rather because of the very choice of terms, to stir our sympathy; and we may suspect that she is calculating on some sympathy from her addressee. It is not hard to discern the psychological motives here: she protests a little too obviously.

Line 4 causes the translator and commentator some difficulty. Ovid has repeated the verb *movere* and evoked a second time the prayer-context, and we ignore the echo at our peril.[1] My suggested translation clarifies the context: 'the prayer I have set in motion.' But there is an added point to make, I believe. By reusing *movere*, by changing it from passive to active, Ovid is revealing the true psychological motivations of the speaker. Despite her pose of hopelessness, she actively combats her fate, setting words in motion that subconsciously she hopes will move her addressee. Ovid has a distinct interest in showing how spoken words reveal intentions that belie or seriously/amusingly qualify the professions of his speakers.

A few words about the ablative phrase *adverso deo*. We all know what the two words mean, that all the activity in *movimus* is futile because a god opposes its success. So the commentators concentrate on defining the god: he must be Cupid, god of love. Yes, in retrospect we might well adopt this limitation on Ovid's generalized phrase. However, if we press the correspondence between lines 3 and 4 (which is all that we have to go on at this early stage in the poem), we should be tempted to interpret the so-far-unnamed addressee as the deity. Dido prays to him as a god in line 3, disclaiming hope; she explains the hopelessness in 4 by calling the god *adversus*. In this prayer context and the ambiguity of *adverso deo*, I suggest, Ovid has initiated one of the fundamental paradoxes of this *Epistle* (as well as of other *Heroides*): the woman looks up to the man with pleading, devoted love, as to a god, while at the same time she struggles with her awareness of the man's ungodlike, even inhuman behaviour towards her. Her words vacillate wildly among prayer, complaint and imprecation. When in line 7 we learn that the speaker is Dido, we must revise *our* estimate of the dramatic situation and the godhead of the addressee. But Dido continues to pray movingly to Aeneas (cf. *precor* 63, 163).

Having disclaimed any hope of moving the addressee, the speaker is now bound to justify her words. This she does in an effective manner which Ovid has enhanced by wit. Ostensibly she gives no real justification; she merely states that she has words or, as we might put it, time to waste. That would seem to reinforce her sense of hopelessness and doom. When, however, Ovid lets her combine the ideas of wasting words and wasting values, he not only increases her pathos, but he also insinuates a discordant note that functions as the transition to the next couplet. Why list all those things she has wasted – good deeds, reputation, chastity? Partly to make *perdere verba* effective by contrast: in rhetorical terms, Ovid has contrived a brilliant anti-climax. Partly, however, she is also reminding the addressee of how he has caused her to waste these values, and, as she reminds him, her own memory harks back to earlier days and stirs her indignation. She cannot grasp how her 'god', to whom she has sacrificed so much, can now be hostile, and by these very words to him, which she labels 'wasted', she obviously wants to stir his compunction. In the end, though, we shall recognize that her expressed words are right. Because the gap between past deeds and sacrifices and present suffering is too great to bridge, for all her pleading words the speaker cannot persuade her addressee: her cause is hopeless; she is wasting those emotional words.

Now at last Ovid is ready to reveal who his speaker is, in a set of angry questions that protest plaintively against Aeneas' decisive return to duty from his idyllic love. She calls herself 'poor Dido', her self-pity calling for pity from Aeneas. How can he leave her alone to her misery after all she has done for him? If he abandons her, he will have violated his promises, she claims; but she voices her dismay with the rhetorical device of zeugma, whereby the one verb *ferent* functions jointly, though in different senses, with its two objects. (Note the alliteration in 8 also.) From Dido's point of view, Aeneas' departure for Italy cannot be justified: it is the rejection of her love, the breaking of his trust.

And what is he seeking? Worse than nothing, in her terms: Italian kingdoms in some unknown region. Once again, in 9–10, Ovid allows her to balance the damage Aeneas causes against the futile goal he pursues. If, by sailing, Aeneas breaks his oath and achieves no positive results, everything must be done to stop him, and Dido rightfully claims our and his pity.

Thus, in ten lines, Ovid has introduced us to a situation and the woman who is struggling to combat it. Although she feels herself doomed, she is too strong a personality to give up yet, and she hurls herself into an energetic effort to stop Aeneas from leaving. Out of her hopelessness she creates an appeal to Aeneas' pity and sense of duty towards her. Building up her own case, stressing Aeneas' immoral behaviour towards herself and his senseless pursuit of an impossible goal in Italy, she tries to prevent the departure which, as she knows only too well, will result in their permanent separation, the end to her hopes that she so dreads.

I need hardly remind my reader that Ovid was placing his audience in a highly familiar drama. Not long after Virgil died in 19 B.C., Augustus saw to it that the *Aeneid* was published and available to the Roman world. We can well imagine that the appearance of Virgil's epic, recognized as a superlative work of genius at the first reading, enhanced the celebration of the Secular Games of 17 B.C. Within a decade it was so well known in Rome that Ovid, fitting the story of Dido to the general plot of the *Heroides*, could exploit his audience's familiarity with Virgil in order to make something new of Dido's wretched fate.

In Virgil's account of *Aeneid*, IV, Dido discovers that the Trojans are preparing to sail, and she angrily accosts Aeneas. Aeneas tries to calm her down, while insisting on the necessity of his departure, and she replies with even wilder wrath, so wild that she faints before completing her tirade. This is the last time the lovers are together. When she recovers consciousness and finds the Trojans still intent on sailing, she makes further attempts, in desperation resorting to messengers like her sister Anna or, as Ovid imagines, a letter such as the elegiac poem we are considering:

> ire iterum in lacrimas, iterum temptare precando
> cogitur et supplex animos summittere amori,
> ne quid inexpertum frustra moritura relinquat.
>
> (*Aen.*, IV. 413–15)

(Again she is forced to tears, again driven to try prayers, to
surrender her pride to passion and beg, so that she might not
leave any possibility untried – a woman doomed to die in
vain.)

It is from these lines and their dramatic situation that Ovid starts
his poem. Dido does not tell us that she is weeping here; but near
the end of her letter she refers to her tears and tries to make one
final pathetic argument from them (185–6). She does refer to her
prayers; she regards herself as *moritura* in the swan-analogy; and
the hopelessness she voices so pathetically catches the sense of
Virgil's *frustra*.

I said, however, that Ovid makes something new of the
Virgilian situation. There are two chief differences between Ovid's
and Virgil's Dido, one of which makes itself felt in these first two
lines and throughout the *Epistle*, the other of which, barely
adumbrated in line 10, gradually impresses us. The best way of
defining the first main difference is to point to the style that Ovid
has given his character. She manipulates words with an elegance
and rhetorical mastery that suggests a supreme self-consciousness,
a desire to dramatize her emotions and her deserts effectively,
perhaps more than to voice them directly. Thus, instead of making
an immediate plea, she starts by comparing herself beautifully
with a dying swan. After we let our imaginations stray to that
lovely pathetic picture, we hear her use the rhetorical ploy of
negating her true purpose in order to present ironically a false
purpose: she has no objection to wasting words! It is easy to let
ourselves be trapped by those carefully weighed – not wasted –
words. However, as I noted earlier, Ovid likes to characterize
through direct speech, to reveal subconscious motivations behind
a speaker's words. Thus, for all her professed hopelessness and
vividness as a dying swan, for all her claim to throw away words
lightly, Dido acts as though these words are her very *raison d'être*,
the last link with Aeneas and with life. Indeed her words provide
the sole means Ovid employs to give his character being; no background details, no dramatic introduction, commentary or epilogue
in any way fill in the portrait.

Now some men object to an articulate woman, and many
Ovidian critics – all men, of course – object strenuously to a Dido
who manipulates rhetoric so ably and so cleverly works upon the

sympathies of Aeneas (and us). Virgil's Dido, they correctly observe, is so immersed in her tragedy that she not only never wastes words in any sense, but also she never seems to pause to calculate effects, to try to arrange details and pictures so as to dramatize herself. It is a triumph of Virgilian poetry that his Dido, who speaks with great power, strikes us as simple, direct, and frequently inarticulate, quite genuinely at the mercy of her emotions. Thus, when before her last plea to Aeneas he describes her as *moritura*, destined to die, we feel that the incoherence and impetuosity of her words belong to a woman who will soon be a suicide. Not that Virgil abandons rhetoric in giving words to his Dido, far from it. But his rhetoric springs integrally from his poetic intentions, which are to represent a woman overcome by emotions, a woman and not the self-controlled queen who so calmly and regally welcomed the Trojans in *Aeneid*, 1. Whatever she says, he has circumscribed it with his narrative frame, and no audience should – although more than one has succumbed – surrender its objectivity and view the epic situation as Virgil's Dido does.

Ovid's purposes are different, and his articulate Dido aims at and can – if we hear her rightly – achieve a success that bears no relation to epic values or the power of a tragic heroine. Take the tragic element. Virgil shows us how Dido falls from queen to mere woman, then follows her to her bitter suicide and death. Ovid abstracts his Dido from that total drama, and freezes her in a single moment. When she opens her letter, she regards herself as a dying swan, and, as she ends it, she self-consciously evokes *scribentis imago* (183), the picture of herself as letter-writer, Aeneas' sword on her lap dripping with tears. Naturally we are to assume that she will use the sword on herself soon, but that is outside the letter. Her mood has not appreciably changed in the course of writing the letter, and the final funereal allusions, repeating the initial ones, also constitute part of her argument against Aeneas' departure. She is using the threat of suicide to weaken Aeneas' resolution; Virgil's Dido never acted so deliberately, and consequently her suicide seemed to be the gradual result of despair, not a dramatic plan that she first formed to win back Aeneas. Ovid's Dido, then, does not pull us into a tragic situation or the character of a tragic heroine caught at the moment of self-realization; his Dido pulls us into a dramatic situation

entirely by her own words, and, by her obvious desire to dramatize herself, invites us to pity her artistically contrived character,
but at the same time to admire the artistry which she (and Ovid)
used to contrive it. She does not die in Ovid's drama; she remains
forever a woman arguing with facts, offering love affectively.
One responds to that woman differently from the way one does
to Virgil's tragic heroine.

Let me put it another way. In the *Aeneid*, Virgil separates his
effects so that, whereas Dido speaks directly out of her tragic
situation and makes on us a clear, undivided impression of a
broken woman, the poet has created a dramatic frame for her that
enables us to put her words in perspective, judge her character,
and in the end accept her suicide as sad but appropriate. In his
Epistle, on the other hand, Ovid combines his effects. His Dido
speaks from her situation, but with such conscious art and
within such circumscribed limits that, at the same time as we
start to respond with the pity she demands, we are stopped by
our awareness that she is exploiting that pity, and we end up by
being charmed, I think, by the tension this one woman produces
in us. Since the poet does not frame Dido's speech or qualify
it by any direct intrusion, we are invited to exercise our own
judgment and sophistication and to discern, on the basis of our
own experience, where Dido ceases, so to speak, to be the purely
pathetic character she represents herself to be and becomes also
the clever woman. We neither go so far in sympathy for Ovid's
Dido as we do for Virgil's, nor on the other hand do we feel
obliged in the end to condemn her. Rather, Ovid seems to be
intent on showing us a familiar feminine personality, warm,
articulate, self-conscious and self-deceiving at the same time. This
appeal to our sophisticated humanity, not to the high seriousness
evoked by Virgil's tragic epic, is one major effect that Ovid aims
at and achieves by his first main innovation, his adoption of an
entirely un-Virgilian style for his Dido.

I believe that many Romans responded favourably to Ovid's
new way of letting Dido speak, that, although he may not have
pleased Augustus or the more confirmed members of the Establishment, he won applause from a large audience that was capable
of the sophisticated response he required. Such sophistication,
however, is not available to all ages, and Ovid's Dido has met
far less consistent appreciation than Virgil's. Chaucer and

Shakespeare would have understood her, and I have hope that our era, precisely because of its complexities, its odd sense of humour, and its new, hard-won attitude towards women, can see and accept Ovid's Dido for what she is. The effects of Romanticism and late-Victorian prejudices have just about worn off, and we should be prepared to realize that spontaneity in art is nonsense, that the *impression* of direct emotion is but one of many optional values. It is not necessary to labour the point about Romanticism's disservice to Roman literature and to Ovid in particular. Instead of citing an obviously horrible example of Victorian incomprehension, let me remind my reader of the experience of John Dryden, who, having translated Ovid's *Epistle* and then later Virgil's *Aeneid*, voiced his open hostility to the former. Wouldn't one have expected better from a leading poet of the Restoration? Shouldn't intelligent Joseph Addison have protested against such prejudice?

In Number 62 of the *Spectator*, which appeared on 11 May 1710, a decade after Dryden's death, Addison quoted with approval some observations of the former, in order to support his contention that poets who lack 'the strength of genius to give that majestic simplicity to nature, which we so much admire in the works of the ancients, are forced to hunt after foreign ornaments, and not to let any piece of wit, of what kind soever, escape them'. Ovid serves Addison as his primary example of such weak genius and misplaced wit, Dryden as his main authority, in the following passage:

> Mr Dryden makes a very handsome observation on Ovid's writing a letter from Dido to Aeneas, in the following words: 'Ovid (says he, speaking of Virgil's fiction of Dido and Aeneas) takes it up after him, even in the same age, and makes an ancient heroine of Virgil's new-created Dido; dictates a letter for her, just before her death, to the ungrateful fugitive; and, very unluckily for himself, is for measuring a sword with a man so much superior in force to him on the same subject. I think I may be judge of this, because I have translated both. The famous author of the Art of Love has nothing of his own; he borrows all from a greater master in his own profession, and, which is worse, improves nothing which he finds: nature fails him,

and being forced to his old shift, he has recourse to
witticism. This passes, indeed, with his soft admirers, and
gives him the preference to Virgil in their esteem.'

It is plain that neither Dryden nor Addison is a 'soft admirer' of
Ovid's Dido.

From what I have said earlier, the reader will understand that
both critics were, in my opinion, using the wrong critical
weapons when they attacked Ovid for lacking strength of genius,
for letting Nature fail him, and for desperately resorting to any
shred of wit in order to cover up his deficiencies. Ovid is most
definitely not making the slightest effort 'to give that majestic
simplicity to nature, which we so much admire in the works of
the ancients'. (Parenthetically let it be said that we might admire
other features, such as sophistication, in certain ancients if we
appreciated more accurately the contributions of Hellenistic
and Roman literature to our total view of 'the ancients'.) But
perhaps the best way to make the point – and at the same time
to review our evaluation of Ovid's style – is to show how Dryden
struggled with his prejudices when he translated Ovid's *Epistle*
for an edition of the *Heroides*, rendered by several poets, that
appeared in 1680. Here are Dryden's lines which parallel the
opening passage that I have less artistically translated, then discussed in detail:

> So, on Meander's banks, when death is nigh,
> The mournful swan sings her own elegy.
> Not that I hope (for, oh, that hope were vain!)
> By words your lost affection to regain;
> But, having lost whate'er was worth my care,
> Why should I fear to lose a dying prayer?
> 'Tis then resolv'd poor Dido must be left,
> Of life, of honour, and of love bereft!
> While you, with loosen'd sails and vows, prepare
> To seek a land that flies the searcher's care.

For all its elegance, this translation makes some interesting
changes in the original Latin and in Ovid's organization that,
in combination, alter Ovid's effects and imply Dryden's em-
barrassment with the Roman poet. Since the Latin contains no
'mournful' and no reference to elegy, Dryden has started by
overstressing the pathos of the scene which Ovid renders by

more concrete details (e.g. *udis abiectus in herbis, albus olor*). In the next three couplets, which Ovid isolated from each other, Dryden drastically revises the organization. Thus, whereas Ovid made careful use, we saw, of the prayer motif in 3–4, Dryden eliminates that in favour of a sentimental parenthesis and the use of 'words' (taken from *verba* 6), but introduces the motif in 6 as a 'dying prayer' (where *verba* had been). What is the result? The attenuation of the very wit which so much offended Dryden for its 'unnatural' quality.[2] Instead of a general supplication, for which we as yet can provide no precise context – an unknown 'you' being implored, as Ovid wrote it – Dryden limits the situation with 'your lost affection to regain'. The clever anti-climax contrived by Ovid, in which the key Roman values of *merita, famam, corpus,* and *animum pudicum* are then capped by *verba,* disappears. In its place, Dryden balances a vague 'whate'er was worth my care' against 'a dying prayer', and indeed tips the balance in favour of the more precise and pathetic prayer. In lines 7 and 8, the same strategy seems to determine Dryden's moves. Ovid used witty zeugma, in his alliterative clause *venti vela fidemque ferent,* to render the simultaneity of effects: the same winds will carry off ship and sacred trust. Apparently unable to stomach the breach of taste, Dryden ignores the Latin and borrows some of the precise terms from 6, to produce an eloquent climactic triad that again asserts too strongly Dido's love and her determination to die. Only in line 9 does Dryden permit Ovid's wit to emerge, when he faithfully renders 'with loosen'd sails and vows'. But even there he reduces its effect by ignoring the anaphora *certus es* and then, in the magnificent metaphorical version of 10, abandoning *nescis*; thus, Dido's sardonic contrast between Aeneas' determination to leave and his uncertainty about his destination vanishes.

What Dryden has done here, whether conscious of it or not, is to revise Ovid's stylistic techniques so as to remove the 'faults' Dryden sensed in the letter: the translator eliminates or reduces 'unnatural' witticism in order to give Dido the 'natural' diction he believes appropriate, or, as Addison described it, 'to give that majestic simplicity to nature, which we so much admire in the works of the ancients'. Far from being unusual, the treatment of these ten lines agrees closely with Dryden's manner of translation throughout the letter. Thus, to note but a few additional examples, Dryden masks the parenthetical force of 25, where Ovid lets Dido's passion erupt into expression, by connecting the line directly with the wife (*uxor*) of 24 and talking of a love that burns bright 'with purer light'. In 29–30, Ovid contrives a witty evocation of Catallus' famous *odi et amo*:

> non tamen Aenean, quamvis male cogitat, odi:
> sed queror infidum, questaque peius amo.

Dryden gratuitously replaces 29 and produces the following couplet:

> Myself I cannot to myself restore;
> Still I complain, and still I love him more.

In 31–2, Ovid allows Dido to break the illusion and wittily address Venus and Cupid: in the Latin, Aeneas is to play the soldier in Cupid's camp (*castris militet ille tuis*). Dryden shuns this coquettish female and so puts in her mouth a pathetic reference to 'my bleeding heart', then totally alters the soldier-image to achieve: 'And pierce thy brother's (sc. heart) with an equal dart.'[3] Whatever the poetic merit, the result in each case is to make the passage less Ovidian.

The critical terminology with which Dryden and Addison were operating – and which unfortunately still continues in use with too many classicists today – opposes witticism or wit to nature. What Addison required of Dido was natural simplicity; what he found in Ovid's Dido was unnatural artificiality in the form of wit. Without going into the somewhat biased definition of 'nature' used by Addison and Dryden, I propose to enlarge the scope of this Dryden–Ovid antithesis and get at the second major difference between Virgil and Ovid, to which I referred earlier. We might best start from that phrase 'majestic simplicity to nature', where, for our purposes, the key word is *majestic*. It is quite correct to call Virgil's portrait of Dido majestic, whereas that adjective cannot fit Ovid's Dido. If we accept the judgment and prejudice of critics like Dryden and Addison, then we can easily introduce a series of laudatory epithets parallel to *majestic* (e.g. grand, heroic, tragic, epic, powerful) to describe Virgil's highly successful portrait of Dido; but we see Ovid as a mere Virgil manqué, either trying and failing to make Dido majestic because of his lamentable witticism or trying to do something different from Virgil and making a silly, unnatural woman of the queen, a trivialized Dido. The problem lies in attributing such value to *majestic* that it becomes the criterion against which Ovid's achievement must be judged. I should rather view Ovid's Dido on his own terms, as unmajestic perhaps, but more importantly as fulfilling Ovid's new conception of the character, for whom he has created appropriate diction and a suitably limited dramatic context. Thus, instead of talking of Ovid's Dido as the negative or faulty version of Virgil's, I should prefer to use neutral terms for both and talk of a contrast between a *heroic* and a *charming* Dido.

Although Virgil's Dido does not confine herself to the decorum set by the Homeric heroines Andromache and Penelope, anyone would agree that his Dido is magnificent, heroic. He allows her occasionally to speak in unheroic terms (for example, when she voices the vain hope that she might have borne a *parvulus Aeneas*, to play in her palace after Aeneas leaves), and thereby he invites us to inspect the values for which Aeneas is supposed to stand, to which she is being sacrificed. The heroic is not for Virgil unequivocally good; it must be criticized and accepted only by conscious decision. For all that, however, Virgil regards it as central to his conception of Dido to insist that she is a queen as much as a woman. So long as she remains faithful to her responsibilities as queen it seems that she is also a successful and happy woman: she is both beautiful (*forma pulcherrima, Aen.*, 1. 496) and happy (*laeta*, 1. 540, *laetissima*, 1. 685 – with some irony). Once, however, she succumbs to passion, Virgil emphasizes her unhappiness (*infelix, miserrima*, starting at the end of Book 1 in line 749) and ignores her beauty.[4] There is no gratification in Dido's love; whereas her womanhood is not enhanced, her status as queen is dramatically undermined. The creative activities which define the building of her realm cease; rumours divide the Carthaginians; and neighbouring enemies see an opportunity to attack. When she makes her pleas to Aeneas, Virgil's Dido recognizes fully that she is a fallen queen as much as a fallen woman. In her judgment, she has lost all right or chance to continue in power, and accordingly she makes her appeals in order to hold on to the man for whom she gave up so much. However, after it becomes obvious that Aeneas will not alter his plans, Virgil allows his Dido to face her despair with grandeur, so that she strikes us as tragically majestic at the time of her suicide.

In her later speeches Dido expresses the national hatred of her Carthaginians for the Romans (IV. 622ff.), and she declares, after estimating her accomplishments, that she still retains *magna mei imago* (IV. 654). Thus, on one important level, Dido's death clearly points to the ultimate destruction of mighty Carthage by the Romans, one great power by another. Virgil is not exclusively interested in the personal pathos of Dido, nor does he concentrate solely on that aspect. Dido functions in subordination to the themes of the epic, which include personal motives and emotions in a larger framework that, in a crisis, requires personal to yield to public values. Moreover, he contrasts Dido's with Aeneas' pathos, her failure with his qualified success. Whereas she forsakes her queenly responsibilities to pursue her passion, Aeneas reluctantly forsakes his lover's duties to pursue his kingdom. Virgil never lets go of these heroic themes or the heroic characters that embody them.

If Virgil moves some distance from Homeric heroism in the direction of fuller psychological perception of his characters and so allows an uneasy tension to exist for a while between Dido the queen and Dido the woman, Ovid, on the other hand, moves right out of the heroic framework. His Dido emerges simply as a woman, a famous woman, but otherwise not to be distinguished from any woman about to be abandoned by the typically selfish male. As she views herself, the fact that she is a queen of Carthage has virtually no significance at the moment; she recognizes no responsibilities either for herself or Aeneas except those of love. Arguing for her love, she expresses a variety of emotions. Since, however, Ovid frees her from the grandeur and majesty Virgil sought, her arguments tend to produce an impression of a charming, even coquettish woman of passion. Nothing matters for her apart from her love for Aeneas. If she carries out her threat of suicide, it will be without shame for her un-queenly behaviour, without concern for her dead husband Sychaeus. Aeneas alone is to blame, she claims, with a final epigram that is more witty than pathetic: *praebuit Aeneas et causam mortis et ensem* (195) (Aeneas provided both the reason for death and the weapon).

Because Ovid deliberately circumscribes the range of Dido's interests and emotions, it is obvious that he produces a clash with Virgil's Dido that his Roman audience was expected to appreciate. By making the heroic queen into a charming woman, he pulls Dido out of her distant epic world and brings her to Augustan Rome. I do not think that we need assume that Ovid therefore negates the epic world and its value, but that he is amused, and expects to amuse us, by his humane and courtly representation of majestic Dido. Whether we emphasize the greater psychological concern of Ovid's portrait or use generic terms to argue that elegiac qualities have replaced the epic, the fact remains that Ovid was not 'measuring a sword' with Virgil (*pace* Dryden), but playing with Virgil's *Aeneid* and extracting from it, as from a capacious source, whatever might be useful. Consider two instances. It was a conventional fashion of conveying another's inhumanity to assert that no human mother bore him but that he was produced by savage beasts or the like. Virgil's Dido reacts violently to Aeneas' defence of his departure by erupting with such a charge of inhumanity (*Aen.*, IV. 365ff.). Ovid's Dido is, as we have noted, less violent and less majestic, so he handles this *topos* differently. In 29–30 Dido reports her dilemma of *odi et amo*. Then, under the spell of love, she appeals to Venus for help. But Ovid plans on using Venus in a double manner: as the goddess of love and as the mother of Aeneas. (Virgil avoids the ambivalence; his Dido appeals to Juno, never to Venus.) Arrogating to herself a false position, Dido asks Venus to spare her 'daughter-in-law' (Dido). She then avails herself of another double relation: Cupid as god of love and brother of Aeneas. (I have indicated above how this wit offended Dryden and was drastically attenuated in his translation.) All this is an innovation on Virgil, yet all the details lay ready in the *Aeneid* for Ovid's novel use. After she has played with these conceits Dido suddenly checks herself (35–6), denies the truth of Aeneas' divine origin and veers off for a while into the opposite extreme of hatred. A couplet suffices to accuse Aeneas of inhumanity (37–8) in Virgilian terms. However, again seeing a clever way of innovation and transition, Ovid adds one final term to the list of inhuman 'parents' and so dazzles us by his inventive transition

> aut mare, quale vides agitari nunc quoque ventis,
> quo tamen adversis fluctibus ire paras. (39–40)

(. . . or the [stormy] sea, such as the one you now watch stirred up by the winds, on which in spite of the hostile waves you are preparing to depart.)

Dido's charge vanishes as soon as she mentions the dangerous
sea, for it connotes more powerfully to her the peril Aeneas
faces. Her own love instinctively denies that the sea could be
related to her lover, for then it would logically be his ally and
assist him in his escape. Whereas Virgil's Dido remains in the
mood of tragic violence which she first expresses in the hyper-
bolical assertion that Aeneas was born of savage beasts in a wild
region, Ovid's Dido reaches this extreme only for a moment, then
reverts to her gentler mixture of love and complaint.

Again, one of Dido's most memorable appeals in the *Aeneid*
comes, located with maximum effectiveness, at the end of her
first attempt to dissuade Aeneas from leaving. 'If only I had had
a child by you, a baby Aeneas crawling happily about the palace
to remind me of you, that would be some comfort' (*Aen.*, IV.
327–30). Virgil has dramatically reduced Dido thereby to the
position of greatest humility, most basic humanity; and consequently the terms in which Aeneas must reply, self-controlled,
polite, tepidly grateful, legalistic, capture sympathy for Dido
and seem to justify her outburst against Aeneas' inhumanity.
Ovid turns this all around, to produce a momentary effect which
then, by an ingenious transition, he manipulates in a new manner.
For his Dido, having a baby by Aeneas represents no consolation
for desertion or for being exposed to surrounding enemies.
Rather, she converts it into a manifestly hypothetical argument
for holding Aeneas. 'Perhaps, you wretch,' she says, 'you are
leaving me pregnant' (133). That works into further innovations.
She pictures, not the happily playing *parvulus Aeneas*, but a
miserabilis infans, exposed to the same dangers as herself and
dying pathetically with her before birth! (135–6). Before this
detail becomes fixed in us, however, she rushes on to an entirely
new device, questioning the truth of Aeneas' divine guidance.

We may say, on the basis of these two passages and many others
like them, that Ovid converts every usable detail, whether from
narrative or direct speech, into an argument for his Dido. This
means that his Dido emerges as a woman signally endowed with
rhetorical ability, not at all incoherent and violent like Virgil's
Dido. It also means that we in the audience enjoy the cleverness
with which she manipulates details that, we know, have been
used differently in the source from which Ovid borrows. In fact,
the more one reads the *Heroides*, the more one realizes that Ovid's

speaker has regularly become a modern woman with a gift for artful argument instead of an antique heroine, and the more one relishes the way Ovid has drawn from noble subjects of epic and tragedy the charming portraits he has created. His is the art both of learned allusion and playful anachronism. Thus, he exploits Homer for the portraits of Penelope (*Epist.*, I) and Briseis (*Epist.*, III), Apollonius and his Roman imitators for Hypsipyle (*Epist.*, VI) and some of Medea (*Epist.*, XII), Euripides for other facets of Medea and for Phaedra (*Epist.*, IV) and Sophocles for Deianira (*Epist.*, IX), Catullus for Ariadne (*Epist.*, X) and probably Laodamia (*Epist.*, XIII), and, I think, Horace, *Odes*, III. 11 for Hypermnestra (*Epist.*, XIV). When reading Homer we would never imagine his Penelope or Briseis speaking in this Ovidian manner; indeed, it is a special *tour de force* for Ovid to have made a character out of Briseis, who in the *Iliad* plays a very subordinate role and speaks a mere fourteen lines – and those over Patroklos' corpse (*Il.*, XIX. 287ff.). But when we listen to Ovid, these famous characters from literary tradition spring to life in a charming new manner.

I said above that there is no need to assume that Ovid calls into question the heroic values of the *Aeneid*, and the same can be said when the source is Homeric epic or Greek tragedy. Ovid's women are not anti-heroic; they are represented as unaware of heroic criteria. It would have been relatively easy for Ovid to put words in his Dido's letter that would effectively attack Aeneas and expose him as the scoundrel that so many Romantics think him to be. After all, Virgil had amply sketched out the lines for such an attack. But Ovid was not interested in Aeneas except in so far as Dido understands him; and it is plain to us that Dido does not have the capacity to comprehend him. Therefore, even though she is writing a letter to him, she is not communicating with him because her words and ideas are basically beside the point. Another poet might take this situation, that of a great woman vainly trying to communicate her deepest feelings to a great man, and make it into noble poetry. Ovid, however, has made sure that we do not react to Dido or his other women as 'great'. As we have seen, his Dido is not viewed as a queen; and similarly she does not try to grasp Aeneas' heroic purposes. Instead, she is a woman of fears, anxieties, tears and complaints, pursuing her love with every feminine means, not by magniloquent appeals. Hopeless though her effort may be, so long as she speaks our attention concentrates on the vitality of this speaker, so clever, so changeable and by implication so hopeful.

Formally speaking, of course, the *Heroides* are composed in elegiac couplets. It would also be true to say that the concerns of these poems are appropriate to the elegiac genre: the irrelevance of heroism, the tearful, plaintive mood, the essential plot of unhappy love. I am not one, however, who believes that elegy and epic are two irreconcilable entities and that one explains all by labelling an Ovidian *Epistle* as elegy. It is obvious that Ovid was fascinated by the task of making grand poetry serviceable for his purposes. And he was not the first. Propertius before Ovid had repeatedly introduced examples from heroic myth into his love elegies in order to playfully 'dignify' his amatory passions and experiences with a heroic quality. That witty combination of pathos and humour which results from such an effort to heroize a mundane sentiment, a hallmark of Propertian elegy, explains in part our reactions to the *Heroides*. But Ovid has changed the tactics of contemporary elegy (including those of his own *Amores*) in two respects: he has concentrated on the girl's feelings instead of those of the poet-lover, and he has chosen to modernize a heroic situation instead of heroizing an everyday erotic situation. Both these changes result in the withdrawal of the presence of the poet-interpreter, who is so dynamically present in Ovid's other poetry.

If Ovid contrives to let the woman speak every line of the poem it is plain that he cannot intrude directly with commentary that influences our reactions. All he can do is to make the woman speak in such a way as to affect our interpretation. Thus the self-conscious and witty aspects of his Dido move us quite differently from the suicidal passions of Virgil's majestic figure. Moreover, since the woman speaks from an experience whose general outline is fixed by well-established myth, the poet cannot tamper radically with the plot. Nor does Ovid want to. That well-established myth serves him excellently: his interest lies in colouring the features of antique myth and early literary renditions with modern sophistication: to give charming eloquence to Homer's simple, faithful Penelope; to put coquettish words into the mouth of Briseis who, in the *Iliad*, had no character whatsoever; to make Phaedra seductive instead of the vengeful tragic female drama-

65

tized by Euripides and later Seneca. So Ovid's audience had the pleasure of encountering epic and tragic heroines as elegiac lovers who woo and complain about their lost loves with the typical strategies found in the elegists from Gallus to Ovid in the *Amores*.

In order to make these poems uninterrupted, unintroduced monologues, in which we come to know the female speaker exclusively through our reactions to her words and without any help from the narrator, Ovid resorted to the fiction of a letter. We are reading the letter, or, to be more accurate, we are peeking over the woman's shoulder as she is writing it. Sometimes the fiction is transparent, or even breaks down. Penelope's letter to Ulysses is apparently one of those she gives to almost every passing sailor, in the hope that it will reach her husband (*Epist.*, I. 61–2); but Ulysses never receives it. Ariadne writes to Theseus without even having someone at hand to deliver the letter. And Deianira, realizing that she has brought about Hercules' death, apparently breaks off her unsendable letter to him in order to express her despair before committing suicide; but the epistolary form remains unaffected.[5] A good part of Ovid's art consists in creating the illusion that we are indeed meeting these women directly; that the letters they write express their feelings with total spontaneity. And although we remain aware of his clever fiction, we are easily trapped into responding sympathetically to their unhappiness in love, especially because we know that these letters will not change in any way the situation that prompts their writing.

In the typical love elegy, the poet-lover, for all his complaints, sputtering anger and unhappiness, is close to a comic figure. He is in love with a dream of his own creation; and when the real woman who has inspired the dream turns out to be all too human (accordingly unfaithful or nasty or selfish or expensive), his disillusion and irrational attempts to cope with cruel reality are ineffective and silly. It is entirely true of Roman love elegy, to borrow the words of Rosalind in *As You Like It*, that no poet-lover ever dies of love. On the other hand, the *Heroides* cannot be called simply comic. I have said that we are charmed by Dido and her fellow letter-writers because we appreciate the clever way Ovid has modernized and humanized (in his special fashion) the ancient female figures of myth and early literature. For a variety of reasons, e.g. the Homeric avoidance of verbalizing feelings, the stereotyped attitude towards women, the decorum of epic and tragedy, none of Ovid's letter-writers was fully realized as a woman before the *Heroides*. Yet even if we recognize the elegiac fitness of viewing Dido's predicament as analogous to that of the lover-poet, and even if we relish the sophisticated argument that she puts together, we cannot completely forget the pre-scribed dramatic outlines within which, for a brief moment, she seems to move so freely. We admire the energy which a Dido can expend to preserve her love, but the myth prescribes that all that striking vitality is doomed. So Ovid has introduced a new note of genuine dramatic pathos into this novel kind of elegy. Dido, Phyllis and Phaedra will die for love as no poet-lover can do. All the heroines suffer radically, not merely in a silly juvenile way.

The closest analogue to Ovid's *Epistles* that we now possess is *Elegy*, IV. 3 of Propertius, in which the poet imagines a Roman wife, Arethusa, writing to her soldier husband in the East, expressing her deep loyalty to him. Like many critics, I consider it the prototype for Ovid's collection. We can see the powerful effect of the inventiveness in Propertius' Book IV not only in the *Heroides* but also in the *Fasti* and the *Metamorphoses*. What parti-cularly excited Ovid in the Arethusa elegy, it seems, was the dramatization of a woman's emotions through a total monologue, to express not the stereotyped Euripidean female fury but the softer sentiments of unhappy but still active love. Ovid then devised a new 'heroic' setting for his letters and a situation that stirs more pathos: instead of the everyday separation of husband and wife because of the man's military duties, we have an in-genious evocation of two mythological lovers, either precariously married or not married at all, whose separation is now usually a hopelessly unbridgeable chasm (as we know from the myth, though the 'heroine' clings to her fond hopes).[6] The antique 'heroic' setting keeps these elegies from being merely comic monologues. On the other hand, the many elegiac tactics which Ovid carried over from his *Amores*, his manifest wit and his patent display of ingenuity in the manipulation of Virgilian or Homeric nuances prevent the 'heroic' situation from effacing Ovid's characteristically sophisticated note. The fifteen mono-logues, therefore, represent a first productive blend of elegiac and grand poetry for Ovid, anticipating by as much as two decades the final masterpiece of blending, the *Metamorphoses*. But long before proceeding to that ultimate development, Ovid experimented with a new and also creative way of extending the range of the *Heroides*.

The Double Letters

Although there is considerable uncertainty as to precisely when Ovid wrote and published the *Heroides*, we are, I think, on safe ground in assuming that he composed the epistle of Dido within a decade of the *Aeneid*'s appearance and that *Heroides*, I–XV were available to the public (perhaps in an edition of three books) by 4 B.C.[7] During the next five years Ovid explored the role of *praeceptor amoris*, Master of Love, and brought out his various didactic works, three books of *Ars Amatoria*, the *Medicamina faciei femineae* and the *Remedia*, all in elegiacs. It is likely, too, that Ovid made his plans during this same five-year period for the *Fasti* and the *Metamorphoses*, but that most of the composition of these major poems took place within the six-year period A.D. 2–8, the years before Ovid was abruptly exiled by Augustus. These are years, then, of amazing creativity. And yet we must also find a place in the same period for six additional epistles that Ovid wrote and published as three pairs. Most scholars today assume that these 'double letters' were produced while Ovid was also involved with the *Fasti* and the *Metamorphoses*. There seem to be enough differences between *Heroides*, I–XV and XVI–XXI to warrant the hypothesis of a definite hiatus of time between the groups, and the expansiveness and narrative techniques of XVI–XXI seem to reflect qualities evident in the later *Fasti* and *Metamorphoses*.[8]

Much scholarly time and effort have been poured into the controversy of whether these double letters are genuinely the work of Ovid.[9] We must not smile contemptuously and declare that all such effort was wasted. However, much of this controversy has been characterized by unpoetic imagination and philological myopia. In defence of the advocates pro and contra genuineness, we may say that the same nineteenth century that concentrated on this kind of problem could hardly tolerate Ovid the poet because of his un-Romantic attitudes, and accordingly, although these scholars laboured in a largely sterile field, at least they did, if for the wrong reasons, keep reading Ovid. Now that *Heroides*, XVI–XXI can be safely credited to Ovid, it is possible – and some beginnings have been made – to appreciate the innovative art that Ovid there displays.[10]

In order to get at what is new in XVI–XXI, we may first summarize the salient aspects of I–XV in terms of a series of elegiac *topoi*. These dramatic monologues are, we recall, letters written by heroines who find themselves in generally similar circumstances: they are separated from the man they love, to whom they have entirely committed themselves, whether as legitimate wife, would-be wife, or lover. Although the reasons for separation vary, the heroines tend to respond to it similarly, feeling abandoned, complaining about the coldness and slowness and cruelty of the absent male. In his *Metamorphoses* Ovid produces an incisive epitome of the situation and the principal *topoi* for the case of Ariadne:

> protinus Aegides rapta Minoide Diam
> vela dedit comitemque suam *crudelis* in illo
> litore destituit. *desertae et multa querenti*
> amplexus et opem Liber tulit. (*Met.*, VIII, 174–7)

(Immediately Theseus seized Ariadne and sailed to Dia [Naxos], where he cruelly abandoned his companion on the seashore. As the deserted girl complained long and loud, Bacchus came to her with kisses and help.)

It is plain that Ovid shows little sympathy for Ariadne's plight in this sketch, but he does not need to. His audience should easily catch the allusions to elegiac *topoi* from *Heroides*, x. The basic tone of *Heroides*, I–XV is complaint; the verb *queror*, which regularly emerges from the lips of the heroines, occurs more frequently in the *Heroides* than in any other Ovidian work. This accords with the standard mood of elegy which, because of its formalized plaintiveness, could be generically defined by Horace, Propertius and Ovid with the word *querela*.[11] The plaintive heroine regards herself as alone, deserted, abandoned (*sola, deserta, relicta*). Deep in her memory is fixed the scene of her parting from her beloved. More often than not, he left after long moments of passionate kisses and fervent promises to return; but occasion-

69

ally the circumstances were different. Nevertheless, all the heroines believe that they have a claim on the man: an explicit or implicit *foedus* or bond links the two, which imposes *fides*, loyalty, on them both. The heroines have remained faithful (*fida*) and regularly represent themselves as still loving (*amans*), but the long absence of the man, perhaps also information about his disloyal behaviour, leads to complaints, unhappy charges that he is anywhere from slow to respond (*lentus*) and iron-hearted (*ferreus*) all the way to cruel (*crudelis*), criminal (*sceleratus*) and faithless (*perfidus*). The heroine hopes, usually in vain as we know, by these complaints to stir the conscience of her beloved and so bring him home, to re-create the *foedus* and the once-glorious context of reciprocal passion.[12]

In *Heroides*, xvi–xxi Ovid creates situations that differ among themselves as well as from the earlier letters, and the basic tone does not match the complaints of I–xv. Moreover, instead of the monologue of an unhappy woman he now devises a context in which first a male writes to a female, then she responds. For xvi and xvii he produces an exchange of letters between Paris and Helen, supposedly written while Paris was a guest in Menelaus' house and just beginning his efforts to seduce his lovely hostess. His letter sounds like that of one who has mastered the lessons of Ovid's *Ars Amatoria*, whereas her reply reveals a clever, reasonably loyal wife who understands fully the character of Paris and will resist his advances for some time. In xviii and xix, on the other hand, Ovid studies two young people who are sincerely in love. Leander writes to Hero to explain why he has been unable to spend another passionate night with her – because of the terrible weather that makes swimming the Hellespont fatally dangerous – and she replies with complaints. We know that her complaints against Leander are groundless and that they will produce the paradoxical result of sending him into the treacherous water and bringing him to Hero as a corpse. None of the *Heroides*, I–xv ever reached its destination or had any effect, least of all this fatal result of a 'tragic return'. Again, xx and xxi take a different direction and concentrate on a young man, Acontius, who for some time has loved Cydippe without her realizing it – she is far less experienced and observant than Helen – and has enlisted the powers of Diana to overcome her resistance, and the girl Cydippe whose letter represents the response of a virginal young maiden to the sudden and totally unexpected declaration of love from a man. She complains because Acontius has caused her to fall sick and she is physically miserable. But she definitely feels none of the emotional torment of Hero, let alone the earlier cast of forlorn women in I-xv. The men's letters, then, are totally new, and the women's letters, because addressed to a tangibly close man, written in reply to his advances and reflecting that early stage of love where the woman has some or all the advantages, must adopt a different manner from that of the complaining abandoned female (*desertae et multa querenti*) in *Heroides*, I-xv.

It is generally noted, and quite correctly, that in these letters which are planned as pairs the poet has subordinated the man's letter to the woman's. Neither Paris nor Leander nor Acontius finds himself in a complex situation, and consequently none of them utters very complicated or penetrating feelings. The main purpose of the man's letter is to propel the woman into a dynamic situation where her feelings must be complex, where, at least in the case of Helen and Cydippe, she must struggle towards a difficult decision in her reply. Although she complains about the pressure to which she is being subjected, about the improper importunities of the male, she obviously does not experience that near-tragic unhappiness of the deserted women of *Heroides*, I-xv, for those very importunities constitute a pleasant experience, too. In some respects, then, Ovid has taken Helen and Cydippe and placed them now in the dominating position of the unresponsive men, addressees of the letters in I-xv. They are making a crucial decision for love, not desperately trying to recapture a love that has long escaped them. Inevitably, then, as Ovid correctly planned it, our interest focuses on the complex way in which the women respond to new and exciting pressures.

The situation of Hero and Leander differs considerably from that of the other pairs, and indeed bears some superficial resemblance to that of the earlier letters. Therefore, before we concentrate on the more complicated emotions of Helen and Cydippe, let us first consider Hero, in order to establish more precisely what new directions Ovid has chosen in these double letters. Leander, who has enjoyed the passionate love of Hero, has left her and promised to return. But he has failed to keep his promise. If we summarize the background in that manner, it might seem that Hero's complaint would fit ideally with those in the earlier elegies. However, we have obviously distorted the situation. In the first place, the lovers have not been separated months or years, but a mere week (cf. xviii. 25). Secondly, Leander is more than eager to rejoin Hero and resume their passionate embraces. It is not his fault, but the violent weather on the Hellespont prevents him from reaching his beloved. Accordingly one result of his letter is to establish beyond question what the myth demanded, that Leander continues to burn with passion for Hero. Thirdly, because their love is so fresh and constant, both tend to remember its supremely happy moments, not its pathetic scenes. Each, in a rapturous portion of his letter, recalls how Leander arrived at Sestos, emerged naked and glistening from the water and rushed into the arms of Hero there on the shore, how arm in arm they moved to her tower and a long night of joyous passion. This emphasis sharply contrasts with the standardized narrative sequence of the earlier letters: the sad parting of lovers at the shore and the woman's misery as she watches her beloved's ship disappear on the horizon. The highpoint of Leander's letter recapitulates this glorious arrival (xviii. 55ff.), starting from the moment he plunged into the tranquil waters beneath a romantic moon. I quote the happy lines that record his landfall and union with Hero:

> cum vero possum cerni quoque, protinus addis
> spectatrix animos, ut valeamque facis:
> nunc etiam nando dominae placuisse laboro   95
> atque oculis iacto bracchia nostra tuis.
> te tua vix prohibet nutrix descendere in altum
> – hoc quoque enim vidi, nec mihi verba dabas –
> nec tamen effecit, quamvis retinebat euntem,
> ne fieret prima pes tuus udus aqua.   100
> excipis amplexu feliciaque oscula iungis,
> oscula, di magni! trans mare digna peti,
> eque tuis demptos umeris mihi tradis amictus
> et madidam siccas aequoris imbre comam.
> cetera nox et nos et turris conscia novit,   105
> quodque mihi lumen per vada monstrat iter.

(When I can be seen, too, then you give me inspiration and strength as you watch. Now I strain to please my beloved by

swimming, and I vigorously move my arms before your eyes.
Scarcely can your nurse prevent you from plunging into the
water – I saw that; you didn't just pretend – and even though
she grabbed you, she could not stop you from getting your
feet wet in the breakers. You welcome me in your arms and
give me rapturous kisses, kisses – o wow – worth a swim
across the ocean! You take a shawl from your shoulders and
give it to me, then dry my dripping hair. As for the rest, the
night and we and the familiar tower know all, as does also
the light which shows me the way to you through the waves.)

That memory, which to Leander is still so vivid that he narrates
it as a present experience, is matched in Hero's letter by her vivid
dream (XIX. 57ff.), a passionate complaint that reveals her own
vivid feelings:

> forsitan invitus mecum tamen, improbe, dormis
>   et, quamquam non vis ipse venire, venis:
> nam modo te videor prope iam spectare natantem,
>   bracchia nunc umeris umida ferre meis,   60
> nunc dare, quae soleo, madidis velamina membris,
>   pectora nunc iuncto nostra fovere sinu.
> multaque praeterea linguae reticenda modestae,
>   quae fecisse iuvat, facta referre pudet.
> me miseram! brevis est haec et non vera voluptas;   65
>   nam tu cum somno semper abire soles.

(Even though perhaps you are unwilling, you wretch, you
still sleep with me; even though you don't want to come,
you do. For I seem to watch you as you are swimming ever
closer, then feel your wet arms go around my shoulders,
then, as I always do, put my shawl on your dripping body
and warm you against me as we hug each other. And there
are many other things which a modest tongue must not say,
a pleasure to have done but shameful to recount. Poor me! It's
a brief insubstantial pleasure, because you always vanish with
my sleep.)

What Ovid represents, then, with Hero and Leander is
genuinely happy, passionate love, not despair. The absence
which Hero complains about above has been brief and in-
voluntary, and all the plaintive terms she uses that seem to echo

the earlier heroines (e.g. *improbe* 57, *lente morator* 70, *socii desertor amoris* 157) serve rather to reveal Hero's misunderstanding of the situation, the result of her consuming passion. Yet it is from these very complaints that Ovid extracts, with supreme irony, the motivation for the death of Leander. No other account of this love story develops this way: we are simply told that Leander eventually met heavy seas that were too much for his swimming and so drowned. Ovid ingeniously makes Hero's half-sincere complaints work so effectively on the already eager Leander that he foolishly commits himself to the stormy Hellespont and is drowned, thus fulfilling the foreboding that both he and Hero have had.[13] Their genuine passion results in a fatal reunion.

Ovid's ingenuity in shaping the story of Hero and Leander is matched by the cleverness with which he adapts the story of Acontius and Cydippe. Scholars have long known that Ovid was working with a very successful elegy that the great Alexandrian poet Callimachus had included in Book III of his *Aetia*. Since the *Aetia* ostensibly accounted for certain ritual practices, odd statues, sayings, and the like, scholars suspected that Callimachus did not concentrate exclusively on a love affair, but also explained something, possibly the use of apples in love or possibly the origin of a clan on the island of Ceos. With the recovery of some valuable papyri from Egyptian Oxyrhynchus it has been possible only in this century to see what Callimachus did with his story. Two extensive fragments, one of fourteen lines from the beginning, the other of seventy-seven lines from the end, help us to reconstruct a typically charming Callimachean narrative. For our purposes the most important fact to know is that Callimachus did not take much interest at all in the personality of Cydippe, and he did work with Acontius in such a way as to make him the typical romantic hero.[14] Cydippe was the standard beauty whom every mother wants for her son, but little else about her was relevant to the Greek elegy. Thus in the long fragment we plunge into the predicament caused by her repeated illnesses on the eve of her wedding. Callimachus merely reported the sickness; he ignored her feelings, if any, and he did not invite us to hear her speak or speculate on her thoughts. Rather than allow Cydippe the chance to reveal her inclinations for Acontius and promote their marriage by some decisive action of her own,

Callimachus gave all the action and decision to her father. Accordingly, when Ovid decided to use the earlier elegy as the basis for double letters, he found ample area in which to exercise his ingenuity.

Ovid makes the occasion of the exchange of letters the period when Cydippe has been sick a third time and her father has sent off to Delphi for advice. Acontius seizes his chance to write to her and reveal his love and the cruel way Diana is punishing her for neglecting her unintentional promise to marry him. The letter does him little credit. He betrays no moral sensibility, few compunctions about the suffering he has caused Cydippe, but we do at least believe that he loves the girl. In his egotistic fashion he acts as though Cydippe must know who he is, and he urges her to confide in her mother how she first met him:

> ordine fac referas ut sis mihi cognita primum,   205
>   sacra pharetratae dum facis ipsa deae,
> ut te conspecta subito, si forte notasti,
>   restiterim fixis in tua membra genis,
> et, te dum nimium miror, nota certa furoris,
>   deciderint umeris pallia lapsa meis.   210

(Be sure you tell her in sequence how I first became
acquainted with you, while you were sacrificing to Diana,
how, as soon as I saw you, in case you noticed, I stood still,
my eyes riveted on your limbs, and, while I admired you
extravagantly, a sure sign of passion, my mantle slipped off
my shoulders.)

In this cleverly indirect description of that standardized situation, love at first sight, Acontius calls to Cydippe's imagination what of course she never noticed earlier.

Whereas Acontius pursues without distraction the simple goal of winning Cydippe, she finds herself in an awkward and painful situation. She has a perfectly eligible fiancé chosen by her father, whom she has been ready to marry without objection until these strange attacks of sickness. And now another man suddenly writes to her to claim her as his rightful bride, guaranteed to him by Diana because of the promise he has tricked from the girl's lips. Cydippe's letter shows how she faces her difficulties. Her first reaction is surprise and indignation, and she attempts some withering wit:

> haec nobis formae te laudatore superbae
>   contingit merces et placuisse nocet?
> si tibi deformis, quod mallem, visa fuissem,
>   culpatum nulla corpus egeret ope. (XXI. 35–8)

(Is this the reward for my proud beauty when you praise it; is it dangerous to have pleased you? If I had seemed ugly to you, as I would prefer, my blemished body would now need no doctor.)

How can he hurt the woman he claims he loves? (59) Then she reviews the unhappy events which have led to Acontius' advantage over her (67ff.). She never admits to having seen him there on Delos. And she protests at this underhand method of 'conquering' her:

> improbe, quid gaudes et quae tibi gloria parta est,
>   quidve vir elusa virgine laudis habes? (117–18)

(Wretch, why do you exult, what glory have you won? What fame do you possess, a man who has tricked a girl?)

She vigorously rejects the legal claims that Acontius has attempted to assert over her.[15] Still, afraid of Diana, she piteously tells of her agony and appeals for sympathy to both goddess and lover. Another bitterly witty paradox acts as transition to a new sequence:

> cur, quae succenset, quod adhuc tibi pacta puella
>   non tua sit, fieri ne tua possit, agit?
> omnia de viva tibi sunt speranda: quid aufert
>   saeva mihi vitam, spem tibi diva mei? (185–8)

(Why does Diana, who is angry that your beloved is not plighted to you as yours, bring it about that she cannot possibly become yours? All your hopes depend on my living. Why does the savage goddess rob me of life and you of the hope of possessing me?)

There may be some indication in these words that Cydippe is beginning to take some interest in Acontius' hopes. At any rate, we next hear her protesting at the false impressions Acontius cherishes about her fiancé (191ff.). While she has been sick in bed, her fiancé has visited her, but she has never encouraged him to take the slightest liberties! Indeed she has turned her back on him and made the poor simpleton believe that she is angry at him. Perhaps she has been disappointed with his timidity; perhaps she now contrasts it unfavourably with Acontius' impetuosity. Aware, however, that she has betrayed her inclinations for Acontius (206), she coyly plays with the etymology of his name, acts coquettishly about her beauty – as if he might now spurn her after her wasting sickness – and finally surrenders: *doque libens victas in tua vota manus* (I freely surrender myself to your will – 242). In short, Ovid has through her letter created a dramatic portrait of a woman slowly responding to love, at first spirited and indignant, then piteous, and finally melting. None of the heroines in i–xv achieves this range of emotions.

Ovid permits Acontius to use a witty reference to Paris that indicates how similarly these two lovers behave:

> non sum, qui soleam Paridis reprehendere factum,
>   nec quemquam, qui vir, posset ut esse, fuit. (xx. 49–50)

(I am not one to criticize the deed of Paris, nor indeed anyone who was a man in order that he might act the part of a man.)[16]

Paris, in the first of the double letters, aims simply and ruthlessly at the same goal as Acontius: to make Helen his wife regardless of her wishes and prior commitments. He, too, talks confidently of the favour of a goddess, for Venus has promised him Helen when he declared her more beautiful than Juno or Minerva. He, too, deprecates the woman's prior responsibilities to another man, even though, in this instance, that man is Helen's husband and Paris' generous host, Menelaus. Naïvely trusting his guest and his wife, Menelaus has gone off on necessary business to Crete. And Ovid imagines that Paris makes his first direct assault on Helen's loyalty in this letter. Since his tactics follow pretty much the familiar ones of Acontius and the earlier *Ars Amatoria*, and since Ovid organized the letter more to set off Helen's reply than to evoke much interest in Paris, let us concentrate our attention, as expected, on Helen.

The portrait of Helen is probably the most sympathetic to emerge from antiquity. This woman, who is about to commit adultery with a mere libertine and thereby bring on an international war that costs incalculable suffering and waste, emerges, in her letter, a sensitive, clever, morally aware, sensual, responsive woman, one whom it is difficult not to like. Unlike Cydippe, she does not weaken, partly because of the obvious pressure of the goddess, for she has experienced none of the debilitating illnesses of the younger girl. And she is not unaware of Paris' intentions nor so naïve as Cydippe in reacting to the man's bold admiration and designs on her virtue. However, when she has discredited most of Paris' arguments, she still cannot veil her interest in the man and encouragement of his advances, for she sees something in Paris that may not in fact be there, but represents what she needs and wants, her idea of love. Ovid in no way defends her adultery; he does attempt to understand her motivations as fully as possible and to show that she was acting from some of the better human principles. To put it somewhat strongly, her inclinations for love entitle her to the role of heroine along with Ovid's other women of the *Heroides*.

Like Cydippe, Helen starts off by complaining about the pressures Paris is exerting on her virtue, but she puts it with greater sophistication:

> nec dubito, quin haec, cum sit tam iusta, vocatur
> rustica iudicio nostra querela tuo. (XVII. 11–12)

(I have no doubt, in your judgment, my complaint would be called rustic, despite its justice.)

As she well knows, Paris will use the typical courtly arguments of Augustan times and try to 'shame' her into compliance by calling her rustic, saying, in our terms, that she is 'not with it'. But she knows how to hold firm against such cavalier devices. Chastity is more important than being 'with it'. Nor does Paris move her by his all too familiar male assertion that other women yield to love: she knows what counts (41ff.). Nor does she feel the slightest excitement over Paris' noble ancestry, his royal family, and the tremendous wealth of Troy (51ff.). What counts with her is feeling and personal commitment, not superficial things like money and reputation. And at this point she betrays a possible interest in the person of Paris, if his trivial arguments, once dispelled, leave behind a man capable of winning her passion:

> sed si iam vellem fines transire pudoris,
> tu melior culpae causa futurus eras.
> aut ego perpetuo famam sine labe tenebo,
> aut ego te potius quam tua dona sequar. (67–70)

(But if I wanted to overstep the limits of chastity, you would have been a better reason. Either I shall keep my reputation forever unblemished, or I shall follow you, not your gifts.)

She has noticed Paris, which means she has appreciated his handsome appearance and been both annoyed and excited by his indelicate and indiscreet attempts to attract her attention even when Menelaus was present (75 ff.). While admitting that, however, she insists on her loyalty to her husband. Of course, if she were unmarried, she would prefer him to any suitor, to any of the thousand suitors who once wooed her (including Menelaus).

> ut tamen optarem fieri tua Troica coniunx,
> invitam sic me nec Menelaus habet. (109–10)

(Even though I might wish to be your wife at Troy, Menelaus has me now not at all unwillingly.)

But her protests ring hollow: she feels unwilling in her marriage. Thus, though she dismisses Paris' casuistry in regard to Menelaus' departure (155 ff.), she encourages him fearfully to take advantage of her husband's gullibility (*simplicis viri* 176).

> et libet et timeo, nec adhuc exacta voluntas
> est satis: in dubio pectora nostra labant. (177–8)

(I am simultaneously inclined towards you and afraid of you, and my wishes are not yet fully worked out: my heart is divided, undecided.)

The rest of the letter elaborates on this hesitation. She wonders how Paris will treat her in the long run, once he knows she can be adulterous. She questions her reception in Troy. She rejects his specious claims that there will be no war or, if war comes,

that Troy will easily prevail. Certainly, Paris will prove no
military hero:

> apta magis Veneri, quam sunt tua corpora Marti:
>   bella gerant fortes; tu, Pari, semper ama.
> Hectora quem laudas pro te pugnare iubeto:
>   militia est operis altera digna tuis.
> his ego, si saperem pauloque audacior essem,
>   uterer; utetur, siqua puella sapit.
> ast ego deposito faciam fortasse pudore
>   et dabo cunctatas tempore victa manus. (253–60)[17]

(Your body is more fit for love than war. Let heroes wage
war; Paris, devote yourself to love at all times. Ask Hector,
whom you praise so highly, to fight for you. A different
service suits your talents. And if I had sense and were a
little bolder, I would take advantage of those talents; any
sensible girl would. Perhaps indeed I shall do so, abandoning
my chastity, surrendering to you after long hesitation.)

Thus, like Cydippe, she is almost ready to capitulate at the end
of her letter.

Helen has a line which may unwittingly allude to the fundamental
situation of *Heroides*, I–XV and mark the innovations Ovid
achieves in his double letters:

> nec quod *abest* hic me tecum mirare *relictam*. (173)

(Just because he is away, don't be surprised that I am left
with you.)

The earlier heroines lamented inconsolably because their lovers
were away and they were left *alone* to their misery. In their
despair they tried to argue for a love to which they had fully,
often tragically, committed themselves, with a man who sooner
or later felt free of such commitment. When he planned the
double letters Ovid wanted to explore this commitment to love,
the fundamental theme of almost all his great poetry, from a
different perspective, namely, at its initial stages. So Hero is
dealing with a lover who has been away for a week, against
his will, and her letter breathes strong physical passion, not the
despair of long privation. And Helen is caught in a triangle,

which Ovid has emphasized in the line cited above by the grouping of the three pronouns. The absence of Menelaus leaves her
not with her despair, but with the all-too-attractive Paris. And
that means that she is caught in the kind of tension between
chastity and love, *pudor* and *amor*, that Ovid finds increasingly
worth studying in his years of greatest achievement. For my part,
I read her letter with greater admiration for her and her poet-
creator than I do the letter of Dido or her complaining sisters
of *Heroides*, i–xv. It may be that I merely respond more readily
to scenes of hopeful love than I do to sentimental pictures of lost
love, but I tell myself, at least sometimes, that Ovid has indeed
made advances in the way he understands the process by which
people do commit themselves to worthwhile feelings regardless
of practical considerations and social taboos. In my opinion, he
is now mature enough to produce his finest stories of the *Metamorphoses*. In that long poem, he would use the epistolary form
to enhance one narrative, the love of Byblis (*Met.*, IX. 515ff.).
And he would have been lucky if that had been his last poetic
epistle. Little did Ovid realize that he himself would soon be
separated from all he loved, forsaken in exile on the Black Sea,
forced to speak once again by epistle in the plaintive tone of
hopelessness in order to bridge the unbridgeable distance between
himself and his wife and friends, between bleak Tomi and vital
Rome.[18] Fate and unappreciative Augustus would reduce him
to the despair of the women in *Heroides*, i–xv which he had once
imagined so brilliantly.

Notes

1 The able nineteenth-century editor, Arthur Palmer, felicitous in textual
criticism but confined by Victorian constraints on poetic imagination,
worked hard to dispose of the line's difficulties. Earlier critics had
voiced disapproval of the pair *moveri-movimus* because, although the
manuscripts solidly guaranteed the readings, the critics, unable to
extract special meaning from the repetition, assumed that their prejudice was right and the reading of *movimus* wrong. So they set about
emending. An easy change to *novimus* makes no sense; but a change
almost as easy to *vovimus* plainly asserts the prayer-context. Heinsius,
the greatest Ovidian scholar of all time, adopted *vovimus*. Now when
Palmer reviewed the emendation, he rightly rejected it, but for the
wrong reasons. He declared: 'There is little likelihood in the conjecture
vovimus; no prayer has been mentioned.' An incredible comment, made
all the worse by Palmer's proposed translation of the received text:

'I begin this letter.' Line 3 has explicitly referred to a prayer (*prece*), and knowing the way Ovid handles his couplets, we have good reason to expect him to continue the context. There is, however, a difference between *prex* and *votum* which justifies the rejection of *vovimus*. The speaker is simply pleading, supplicating, here; she is not trying to bribe the deity by vowing an offering (*votum*) so that he will grant her a favour. Therefore, while rejecting *vovimus* for its wrong kind of prayer, we must try to make sense of *movimus* in the context of supplication. See A. Palmer, *P. Ovidi Nasonis Heroides* (Oxford, 1898), 339, in his note on line 4.

2 Dryden relied on a text rendered popular by Heinsius. He read *vovimus* in 4 and marked no questions in 8 or 10.

3 Throughout his translation Dryden reduces Ovidian wit (e.g. at 61–2, 73, 149) and expands the Latin in order to stress a pathos not in the original (e.g. at 91, 95, 99).

4 Only to emphasize how once-beautiful Dido has disgraced herself does Virgil refer to her as *pulchra* after the end of Book I (in IV. 192).

5 For the change in Deianira, see *Epist.*, IX. 143ff.

6 For a valuable comparison of Propertius' techniques in IV. 3 and Ovid's in *Epist.*, XIII, see H. Merklin, 'Arethusa und Laodamia', *Hermes*, 96 (1968), 461–94.

7 The second edition of Ovid's *Amores* appeared in 4 B.C. In II. 18. 21ff. of that collection, Ovid refers to *Epistles* 1, 2, 4, 5, 6, 7, 10, 11 and 15.

8 The fundamental work on the relative chronology of I–XV and XVI–XXI remains that of W. Kraus, 'Die Briefpaare in Ovids Heroides', *Wiener Studien*, 65 (1950), 54–77; now reprinted in *Wege der Forschung* (1968), 461–94.

9 See, for example, W. Zingerle, *Untersuchungen zur Echtheitsfrage der Heroiden Ovids* (Innsbruck, 1878); S. B. Clark, 'The Authorship and the Date of the Double Letters in Ovid's Heroides', *Harvard Studies in Classical Philology*, 19 (1908), 121–55; B. Latta, *Die Stellung der Doppelbriefe (Heroides 16–21) im Gesamtwerk Ovids* (dissertation, Marburg, 1963); E. Courtney, 'Ovidian and Non-Ovidian Heroides', *Bulletin Institute of Classical Studies*, 12 (1965), 63–6; and now V. A. Tracy, 'The Authenticity of *Heroides* 16–21', *Classical Journal*, 66 (1971), 328–30.

10 See especially E. J. Kenney, 'Liebe als juristisches Problem: Über Ovids Heroides 20 and 21', *Philologus*, 111 (1967), 212–32.

11 In his elegiac works Ovid employs the verb *queror* as follows: *Amores*, ten times; *Ars*, nine; *Fasti*, eleven; *ex Ponto*, fifteen; *Tristia*, ten; but *Heroides*, forty-one. There are twenty-six instances of *queror* in the *Metamorphoses*, of which some, such as the lines quoted from VIII. 174ff., refer to a standard lament of amatory elegy (cf. X. 76). For *querela* in a generic sense, see Horace, *Odes*, II. 9. 18, Propertius, I. 6.11.

12 There are of course exceptions to this typology: Phaedra (*Epist.*, IV) has never enjoyed Hippolytus' love, but attempts to seduce him through her letter; Canace (*Epist.*, XI) makes no accusations against Macareus as she prepares to kill herself in obedience to her father's command; and Hypermnestra, who has saved Lynceus (*Epist.*, XIV), obviously

cannot accuse him of deserting her. Any typology involves distortions, as can be seen in the otherwise valuable article of H. Dorrie, 'Die dichterische Absicht Ovids in den *Epistulae Heroidum*', *Antike und Abendland*, 13 (1967), 41–55.

13 Cf. XVIII. 191ff. and XIX. 191ff.

14 We know from surviving Callimachean fragments and from the imitative account of Aristaenetus that the Greek elegy portrayed Acontius languishing for love in the forest, writing Cydippe's name on the trees. This emphasis would be natural if, as seems likely, Callimachus was accounting for the Akontiadae on Ceos.

15 Kenney has ably analysed this theme in the article cited above in note 10.

16 Ovid uses *vir*, in two senses, to refer to man with respect to bravery and boldness and to allude to the sexual rights of a husband (also *vir*). My translation attempts to preserve the wit.

17 In 259 I accept the emendation *ast* of Bornecque and in 260 *cunctatas* of Palmer.

18 On the *Tristia* and *ex Ponto* as a continuation of themes from the *Heroides*, see H. Rahn, 'Ovids elegische Epistel', *Antike und Abendland*, 7 (1958), 105–20.

III

The Ars Amatoria *and* Remedia Amoris

A. S. Hollis

Until recently the *Ars Amatoria* has been more or less taboo, and conspicuously absent from school and university classical courses. As a result many literate non-specialists consider it a very naughty poem; they cannot be blamed for this opinion when professional scholars have thrown out such comments as 'shameless compendium of profligacy' or 'vade mecum in wantonness'.[1] Fulminations of this kind, besides being unfair to Ovid, are liable to distort the understanding of those who do penetrate to reading the *Ars* – finding it not such a naughty piece after all, they may think it poor stuff and overlook the real qualities of the gayest and wittiest among Ovid's love poems. But since the *Ars Amatoria* is known to have been a partial cause of Ovid's exile and thereafter was removed from the public libraries,[2] perhaps we should examine briefly the charges which might be or actually were brought against it; in the end we may be led on to a truer appreciation of the poem's nature. Most of our information derives from the remarkable 'open letter to Augustus' (*Tristia*, II) composed in exile. We must remember the varying pressures on Ovid, to offer a defence without implying that Augustus had made a fool of himself in condemning him and to plead not so much for restoration to Rome (which would have been unrealistic) as for a more hospitable place of banishment. Personally I think that Ovid's defence of the *Ars* is on the whole well-founded, and that the most striking parts of *Tristia*, II are those where he warms to his task and even says more than prudence would dictate in such circumstances.

First of all we can clear out of the way one possible objection to the *Ars*. No Roman could well have considered it obscene; their tradition, both in oratory and verse, was for considerable frankness in sexual matters. Indeed the future emperor Augustus as a young man had written lines against Antony expressed with what Martial[3] calls 'Roman simplicity'. For the Latin equivalent of four-letter words one must go to Catullus, and for a technical description of sexual intercourse to Lucretius, IV. Ovid does not approach either; certainly his *Ars Amatoria* is not a manual of sexual technique, but rather an 'Art of Courtship'.[4]

A charge that the poem undermined marriage was definitely made (*Tristia*, II. 345–6). Ovid foresaw this, and tried to forestall it by the statement that he was writing only about *hetaerae* (high-class courtesans who would probably be freedwomen), not about respectable married women (*A.A.*, I. 31–4):

> este procul, vittae tenues, insigne pudoris,
> quaeque tegis medios instita longa pedes:
> nos Venerem tutam concessaque furta canemus
> inque meo nullum carmine crimen erit.

(Away, away, all who wear narrow head-bands, symbols of modesty, and long skirts which cover half the feet. Our subject will be safe love-making, and amusements allowed by the law, so my poem will contain nothing objectionable.)

In defending himself Ovid constantly returns to these lines.[5] One could object that married women still might profit from instruction meant for others (*Tristia*, II. 253ff.), but this takes the *Ars* too seriously. It was not really intended as a practical guide to ensnaring the opposite sex, any more than Virgil really intended his *Georgics* to be a practical handbook of farming which would supplant Varro's prose treatise. The work's didactic form was something of a façade; as for the subject-matter, this rested for the most part upon a background of Greek epigram and Roman love-elegy which itself contained a high degree of convention. So on two counts the *Ars* had only a tenuous and intermittent connexion with real life. Ovid makes both these points in *Tristia*, II, but Augustus either failed to understand, or, more probably, pretended not to understand. Similarly Cicero, when attacking L. Piso, pretended that the erotic epigrams of his protégé Philodemus accurately represented the goings-on in Piso's household, although he must have been aware that the poems were merely conventional.[6] The most one can fairly say is that the general atmosphere of the *Ars* was unhelpful to Augustus' policy of moral reform.

Could it be that Ovid is basically opposed to the Augustan régime, and showed it in his writings, so that the charge against his poetry did not rest on moral grounds alone? This theory has gained a number of adherents among modern scholars and certainly deserves a run for its money. When Ovid advises the girls to arrange their admirers in the same way as the emperor makes his military appointments, the introductory couplet hardly lessens his cool audacity (*A.A.*, III. 525ff.):

> quis vetat a magnis ad res exempla minores
> sumere nec nomen pertimuisse ducis?
> dux bonus[7] huic centum commisit vite regendos,
> huic equites, illi signa tuenda dedit:
> vos quoque, de nobis quem quisque erit aptus ad usum,
> inspicite et certo ponite quemque loco.
> munera det dives; ius qui profitebitur, adsit . . .

(Why should I not illustrate my trivialities from great affairs, and dare to mention the Leader's name? Our good Leader makes one man a centurion, another a commander of cavalry, yet another a standard-bearer. You too must observe what profit you can derive from each of us, and arrange each in the appropriate place. Let the rich man give you presents, and the lawyer represent you in court . . .)

After a charming digression on the Rape of the Sabine Women, whereby Romulus provided a wife for his soldiers, Ovid adds in conclusion (I. 131–2):

> Romule, militibus scisti dare commoda solus:
> haec mihi si dederis commoda, miles ero.

(Nobody has ever seen to his soldiers' comforts like you, Romulus. Offer me comforts like that, and even I will join up!)

Now *commoda* was the technical prose term for the 'fringe-benefits' of military life, in addition to regular wages, and at this very time Augustus was having difficulties in filling his legions due to the lowness of these extra rewards.[8] Another respectable Roman profession, the Law, does not escape (its terminology parodied

at 1. 79ff.). There were further pin-pricks: when is a good time
to start courting your girl? Answer, the anniversary of a national
disaster (1. 413–14), because the shops are shut and you will not
have to buy her a present. Should the young receive a liberal
education? Yes, but not only to protect the innocent and make
powerful speeches before the people, the courts or the senate
(time-honoured occupations of a public-spirited noble). Oratory
will be just as useful for winning a girl-friend (1. 459–62). To
praise the unequalled variety and quality of native Italian products
was a stock theme of patriotic literature at this time,[9] but the
compliment becomes two-edged when extended to feminine
beauty (1. 55–6):

> tot tibi tamque dabit formosas Roma puellas,
>   'haec habet' ut dicas 'quicquid in orbe fuit.'

(Rome can offer you so many girls of such beauty that you
will say 'The fruits of the whole world are here.')

Yet we should not exaggerate the significance of such points
(many of which do not touch Augustus directly), and at the same
time Ovid will turn his pen to a facile panegyric of the imperial
house (1. 177ff.). Our poet hardly fits into any recognizable
category of men who opposed the Augustan régime. Born in
43 B.C. he was not one who, in Tacitus' phrase,[10] had 'seen the
Republic', even in its last convulsions, nor would the austere
ideals represented by the elder Cato have much appeal to him on
the intellectual level. In my opinion the passages mentioned above
can be explained by Ovid's unrivalled sense of the ridiculous.
He enjoyed nothing more than deflating pomposity, and the
Augustan establishment, like other establishments, offered a good
measure of that. It has been said that Ovid's attachment was to
personal rather than public values. This trait may be discerned
in his poetry and supported by his abandonment of a political
career; it might make him impatient of any government. But
when one considers the régimes which Rome had endured in the
past, or any alternative which might have seemed feasible to a
contemporary, I doubt whether Ovid should be reckoned as
specifically anti-Augustan.[11]

All the same the *Ars Amatoria* clearly upset traditional Roman
sentiment, and it is important to discover where exactly it hurt.

If the opinions against which Ovid reacted seem a little stuffy and old-fashioned, yet they must still have had force. Perhaps the main irritation lay in the poem's frivolity; several stages of disrepute are involved here. In the first place Romans had strong feelings about what was worthwhile and what was a waste of time. Literary pursuits were still not wholly respectable – it may surprise us that even historians could be represented as 'genus ignavum quod lecto gaudet et umbra' ('an idle breed, given to putting their feet up out of the sun', Juvenal, VII. 105), and Sallust felt it necessary to excuse his withdrawal from practical affairs.[12] For a man of the administrative class (to which Ovid belonged) a public career was expected, with literature confined to spare moments or retirement. Poetry had less obvious use than prose history, and the opening of *Amores*, I. 15 indicates that Ovid was criticized for his passionate belief in poetry as a full-time occupation:

> quid mihi, Livor edax, ignavos obicis annos
> ingeniique vocas carmen inertis opus,
> non me more patrum, dum strenua sustinet aetas,
> praemia militiae pulverulenta sequi
> nec me verbosas leges ediscere nec me
> ingrato vocem prostituisse foro?

(Why, consuming Jealousy, do you charge me with a life of idleness, and call poetry an occupation for sluggish spirits, complaining that I do not seek the usual hard-won rewards of soldiering, while the prime of life gives me strength, or learn by heart long-winded laws or prostitute my voice in the thankless courts?)

But, if you must write poetry, some types were more worthy than others. Epic and tragedy could be patriotic and morally uplifting. On the other hand Cicero said that not even if his lifespan were doubled would he find time to read the lyric poets[13] – this is revealing from a man who could once have been reckoned the leading Roman poet of the day. Place epic and tragedy at the top, and love poetry will rate low in the scale of utility. Furthermore, by the same convention according to which a pastoral poet must himself be a shepherd, the full-time love poet must himself be a full-time lover, which was no way for a Roman to spend his life. And the worst is still to come. In the *Ars Amatoria*, as earlier in the *Amores*, Ovid provocatively reverses the usual moral categories, presenting love as a worthy and strenuous occupation, like farming or hunting, in which all his fellow-citizens should be expert. Let us see the germ of this idea in Ovid's 'testimony' at *Amores*, I. 9. 41–6:

> ipse ego segnis eram discinctaque in otia natus;
>   mollierant animos lectus et umbra meos;
> inpulit ignavum formosae cura puellae,
>   iussit et in castris aera merere suis.
> inde vides agilem nocturnaque bella gerentem:
>   qui nolet fieri desidiosus, amet.

(Personally I used to be a shirker, fit only for slackness and ease; shade and the couch had enfeebled my spirit. Love for a pretty girl shook me out of that state, and made me enlist in Cupid's service. From that day on, as you see, I have been a man of action and a warrior by night; if you don't want to become lethargic, you should be a lover!)

Otium had disreputable connotations to a traditionally-minded Roman[14] – even more so *lectus* and *umbra* (e.g. Juvenal, VII. 105, quoted above), and no-one would have deserved these terms of opprobrium more thoroughly than a love poet. Yet Ovid applies the words to himself *before* he enlisted in Cupid's army (i.e. began to write love poetry). Now by contrast he is engaged in warfare by night and *agilis*, which suggests the Greek *praktikos*,[15] applied particularly by the Stoics to a man who embroiled himself in politics. So in a paradoxical way Ovid has become active in both political and military affairs, refuting the criticism of *Livor* (*Amores*, I. 15, above).

I mentioned earlier that the *Ars Amatoria* has the superficial appearance of a didactic or instructional poem, and now is the time to consider this didactic tradition and how it affected the *Ars*. Later poets in this style, both Greek and Roman, looked back to the *Works and Days* of Hesiod as the original of the genre. Hesiod, writing in the eighth or seventh century B.C. was giving advice on agriculture, interspersed with many moral maxims of a homely and down-to-earth type. But it was not until the third century B.C. that this Hesiodic tradition really flourished and became self-conscious. An important figure was Aratus, with his astronomical poem *Phaenomena* which Callimachus praised as being 'in the manner of Hesiod'.[16] Aratus wrote competently, sometimes even elegantly, although his popularity and influence in later times seem to us excessive. Little can be said in favour of Nicander (c. 135 B.C.), who in addition chose the most unpromising subjects for his verse, such as venomous reptiles (*Theriaca*) or antidotes to poison (*Alexipharmaca*), but even Nicander had his followers. Aratus and Nicander illustrate the characteristics of this genre quite well. Their language is archaic and often obscure beyond the demands of a technical subject; these features show them trying to re-create the style of Hesiod, as well as following the taste of their own age. Hesiod inspires the digressions from the main theme, usually of a mythological character, and a sparing use of 'poetical' embellishment, which might have been a genuine feature of country speech in the eighth century B.C., but seems an affectation after Alexander the Great – e.g. Hesiod had called the snail 'the house-carrier' and Aratus and Nicander follow him when they describe frogs by a periphrasis as 'the fathers of the tadpoles'.[17] Also from Hesiod comes a certain melancholy attitude towards life, manifest when Aratus considers the dangers of sea-faring at the wrong time of year, or when Nicander depicts a particularly horrible kind of reptile. All this may make us wonder where the appeal of didactic poetry lay. From the poet's point of view there was a severe technical challenge in moulding the recalcitrant material (often by versifying a prose treatise) and gathering together so much information in an age dedicated both to poetic craftsmanship and scientific inquiry. The audience would share many of the poet's preoccupations; also there must have been a belief, however misguided, that such works did have practical utility. Several serious astronomers made their contribution by commenting on Aratus' *Phaenomena*; but it has been well said that if you were bitten by a poisonous snake and had only Nicander to help you, your prospects would be poor.

Among the Romans didactic poetry found two practitioners whose talent was immeasurably superior to that of Aratus or Nicander – Lucretius with his *De Rerum Natura* and Virgil in the *Georgics*. Lucretius, admittedly, drew on a rather different tradition of philosophical poetry going back to such men as Empedocles, but he exhibits similar features, e.g. in his love of archaism, being a great admirer of Ennius and the old epic and tragic style of Roman poetry, and in his digressions. Both Lucretius and Virgil stood to Ovid in the *Ars Amatoria* in much the same relationship as Hesiod to Aratus and Nicander – they provided for him a fount of dignified and old-fashioned language which gave the colouring appropriate to this genre. One must say, however, that there is no question of our poet mocking Lucretius or Virgil in any hostile spirit; in *Amores*, I. 15 he states his admiration for the pair of them, and shows it in practice elsewhere.[18] Two lesser Roman didactic poems offer some illuminating parallels to Ovid, the *Cynegetica* of Grattius (on hunting), perhaps composed a little before the *Ars*, and the *Astronomica* of Manilius, written soon afterwards. Since Grattius in particular lacks all the genius of Lucretius and Virgil, we can appreciate both the pompous nature of the genre and Ovid's delightful parody. He makes use of didactic language mainly when introducing, closing, or passing from one section to another; here we find formulae like *nunc age*, *adde quod*, *principio*, *praeterea*, familiar from Lucretius and Virgil.[19] Other features belonging to the same tradition are the summary of proposed contents (I. 35–40), a recapitulation showing how far we have progressed (I. 263–6), and the personal 'seal' which closes both Books II and III, since the work was originally planned in only two books. Of course the joke could easily be overdone, and Ovid avoids that temptation.

The influence of Virgil's *Georgics* appears more widely in the constant analogies from farming, hunting or animal life in general, e.g. I. 93ff., lines redolent of Virgil:

> ut redit itque frequens longum formica per agmen,
>   granifero solitum cum vehit ore cibum,
> aut ut apes saltusque suos et olentia nactae
>   pascua per flores et thyma summa volant,
> sic ruit ad celebres cultissima femina ludos . . .

(Just as thickly-congregating ants travel to and fro along a path, bearing in their mouths their usual meal of grain, or as bees after reaching fragrant pastures and their favourite glades hover around the flowers and above the thyme, so all the most elegant women make for the crowded games . . .)

91

Virgilian tricks may affect the structure of the *Ars*. When Ovid has finished telling his young man the best places to meet a girl, we expect him, as promised, to reveal straight away how to win her. But instead three preliminary sections follow: (a) you must believe that she can be caught; (b) it is useful to get to know her maid; (c) some times are better than others for making an approach. One should probably see here Virgil's insistence on the manifold preparations necessary before attempting the main task.[20] Again, Hesiod urged the necessity of 'work on top of work' (*Works and Days*, 382), echoed by Virgil (*Georgics*, I. 145–6):

> labor omnia vincit
> improbus.

(Relentless toil overcomes everything.)

In love too, all is not plain sailing (*A.A.*, II. 236):

> labor omnis inest

('a love affair is not really a soft option' [tr. Paul Turner]).

Some parts of the *Ars* turn out quite unexpectedly to be at home in didactic verse. What could be more authentically Roman, more up to the minute than the advice to young men on how to turn themselves out when courting (I. 513ff.)?

> munditie placeant, fuscentur corpora Campo;
>   sit bene conveniens et sine labe toga.
> lingula[21] ne rigeat; careant rubigine dentes;
>   nec vagus in laxa pes tibi pelle natet;
> nec male deformet rigidos tonsura capillos:
>   sit coma, sit trita barba resecta manu.

(A man's person should win approval by being well
groomed, with a sun-tan from exercise in the Campus
Martius. Your toga must be well-fitting and spotless. The
tongue of your shoe should not be too tight, nor its buckle
rusty; and your feet should not swim about in too large a
sole. Your hair must not be cut so that it stands hideously
on end; it should be trimmed (together with the beard) by
an expert hand.)

Yet to prescribe the dress and even the physical requirements for
success had its place in the didactic tradition.[22]

The idea of writing a frivolous didactic poem was not new.
Ovid himself had composed one on female cosmetics (*Medicamina
Faciei Femineae*), from which a hundred lines survive. And, when
defending himself at *Tristia*, II. 471ff., he mentions several others,
e.g. on indoor and outdoor games, etiquette or the bottling of
wine. All these are described as 'amusements for the fireside in
December' (*Tr.*, II. 491). But none had the high possibilities of
an *Ars Amatoria*. The very title promises a delicious incongruity
and tension between form and content. It is not merely a case of
pedantry against passion – one might reasonably hold that love,
like virtue, is not teachable, not to be governed by rules and
prescriptions. This particular tension had never been exploited
before, although earlier Latin elegy contains a fair amount of
instruction in love, and the background deserves to be mentioned briefly.[23] Among the influences on Roman elegy, Greek
New Comedy together with its Latin followers played an important part, and one stock scene in Comedy showed the un-
savoury old *lena* advising a girl how to attract men. Both Propertius (IV. 5) and Ovid (*Amores*, I. 8) write elegies on this theme
which betray their antecedents clearly. A still closer parallel to
the *Ars* exists at Tibullus, I. 4. The poet has a conversation with
Priapus (in itself a 'learned' touch – compare Hesiod's visit from
the Muses and the appearances of Cupid, Venus and Apollo in
Ovid) wherein the god gives advice for success in love; his tone
is pompous, with an occasional hint of Ovid's mannerisms. At
the end Tibullus foresees a time when the eager young will crowd
round him for instruction (I. 4. 79–80):

> tempus erit cum me Veneris praecepta ferentem
> deducat iuvenum sedula turba senem.

(The day will come in my old age when an attentive crowd of
youths follows me about as I impart to them guidance in
love.)

Propertius too instructs his readers, not only in the *lena*-poem:
'invenies eadem blandi praecepta Properti' ('You will find that
graceful Propertius teaches the same', *Tristia*, II. 465).

But neither Tibullus nor Propertius allowed the didactic tradi-

tion to influence the way they depicted love; that was a master-
stroke of Ovid himself. To appreciate it fully we must understand
the conception of love which is regular in Roman elegy and which
broadly speaking, Ovid followed in the *Amores*. Love appears as
an overwhelming force, even a disease or madness, which carries
the poet by storm; he has little choice as to whom he falls in love
with (the woman may well take the initiative) and little freedom
of manœuvre once he has succumbed. Often the painful rather
than the pleasurable side of love is uppermost. If this seems too
searing a picture, it can easily be exemplified from the very first
poem of Propertius[24] – and there are indications that the lost
elegies of Cornelius Gallus possessed the same colouring in even
greater degree. Consider the opening line of Propertius, I. 1:

> Cynthia prima suis miserum me cepit ocellis

(Cynthia was the first to trap me helpless with her gaze.)

Propertius himself is no more than a powerless victim, who has
no chance of escape once the fateful glance has fallen upon him.
And a few lines below:

> et caput impositis pressit Amor pedibus

(Love trod upon my head and bore me down.)

Certain conventional images in love elegy reinforce this attitude.
For example, the lover may be spoken of as the captive of Cupid,
as at *Amores*, I. 2 where Ovid imagines a Roman-type triumphal
procession in which he himself is paraded through the streets as
a prisoner. Particularly revealing is the figure of *servitium amoris*[25] –
the lover is a slave of his girl-friend and forced to perform duties
which degrade a free man. Often this is expressed in strongly
Roman terms, to make his disgrace feel all the more sharp, as at
Tibullus, II. 4. 1–2:

> hic mihi servitium video dominamque paratam;
> iam mihi, libertas illa paterna, vale.

(Here I see slavery and a mistress await me; farewell to the
freedom which my family enjoyed from of old!)

The very word *domina*, standard in elegy for the girl, points this

theme: to a free-born Roman *dominus* and its derivatives had un-
pleasant connotations. Propertius too exclaims indignantly
(II. 23. 3):

> ingenuus quisquam alterius dat munera servo . . .?

(Will a free man bribe another's slave . . .?)

Of course Ovid's more flippant approach tends to diminish the
heat, but even he writes (*Amores*, II. 17. 1–2):

> si quis erit, qui turpe putet servire puellae,
> illo convincar iudice turpis ego.

(If anyone thinks it disgraceful to be a girl's slave, in that
man's verdict I will be convicted of disgrace.)

All in all love, as presented by the elegists, might seem thoroughly
unsuitable to be the subject of a didactic poem. How can one
lay down rules for something so chaotic, over which the individual has so little control? Borrowing the words of Parmeno
to his love-sick young master (Terence, *Eunuchus*, 61–3):

> incerta haec si postules
> ratione certa facere, nihilo plus agas
> quam si des operam ut cum ratione insanias.

(If you wished to conduct these random affairs by a fixed
system, you would achieve no more than if you decided to
rave systematically.)

Theophrastus had defined love as 'an emotion which seizes the
unoccupied spirit'. But in what we might call the didactic view,
love is not so much an emotion as an activity; feelings hardly
matter, performance is all-important. The *Ars* will sometimes
echo conventional themes of elegy like *servitium amoris*, e.g. II.
215–16:

> nec tibi turpe puta (quamvis sit turpe, placebit)
> ingenua speculum sustinuisse manu.

(Do not consider it below your dignity as a free man to hold
her mirror – that it may be, but it will give pleasure.)

At other times, however, the young man seems to be playing a game – whether he is 'in love' or not becomes at least doubtful – e.g. I. 611:

> est tibi agendus amans imitandaque vulnera verbis.

(You must play the lover, and by your speech give the impression of a grievous wound.)

Some of the most delightful moments in the whole poem occur when these two conceptions are juxtaposed, as at I. 41–2:

> dum licet et loris passim potes ire solutis,
> elige cui dicas 'tu mihi sola places.'

(While your eye is free to rove wherever it wishes, choose to whom you will declare 'You are the only girl who pleases me.')

'Tu mihi sola places' represents the typical declaration of an elegiac lover (in fact this half-line is found twice elsewhere in Augustan elegy[26]), and *sola* implies that he has no choice which girl he loves. On the other hand *elige* suggests cool and deliberate selection after surveying all the possible candidates. But Ovid adds the cautionary *dum licet* – there may come a time when you are really in love and no longer a free agent.

Another notable feature of the *Ars* is the wealth of contemporary Roman colouring. Earlier elegy had for the most part been conducted in a nebulous half-Greek, half-Roman world; a poem like *Amores*, III. 2, set at a race-meeting in the Circus Maximus, is a rarity (and all the more effective for that). But from the first line of the *Ars*:

> si quis *in hoc* artem *populo* non novit amandi . . .

(Any fellow-citizen of mine who has not learnt the art of love . . .)

we are firmly in the capital. To Ovid's young hero, conventionally poor but leisured, it is 'tua Roma' (I. 59). So there are frequent glimpses of the city which Augustus boasted that he had transformed from brick to marble, its temples and fountains

> . . . subdita qua Veneris facto de marmore templo
> Appias expressis aera pulsat aquis.[27]

(. . . where below Venus' marble temple the Appian fountain
sends a jet of water into the air.)

Whether the emperor would approve of his splendid new buildings being recommended for meeting elegant females is another
matter. The full round of Roman social activity is here: theatres,
festivals, markets, law-courts, race-meetings, gladiatorial displays,
a triumph, a naval spectacular, exercises in the Campus Martius.
I have mentioned the section on what the well-dressed man was
wearing in 2 B.C., and Ovid offers plenty of corresponding advice
to young ladies.

This much sharper definition of a Roman milieu in the *Ars*
did, however, bring a problem which eventually proved fatal
to its author. His girls must also be set more recognizably in real
Roman society, and this was likely to raise moral objections.
Orthodox scholarly opinion nowadays holds that the typical
heroine of Roman love poetry should be considered a *hetaera*,
but in my view Gordon Williams[28] is basically right in arguing
that some of the most famous figures over whose reality we feel
we have most grasp (particularly Catullus' Lesbia, also Propertius' Cynthia) were women of some social standing, maybe
married, who played fast and loose in the chaotic conditions of
the late Republic. Ovid's heroines in the *Amores* often seem to be
pale reflections of this type. So there was a real danger that our
poet would be accused of undermining marriage. He tried to
avoid this by making the women more obviously *hetaerae* (e.g.
I. 31–4, 435) of the class of freedwomen (III. 615). Thereby he
adhered more closely to his models in Greek Comedy and
epigram, and at the same time ranged himself with a long-
standing Roman view (indeed the 'inspired pronouncement of
Cato', Horace, *Sat.*, I. 2. 32) that irregular affairs were quite
acceptable as long as they did not involve other people's wives.
None the less Ovid has retained in the *Ars* a conventional figure
of earlier elegy – it might have been advisable to remove him –
the girl's 'husband', who is a rival to the hero.

So far we have looked individually at three main elements in the
Ars: the didactic tradition, material taken from straight love
elegy and the added colouring of Roman social life. Now observe
how Ovid interweaves all of them in a longer passage (I. 399–
418): he is telling the lover that some times are better than others

97

for starting a courtship (an idea derived ultimately from the *Days* of Hesiod's *Works and Days*). The point in every case is that the young man, conventionally poor, must avoid times when he will be expected to bring a present, and make a move only when the shops are shut. This results in a grim sort of humour – cheerful festivals are out, but days of national mourning excellent. Altogether the lines are unusually intricate and sometimes obscure due to our defective knowledge of the Roman festivals.

> tempora qui solis operosa colentibus arva,
>   fallitur, et nautis aspicienda putat.   400
> nec semper credenda Ceres fallacibus arvis
>   nec semper viridi concava puppis aquae,
> nec teneras semper tutum captare puellas:
>   saepe dato melius tempore fiet idem.
> sive dies suberit natalis sive Kalendae,   405
>   quas Venerem Marti continuasse iuvat,
> sive erit ornatus non, ut fuit ante, sigillis,
>   sed regum positas Circus habebit opes,
> differ opus: tunc tristis hiems, tunc Pliades instant,
>   tunc tener aequorea mergitur Haedus aqua;   410
> tunc bene desinitur; tunc si quis creditur alto,
>   vix tenuit lacerae naufraga membra ratis.
> tum licet incipias, qua flebilis Allia luce
>   vulneribus Latiis sanguinolenta fuit,
> quaque die redeunt rebus minus apta gerendis   415
>   culta Palaestino septima festa Syro.
> magna superstitio tibi sit natalis amicae,
>   quaque aliquid dandum est, illa sit atra dies.

(Anyone who thinks that only those who work the land or sailors need observe the seasons is making a mistake. Just as any and every season is not right for entrusting seed to the deceitful ground or curved ships to the dark ocean, so it is not always safe to hunt dainty girls; often the same action will be improved by correct timing. If her birthday is at hand, or those merry Kalends which join the months of Mars and Venus, or if the Circus, no longer decked out with statuettes as in the old days, displays items from a maharajah's collection, you should postpone operations. Then ugly storms and the Pliades threaten, and the Kids

98

are sinking below the horizon. On such occasions one does well to stay at home; anyone who takes to the deep can barely save himself by clutching a spar from his shattered vessel. But it will be quite appropriate for you to start on that day when the grim Allia was stained red with Latin blood, or on the recurring weekly festival celebrated by Jews from Palestine when business should cease. You should view your girl-friend's birthday with the utmost dread, and any occasion when a present is due must be accounted a black day.)

Analysing this passage we see that Ovid first of all stresses the didactic element by his comparison with farming and sailing (both regular subjects for didactic poetry) and two definite echoes of Virgil's *Georgics*: 1. 204-7:

> praeterea tam sunt Arcturi sidera nobis
> Haedorumque dies servandi et lucidus Anguis
> quam quibus in patriam ventosa per aequora vectis
> Pontus et ostriferi fauces temptantur Abydi.

(Furthermore we farmers should pay as much attention to Arcturus, the times of the Kids and the bright Serpent as do those who, sailing homewards over stormy seas, attempt the Pontus and the straits of oyster-bearing Abydos.)

and 1. 224:

> . . . invitae properes anni spem credere terrae

(. . . before you hurry to entrust the hope of the year to the reluctant earth.)

Then he cleverly introduces Roman colouring – birthdays, which were celebrated with great attention, and the festival of Venus (April was sacred to the goddess and she received special worship on the first of the month). Lines 407-8 refer to the time of the great December holiday, the Saturnalia, but some details are puzzling. During the period of the Saturnalia a fair took place, called Sigillaria from the clay statuettes (*sigilla*) originally given as presents then. In my opinion 'non ut fuit ante' probably contrasts the old days, when people were content with such token gifts, and the present, when something much more costly

99

is expected.[29] Ovid seems to indicate that in his time the market took place in the Circus (Circus Maximus or Circus Flaminius?) – apparently no other evidence survives on this point.[30]

But the full complexity of the writing only emerges with lines 411–12. In the first place we see a melancholy reflection on the dangers of seafaring (prepared by the metaphorical references in 409–10), descending from Hesiod through Aratus and Virgil. One can compare *Georgics*, 1. 456–7:

> non illa quisquam me nocte per altum
> ire neque a terra moneat convellere funem

(On that night let no-one urge me to voyage over the deep or cast off my rope from the land.)

and particularly an isolated line from Cicero's adaptation of Aratus[31] probably describing, as does Ovid (cf. 410), the fate of those who go to sea when the Kids are setting:

> . . . navibus absumptis fluitantia quaerere aplustra

(. . . to search for floating stern-ornaments after their ships have been destroyed).

At the same time Ovid is using a favourite image of love poetry. The lover who comes to grief is said to be 'shipwrecked on the sea of Venus',[32] and his success or failure may be described in terms of a ship which either comes safely to port or founders in mid-ocean. Lines 413–14 introduce the blackest day in the whole Roman calendar, 18 July, anniversary of Rome's defeat by the Gauls in 390 B.C. – but for the lover an excellent prospect since he would face few dangers of spending money. Finally, an interesting glimpse of the extent to which Judaism had affected Roman society. Although there was a large Jewish colony in the capital, Ovid need not be referring specifically to Jewish shop-keepers. We know from other sources that many Gentiles would observe some of the basic Jewish prohibitions, such as not doing business on a Sabbath.

Now of course one can enjoy the *Ars* in a simple way without appreciating the background and complexity of themes, as many people have enjoyed this poem in the past. The learning is unobtrusive and never diminishes gaiety. But undoubtedly Ovid wanted and expected his readers to follow him in such an amazing *tour de force*, and I think one has a certain duty to respect the author's intentions. Also the result is surely a gain in pleasure. Writing on more than one level is a constant feature of Ovid's style, but in this poem he surpasses himself.

The *Ars* shows clear signs of having originally been planned in two books, addressed to men only.[33] Before long Ovid decided on a third, for the benefit of young women, but did not obliterate signs of the original two-book scheme. The *Remedia Amoris*, addressed almost solely to men but said to be equally applicable to both sexes, may belong to this second stage; in any case the complete work, *Ars Amatoria* in three books together with its companion piece, must have seen the light of day about A.D. 1.[34] Ovid's final conception gave him the chance to handle the stock themes of love poetry in a number of ways: straightforwardly in Books I and II, from another angle for the girls in Book III, and completely in reverse for the *Remedia*. Let us see how he does this, selecting as an example a favourite theme, how a girl can excite her lover's admiration by all her accomplishments and manners of dress. An unknown minor Augustan poet provides a good illustration:[35]

> illam quidquid agit, quoquo vestigia movit
> 　componit furtim subsequiturque decor.
> seu solvit crines, fusis decet esse capillis,
> 　seu compsit, comptis est veneranda comis.
> urit, seu Tyria voluit procedere palla,
> 　urit, seu nivea candida veste venit.

(Whatever she does, wherever she goes, charm imperceptibly follows and adorns her. If she lets down her hair, that suits her; if she combs it, she is majestic with combed hair. She sets alight whether she chooses to come forth in a gown of Tyrian purple or to appear gleaming in a snow-white dress.)

First, Ovid's advice to men (II. 297ff.):

> sive erit in Tyriis, Tyrios laudabis amictus;
> 　sive erit in Cois, Coa decere puta.
> aurata est: ipso tibi sit pretiosior auro;
> 　gausapa si sumit, gausapa sumpta proba.

astiterit tunicata: 'moves incendia' clama,
    sed timida, caveat frigora, voce roga.
conpositum discrimen erit: discrimina lauda:
    torserit igne comam: torte capille, place.
bracchia saltantis, vocem mirare canentis,
    et, quod desierit, verba querentis habe.

(If she wears Tyrian, you will praise her Tyrian gown, or if
Coan, you must think that Coan suits her best. Suppose
she has cloth of gold; let her be more precious to you
herself than gold; if she chooses a woollen dress, applaud
the woollen dress she chooses. Perhaps she will present
herself to you in a tunic: cry out 'You set me on fire!'
(but express the anxious hope that she should be careful of
the cold). She has arranged her parting – then you should
praise her parting; alternatively, she has curled her hair –
then you must applaud the way she has done it. Admire her
arms when she dances and her voice when she sings, and
show disappointment if she stops.)

Book III naturally contains much advice to women on doing and
wearing what suits them (and avoiding the opposite). But the
wittiest variation comes at *Remedia*, 331ff. (how to fall out of
love):

quin etiam, quacumque caret tua femina dote,
    hanc moveat, blandis usque precare sonis:
exige uti cantet, si qua est sine voce puella;
    fac saltet, nescit si qua movere manum;
barbara sermone est, fac tecum multa loquatur;
    non didicit chordas tangere, posce lyram.

(Furthermore you must continually press your girl to exercise
whatever gift she lacks. If she has no voice, demand that she
sing; if she cannot move her arms gracefully, make her dance.
Is her speech uncouth? Engage her in long conversations.
Has she never learnt music? Call for the guitar!)

There is a ruthless inevitability about this procedure which
itself can be reckoned as a sort of dry humour. But Ovid shows
good judgment in not overdoing the trick; when he does echo

an earlier precept it is nearly always with elegance. Thus, I. 631:

> nec timide promitte: trahunt promissa puellas

(Do not hesitate to make promises: promises lead girls on.)

finds its antidote at III. 461:

> si bene promittent, totidem promittite verbis

(If they make fine promises, make as many in reply.)

I. 741-2:

> ei mihi, non tutum est, quod ames, laudare sodali:
> cum tibi laudanti credidit, ipse subit.

(Alas! you cannot safely praise your love to a friend: the moment you convince him he will take your place.)

is ruefully recalled at III. 659-60:

> questus eram, memini, metuendos esse sodales;
> non tangit solos ista querela viros.

(I remember complaining that one must beware of friends; unfortunately this does not apply only to men.)

A danger to one side will be profit to the other: at a party (a) I. 245-50:

> hic tu fallaci nimium ne crede lucernae:
> iudicio formae noxque merumque nocent.
> luce deas caeloque Paris spectavit aperto,
> cum dixit Veneri 'vincis utramque, Venus.'
> nocte latent mendae vitioque ignoscitur omni,
> horaque formosam quamlibet illa facit.

(On these occasions do not put too much trust in the deceptive lamp-light; darkness and wine can spoil your judgment of beauty. It was in daylight and under the open sky that Paris inspected the goddesses and said to Venus: 'You are better than both of them.' At night-time faults are unnoticed, and every defect escapes censure; any woman may pass as a beauty then.)

But (b) III. 753-4:

> etsi turpis eris, formosa videbere potis,
> et latebras vitiis nox dabit ipsa tuis.

(However ugly you may be, the men will think you beautiful when they are drunk, and the very darkness will conceal your faults.)

The idea that lovers hide the defects of those whom they love by using the nearest complimentary term (II. 657ff.) was already a commonplace, but to recommend the converse as a way of overcoming love is highly original and amusing (*Remedia*, 323ff.):

> et mala sunt vicina bonis: errore sub illo
> pro vitio virtus crimina saepe tulit.
> qua potes, in peius dotes deflecte puellae
> iudiciumque brevi limite falle tuum.
> 'turgida', si plena est, si fusca est, 'nigra' vocetur;
> in gracili 'macies' crimen habere potest.
> et poterit dici 'petulans', quae rustica non est;
> et poterit dici 'rustica', si qua proba est.

(Merits are narrowly separated from faults; this has often led to virtue being mistakenly attacked as vice. Wherever possible, disparage your girl's good points and distort your judgment by this fine division. If she has a full figure, you should call her overblown, or if she is dark, call her swarthy; if she is slender, 'emaciated' is a useful term of reproach. An uninhibited girl can be called forward, a decent one inhibited.)

I have not yet spoken about one of the work's chief delights, its digressions. As mentioned earlier, these derive from the didactic tradition; they appear occasionally in Aratus and Nicander, but with much greater frequency and brilliance in Lucretius and Virgil's *Georgics*. For us, with our knowledge of the poet's later development, there is a tendency to see them as a testing-ground for the *Metamorphoses*, and in fact two stories (Daedalus and Icarus and Cephalus and Procris) recur in the hexameter poem. Ovid overcomes the slight restrictions of the elegiac couplet and for the first time gives free rein to his talent for narrative, a talent fulfilled in the *Fasti* as well as the *Metamorphoses*. Every trait which endeared the poet to later generations is here: economy of means, visual brilliance, simplicity masking sophistication and restrained wit. I can only point to some of my own favourite episodes, and give the reasons why I like them. First of all, the Rape of the Sabine Women (I. 101–34). This is amusingly presented in the learned Hellenistic manner as an aetiological story, explaining why the theatre is still a dangerous place for pretty girls (the formal conclusion at 133–4). It must surely have aroused conflicting emotions in a traditionally minded Roman; on the one hand the Rape was a firmly established legend of infant Rome, but it does not show the ancestors in too favourable a light. Ovid enthusiastically endorses Romulus' actions, claiming in effect that the great Founder had anticipated his own doctrines! He sets the scene at a theatrical performance rather than a race-meeting, as was usual, perhaps to give extra spice because conservative Roman sentiment had disapproved of the theatre.[36] I have already mentioned the sly hit at contemporary recruiting difficulties in the army (131–2). For the rest, Ovid constantly makes fun of the primitive conditions of early Rome – in the theatre itself, the entertainment and even the hair-styles. But notice that seating arrangements are as the emperor Augustus prescribed, with women in the back rows (109).[37]

> primus sollicitos fecisti, Romule, ludos,
>   cum iuvit viduos rapta Sabina viros.
> tunc neque marmoreo pendebant vela theatro,
>   nec fuerant liquido pulpita rubra croco;
> illic quas tulerant nemorosa Palatia frondes   105
>   simpliciter positae scena sine arte fuit;
> in gradibus sedit populus de caespite factis,
>   qualibet hirsutas fronde tegente comas.
> respiciunt oculisque notant sibi quisque puellam
>   quam velit, et tacito pectore multa movent;   110
> dumque rudem praebente modum tibicine Tusco
>   ludius aequatam ter pede pulsat humum,
> in medio plausu (plausus tunc arte carebant)
>   rex populo praedae signa petita[38] dedit.
> protinus exiliunt animum clamore fatentes   115
>   virginibus cupidas iniciuntque manus;

ut fugiunt aquilas, timidissima turba, columbae
   utque fugit visos agna novella lupos,
sic illae timuere viros sine lege ruentes;
   constitit in nulla qui fuit ante color.   120
nam timor unus erat, facies non una timoris:
   pars laniat crines, pars sine mente sedet;
altera maesta silet, frustra vocat altera matrem;
   haec queritur, stupet haec; haec manet, illa fugit.
ducuntur raptae, genialis praeda, puellae,   125
   et potuit multas ipse decere timor.
si qua repugnarat nimium comitemque negarat,
   sublatam cupido vir tulit ipse sinu
atque ita 'quid teneros lacrimis corrumpis ocellos?
   quod matri pater est, hoc tibi' dixit 'ero'.   130
Romule, militibus scisti dare commoda solus:
   haec mihi si dederis commoda, miles ero.
scilicet ex illo sollemni[39] more theatra
   nunc quoque formosis insidiosa manent.

(Romulus first introduced this danger into the games, on the occasion when the Rape of the Sabine Women brought his men the solace of a wife. At that date there was no awning suspended over the marble theatre, no stage gleaming with saffron-water. Leafy branches from the Palatine artlessly arranged formed a rudimentary back-cloth. The seats on which the people sat were simply the grassy slopes, and above their ill-combed heads any old boughs kept off the sun. Each man looks behind him to mark out the girl he would like, and silently broods over his plans. And while the performer pounded the earth (levelled for the occasion) to the crude accompaniment of a Tuscan flute-player, in the middle of the applause, which at that time was quite unorganized, the king gave his people the long-awaited signal for action. Immediately they leapt up – the cries left no doubts as to their enthusiasm – and eagerly laid hands upon the girls. Just as that most timorous bird, a dove, tries to escape from an eagle, or as a young lamb sets off at one glimpse of a wolf, so they were terrified by the men's pell-mell pursuit; in no case did their complexion remain unaltered. But, while they were all frightened, they showed it

in different ways; some tore their hair, others remained in
their seats not knowing what to do; some were silent and
sadfaced, some called in vain for their mothers; this one
protests, that one is bewildered; one here stays put, one there
makes off. Eventually, though, all of them are hauled away to
the Registrar (in many cases no doubt looking all the prettier
for their fear). Perhaps the odd one put up more than a token
resistance and refused to go along, but then the man lifted
her up bodily, saying 'There's no need to spoil your pretty
eyes by weeping; I will treat you just as your father treats
your mother.' Romulus, no other general has ever been so
understanding about his men's comforts; offer me comforts
like that and even I will enlist! So you see, from that day till
the present the theatre has by hallowed custom been a
dangerous place for attractive girls.)

Also from the first book the Rescue of Ariadne (525–64) is outstanding for vigour and gaiety, though rather too long to quote
in full here.

Book II is concerned with keeping your girl once you have
caught her. For this purpose, says Ovid, good looks are not
enough; you must cultivate your mind as well, following the
example of Ulysses (II. 123ff.). Here we can enjoy the oblique
glance at Homer:

> non formosus erat, sed erat facundus Ulixes,
> et tamen aequoreas torsit amore deas.
> o quotiens illum doluit properare Calypso
> remigioque aptas esse negavit aquas!
> haec Troiae casus iterumque iterumque rogabat;
> ille referre aliter saepe solebat idem.
> litore constiterant; illic quoque pulchra Calypso
> exigit Odrysii fata cruenta ducis.
> ille levi virga (virgam nam forte tenebat),
> quod rogat, in spisso litore pingit opus.
> 'haec' inquit 'Troia est' (muros in litore fecit),
> 'hic tibi sit Simois; haec mea castra puta.
> campus erat' (campumque facit), 'quem caede Dolonis
> sparsimus, Haemonios dum vigil optat equos.
> illic Sithonii fuerant tentoria Rhesi;
> hac ego sum captis nocte revectus equis – '

pluraque pingebat, subitus cum Pergama fluctus
abstulit et Rhesi cum duce castra suo;
tum dea 'quas' inquit 'fidas tibi credis ituro,
perdiderint undae nomina quanta, vides?'

(Ulysses made up by his eloquence for what he lacked in good looks, and caused heart-ache to more than one sea-goddess. How often Calypso grieved at his haste to be off, and said that the ocean was too dangerous for sailing! Time and time again she used to ask about the events at Troy, and he often told her the same story in different words. Even on the sea-shore, where they were standing, fair Calypso pressed him about the violent end of the Thracian king Rhesus. So with a light staff, which he happened to be carrying, Ulysses made a diagram in the dense sand. 'Here' he said (drawing city walls) 'is Troy; take this to be the river Simois, and this my camp. There was a plain' (and he drew the plain) 'which we sprinkled with the blood of Dolon, while he was on a night expedition in the hope of winning Achilles' Thessalian horses. The tents of Rhesus were just here, and this was the route of my journey back in the darkness with the horses.' He was filling in more details when a sudden wave obliterated Troy and Rhesus with his camp. Whereupon the goddess said 'Don't you see what great names the sea has destroyed – and you are prepared to trust it for your journey!')

Usually the point which the illustration makes is explicitly stated, or else quite obvious. We may think the connexion in the Daedalus and Icarus episode (II. 21ff.) far-fetched – Minos could not confine Daedalus, so to control the winged love-god will prove even more difficult – but Ovid goes out of his way to make it plain. On one occasion, however, he seems to be deliberately puzzling the reader. When arguing that love is the best medicine for a quarrel, he adds a natural enough illustration (II. 465–6):

quae modo pugnarunt, iungunt sua rostra columbae,
quarum blanditias verbaque murmur habet.

(Immediately after fighting, doves join together their beaks, and their murmurs contain words of endearment.)

But then, without further ado, he launches into a 'cosmogony', or account of the creation of the Universe:

prima fuit rerum confusa sine ordine moles
    unaque erat facies sidera, terra, fretum;
mox caelum impositum terris, humus aequore cincta est,
    inque suas partes cessit inane chaos.

(The original state of the Universe was a confused and
shapeless mass; earth, sea and stars all presented the same
appearance. In time the sky was laid over the earth, the land
surrounded by sea, and the void of Chaos separated into its
elements.)

Poetic accounts of the creation of the Universe and the earliest
human society were not so rare – Roman readers would think
first of Lucretius, v – though it is a surprise to find one in elegiacs
rather than hexameters. But what has all this got to do with the
matter in hand? Ovid's original audience must have been as
puzzled as we are, and the following lines do not make things
much clearer:

silva feras, volucres aer accepit habendas;
    in liquida, pisces, delituistis aqua.
tum genus humanum solis errabat in agris
    idque merae vires et rude corpus erat;
silva domus fuerat, cibus herba, cubilia frondes,
    iamque diu nulli cognitus alter erat.

(The forest received wild animals, and the air birds, while
fish found their refuge in clear waters. The human race –
which possessed little more than brute force and a body
without intelligence – led a nomadic existence on the empty
plains. Until then their home had been the forest, their food
grass, and their bedding leaves; for long no man knew his
neighbour.)

The Lucretian atmosphere has become more noticeable, but the
real point of the digression only emerges with the next couplet:

blanda truces animos fertur mollisse voluptas:
    constiterant uno femina virque loco.

(Sweet pleasure, so we are told, softened their ferocious
spirits; men and women made their dwelling together.)

Lucretius had placed sexual union and family life among the soft-ening influences on the brutality of early mankind. The relevant lines are *De Rerum Natura*, v. 1011ff., particularly 1017–18:

> et Venus imminuit viris, puerique parentum
> blanditiis facile ingenium fregere superbum.

(Love-making sapped their strength, and the winning ways of children easily broke down the overbearing temper of their parents.)

So, by recalling Lucretius, Ovid ingeniously suggests that in a more civilized age, too, love-making can overcome quarrels and ill-temper.

The *Remedia Amoris* deserves more than the brief consideration which space will allow here. Nobody nowadays would hold that it was prompted either by an attack of bad conscience for having written the *Ars*, or a desire to avert the wrath of the emperor. But there remains a feeling that poetically it is somewhat inferior to the *Ars*, and I am not sure that this is fair. The title *Remedia Amoris* takes Ovid's didactic joke one stage further: in adding the piece on antidotes he probably had in mind the example of Nicander, whose *Alexipharmaca* (remedies for poisons) was to some extent a companion to his *Theriaca* (on poisonous reptiles). As with the *Ars*, we can find the germ in earlier elegy. I have mentioned that love is often presented as a disease or madness; Propertius may ask his friends for any patent medicines, pre-scribe a course of treatment for himself, and finally pronounce the patient cured.[40] Sober philosophers too had pondered the best way to deal with such a grave threat to mental stability: 'On occasion he should be diverted to other interests, concerns, pursuits and occupations; often, like invalids who do not respond to medicine, he must be treated by a change of climate. Some authorities believe in driving out an old love with a new one, on the principle of knocking out one nail with another.'[41]

Even if Ovid's heart was not in the *Remedia*, his mind and wit were, as usual, actively engaged. We have already seen some examples of the way he reverses precepts from the *Ars*. Perhaps more entertaining are those passages where he argues against his own, or at least customary elegiac attitudes. One way to free yourself from love, says Cupid (559ff.), is to concentrate on money problems:

ad mala quisque animum referat sua, ponet amorem:
  omnibus illa deus plusve minusve dedit.
qui Puteal Ianumque timet celeresque Kalendas,
  torqueat hunc aeris mutua summa sui;
cui durus pater est, ut voto cetera cedant,
  huic pater ante oculos durus habendus erit;
hic male dotata pauper cum coniuge vivit:
  uxorem fato credat obesse suo;[42]
est tibi rure bono generosae fertilis uvae
  vinea: ne nascens usta sit uva, time;
ille habet in reditu navem: mare semper iniquum
  cogitet et damno litora foeda suo;
filius hunc miles, te filia nubilis angat;
  et quis non causas mille doloris habet?

(To free himself of love a man need only concentrate on his
problems (which heaven sends to everyone in greater or
lesser measure). If you are worried by money-lenders and the
first of the month which comes round so quickly, let the
size of your debt prey on your mind. The man who has an
unsympathetic father (however well his other affairs may go)
should conjure up a picture of that unsympathetic father.
Another lives in straitened circumstances with a wife whose
dowry is small; let him think that his wife stands between
him and his destiny. Or do you have a vineyard in a fertile
part of the country which produces a high-class grape? In
that case you must fear that the crop might be withered by
frost before it is ripe. The man with a ship sailing homewards
should imagine the sea always rough and the coastline
strewn with the remains of his fortune. Whether it is a son
in the army or finding a husband for your daughter, who has
not a thousand causes for anxiety?)

Positively the greatest danger is to have no proper business
with which to occupy yourself (139ff.). Therefore, to avoid love,
you should plunge into politics, the law, or the army. Here, for
once, Ovid is arguing like a traditionally minded Roman, using
the stock terms of abuse like *otium* and *desidia*.[43] This is proved
by a famous example from mythology: the anachronistic Roman
colouring has a particular spice (161ff.):

quaeritis, Aegisthus quare sit factus adulter?
    in promptu causa est: desidiosus erat.
pugnabant alii tardis apud Ilion armis;
    transtulerat vires Graecia tota suas.
sive operam bellis vellet dare, nulla gerebat,
    sive foro, vacuum litibus Argos erat.
quod potuit, ne nil illic ageretur, amavit.
    sic venit ille puer, sic puer ille manet.

(Can you wonder why Aegisthus became an adulterer? The
explanation is obvious – he had nothing to occupy him! The
others were engaged in a protracted struggle round Troy –
in fact the flower of Greece had gone on service overseas.
Suppose he wished to concentrate on war, Argos was not
waging one; suppose it was the law, the courts were in vacation.
So he seized his only chance of avoiding complete idleness
and played the lover; that is how Cupid gains a foothold
and cannot be ejected.)

Unlike Tibullus Ovid does not in the *Amores* regularly depict
the countryside as an ideal setting for love. So in the *Remedia* he
suggests that country pursuits are an effective *antidote* to love, and
shows incidentally that he can write just as prettily as Tibullus
(177–84, an extract from a longer section):

aspice labentes iucundo murmure rivos;
    aspice tondentes fertile gramen oves.
ecce, petunt rupes praeruptaque saxa capellae:
    iam referent haedis ubera plena suis.
pastor inaequali modulatur harundine carmen,
    nec desunt comites, sedula turba, canes.
parte sonant alia silvae mugitibus altae
    et queritur vitulum mater abesse suum.

(Watch the streams slipping by with an agreeable sound,
and sheep cropping the fertile grass. See how the goats make
for the crags and sheer rocks; soon they will bring back full
udders for their kids. A shepherd with his attentive retinue
of hounds is playing a tune on the irregular pipe; elsewhere
the deep woods re-echo with lowing as a heifer chides her
absent calf.)

The main features of the *Ars* and *Remedia* stressed in this chapter have been the sharpness and detached, ironical humour. To pinpoint these might be thought no service to a poet who has often been condemned for his lack of sincere feelings. Personally I can believe that Ovid was himself a man of genuine humanity, capable both of giving and inspiring affection; only on rare occasions, however, does such a quality break through the glittering surface of the *Ars*, because this poem, while containing much shrewd psychological insight, is in every sense the most artificial of Ovid's creations.[44] But need 'artificial' be nothing but a term of abuse? If in the last analysis we must admit that Roman traditionalists who objected to the frivolity of the *Ars* had more than a grain of truth on their side, we can still be grateful for this link across the centuries to the intricate workings of a lively and brilliant mind.

Notes

1 Respectively S. G. Owen and J. Wight Duff. However, Owen's overall verdict in his edition of *Tristia*, II (Oxford, 1924) is fairer to Ovid than this quotation would suggest.

2 E.g. *Tristia*, II. 207: 'perdiderint cum me duo crimina, carmen et error.' I do not wish to re-open the tangled question of Ovid's mysterious 'mistake', although suspecting that it was of at least equal weight to the *Ars* in the case against him (cf. *Ex Ponto*, III. 3. 72). Everything that can be gathered from Ovid's own writings, together with much speculation both ancient and modern, is collected by J. C. Thibault in his book *The Mystery of Ovid's Exile* (University of California Press, 1964). For the banning of the poem, see Owen's note on *Tristia*, II. 8.

3 XI. 20. 10.

4 L. P. Wilkinson, *Ovid Recalled* (Cambridge, 1955), 121. 'The prurient will read on with increasing disappointment, and may never reach their first meagre reward at the end of Book II.' (Ibid.)

5 *Tristia*, II. 247–50, cf. ibid., 303–4, *Ex Ponto*, III. 3. 51–2.

6 Cicero, *In Pisonem*, 70 (cf. R. G. M. Nisbet's edition [Oxford, 1961], Appendix 3).

7 I am surprised that translators and commentators should have missed the allusion to Augustus, without which 'nec nomen pertimuisse ducis' loses its point. A. W. J. Holleman (*Historia*, 20 [1971], 458 n. 2) interprets correctly. For 'dux bonus' of the emperor, cf. Horace, *Odes*, IV. 5. 5 and 37.

8 Hans Petersen, *Transactions of the American Philological Association* (*T.A.P.A.*), 92 (1961), 446 (but he exaggerates in writing that the lines 'are in themselves perhaps sufficient to explain, if not to justify Ovid's exile'). Compare P. A. Brunt, 'Pay and Superannuation in the Roman Army', *Papers of the British School at Rome*, N.S., 5 (1950), 63.

9 E.g. Propertius, III. 22. 17–18 (which Ovid has particularly in mind), Virgil, *Georgics*, II. 136ff.

10 *Annals*, I. 3.

11 The above paragraphs represent my own personal judgment: needless to say, there is plenty of scope for varying opinions. Many modern scholars consider Ovid not so apolitical after all, and even those most sympathetic to the poet may admit the justice of the régime's complaint against the *Ars* – 'There can be no doubt of the view which Roman officialdom must have taken of the *A.A.*: it was an immoral and subversive work, and not all the specious pleading of *Tristia*, II. can disguise that it would tend to foster adultery' (E. J. Kenney in *Ovidiana* [ed. N. Herescu, Paris, 1958], 208). It seems to me, however, that Ovid's defence, though a delicate one and very easily misrepresented, can be upheld.

12 *Jugurtha*, 4.

13 Seneca, *Epist.*, 49. 5.

14 Charles Segal, *Greece and Rome*, N.S., 17 (1970), 25–31, with further bibliography; J. P. V. D. Balsdon, *Life and Leisure in Ancient Rome* (Bodley Head, 1969), 136–41.

15 As at Horace, *Epist.*, I. 1. 16.

16 *Epigram* 27, Pfeiffer.

17 Hesiod, *Works and Days*, 571; Aratus, *Phaenomena*, 947, cf. Nicander, *Ther.*, 620, *Alex.*, 563.

18 Compare Kenney in *Ovidiana*, 201: 'When Ovid writes "hoc opus, hic labor est, primo sine munere iungi" (*A.A.*, I. 453) he is mocking not so much Virgil (*Aeneid*, VI. 129) as his own pretensions.'

19 Kenney in *Ovidiana*, 201–9, and more widely Eleanor Leach, *T.A.P.A.*, 95 (1964), 142–54 with reference to the *Georgics*.

20 E.g. *Georgics*, II. 259ff.

21 In text and interpretation I follow G. P. Goold, *Harvard Studies in Classical Philology*, 69 (1965), 65–6, without feeling that certainty has been achieved.

22 Hesiod, *Works and Days*, 536ff., and, much later, Oppian, *Halieutica*, III. 21ff. (a fisherman must be strong, swift-footed, neither too fat nor too thin), *Cynegetica*, I. 81ff.

23 A. L. Wheeler, *Classical Philology*, 5 (1910), 28–40; 6 (1911), 56–77.

24 A. W. Allen, *Yale Classical Studies*, 11 (1950), 255–77. P. Sullivan, *T.A.P.A.*, 92 (1961), 528–36, argues that a more positive and healthy attitude to love can also be found in Catullus and the elegists.

25 F. O. Copley, *T.A.P.A.*, 78 (1947), 285–300.

26 Propertius, II. 7. 19; *Corpus Tibullianum*, III. 19. (= IV. 13.) 3.

27 I. 81–2. We are in the Forum Iulium, where lawyers practised. Behind the fountain of the Appiades, steps lead up to the temple of Venus Genetrix.

28 *Tradition and Originality in Roman Poetry* (Oxford, 1968), 528ff.

29 As suggested to me by Mr N. J. Richardson. Compare Balsdon, *Life and Leisure in Ancient Rome*, 124.

30 Later in the Colonnade of the Argonauts, and then a colonnade of Trajan's Baths (scholiast on Juvenal, VI. 154).

31 Cicero, *Aratea*, fr. 25, Buescu.

32 Material in R. G. M. Nisbet and M. Hubbard commenting on Horace, *Odes*, I. 5. 16 (Oxford, 1970).

33 The original publication date seems to have been towards the end of 2 B.C., since the mock sea-battle of August 2 B.C. is said to have occurred 'recently' (I. 171).

34 Note *Remedia*, 155-6. Gaius is in the East, but has not yet had his summit conference with the Parthian king Phraataces, which took place in the spring of A.D. 2.

35 *Corpus Tibullianum*, III. 8. (= IV. 2.) 7-12.

36 A. E. Wardman, *Classical Quarterly*, N.S., 15 (1965), 101-3.

37 Suetonius, *Div. Aug.*, 44.

38 Accepting Bentley's emendation as probable.

39 Mr Kenney would now adopt Madvig's emendation, which is in fact read by the eleventh-century *Codex Berolinensis Hamiltonensis*, 471.

40 Propertius, I. 1. 25-6; III. 21. 9-10; III. 24. 17-18.

41 Cicero, *Tusc. Disp.*, IV. 74-5 (M. Pohlenz in *Hermes*, 41 [1906], 321ff., discusses the Greek background). All these precepts recur in Ovid.

42 There are problems concerning the text and interpretation of this couplet; see Kenney's note in his Oxford Text. Goold (*H.S.C.P.*, 69 [1965], 49-50) considers the lines spurious.

43 Contrast his usual attitude, discussed on p. 88 above.

44 This is not to maintain that the *Ars* never speaks of kindness and consideration between the sexes (e.g. I. 767-70, II. 663-6). Some consider Book III more ruthless than the previous two; the explanation might be that Ovid, having turned traitor to his sex, is determined to do the job thoroughly – hardly, I think, that his attitude to the work had changed.

IV

The Style of the Metamorphoses

E. J. Kenney

I

Judgments on Ovid's style have tended to exemplify something of the facility which they purport to expose. Often he has in effect been criticized for not being Virgil. So Mackail speaks of 'the tripping movement . . . into which [the hexameter] was metamorphosed . . . by the facile adroitness of Ovid'.[1] Similarly Green's verdict that Ovid's verses are 'under-enjambed' and 'over-dactylic'[2] can only mean 'compared with Virgil's'.[3] Glover called them 'often only elegiac couplets in disguise',[4] a sentence echoed by Wilkinson,[5] though with an important qualification: for having duly quoted the famous criticism of Dryden that 'Ovid with all his sweetness, has as little variety of Numbers and sound as [Claudian]: He is always as it were upon the Hand-gallop, and his Verse runs upon Carpet ground',[6] he goes on to add the rider 'Yet may not Ovid perhaps have been right, for the purpose in hand?'[7] That surely is the crux of the matter.

What was that purpose? Much ink has been spilt on the question whether the *Metamorphoses* is or is not an epic. von Albrecht's careful analysis of the surprisingly brief proem shows that Ovid's declared pretensions are those of an epic poet;[8] and Herter has rightly insisted on the significance of the word *perpetuum* (1. 4), with its oblique but unambiguous anti-Callimachean implication that the *Metamorphoses* was a single poem intended for continuous reading, and not merely a collection of epyllia.[9] There is of course in this attitude a touch of deliberate paradox, perhaps verging on defiance, since when all is said and done, the resemblance to the *Aetia*, metre apart, is immediately obvious; and whatever thematic architecture Ovid's ingenuity might devise or the percipience of modern critics detect, the poem is bound to appeal to most readers as a collection of stories. It is indeed, as von Albrecht has said, 'an epos *sui generis*',[10] and that uniqueness is, as he has also said, the decisive point. In setting out to write the *Metamorphoses* Ovid was attempting something for which, as he envisaged the undertaking, no precedents existed; and those readers who instinctively sense in the first four words of the poem, *in noua fert animus*, read autonomously, a proclamation by the poet to that effect are, I think, following a hint intended by him. However that may be, precisely what was he attempting? What is the special *genus* of which the *Metamorphoses* is sole representative? To this question very various answers have been returned. One critic sees the poem as an example of 'Kollektivgedicht',[11] another as an 'anti-epic' protest,[12] another as a playful variation of epic,[13] another as an epic of love,[14] yet another as an epic of rape;[15] and I have myself elsewhere offered epic of *pathos*.[16] The search for a label may or may not be a profitable exercise; the diversity of labels suggested at all events serves to emphasize the special character of the poem. However, there is one point on which the interpreters seem to be unanimous, and that is the dominant importance of narrative in the *Metamorphoses*, its status as what has been called 'the very soul of the work'.[17] To describe Ovid's verse medium as 'a comfortable, well-sprung, well-oiled vehicle for his story'[18] is perhaps to relegate it to too subordinate and separate a role: the medium and the message can hardly be distinguished in quite the way suggested by this metaphor. Nevertheless the idea of a vehicle is helpful as a reminder of the necessity for keeping this long poem moving and for sustaining its character as a *perpetuum carmen*. The reader of the *Metamorphoses* is always being carried on; the ingenious transitions from episode to episode, abused by Quintilian and variously criticized or justified by later critics,[19] are fundamentally a functional device (whatever extravagances Ovid may have committed in the application of it) to ensure a steady progress through the poem. Smoothness and speed are likewise the salient characteristics of Ovid's hexameter. Critics who merely miss in Ovid the weight, sonority and expressiveness of Virgil are failing to recognize the great difference, not only between the two poets, but between their two undertakings.[20] The comparison with Virgil is by no means misguided; but it is illuminating precisely as it directs attention to this difference.

The existence and instant canonization of the *Aeneid* confronted all subsequent aspirants to epic honours with a most intractable problem. Of surviving Latin epicists only Ovid and Lucan can be said to have tackled it with originality and anything approaching success. It is relevant to bring in Lucan at this point because the very different nature of his attempted solution and of the stylistic means by which he executed it helps to illustrate the originality of both the *Metamorphoses* and the *Bellum Civile*. Both poems were brilliant essays in a modern, or contemporary, style of epic which might legitimately challenge comparison with Virgil, not on his own ground (which Ovid, who obviously admired him, must have seen to be impossible),[21] but on a new and independent footing. In material, structure and intention Ovid's independence from Virgil is almost complete. In language it seems at first sight to be otherwise: for all Ovid's work is shot through and through with Virgilian reminiscences.[22] Closer analysis, however, shows that this is not a matter of straightforward borrowing and adaptation, but rather that what might be called a consistent and calculated process of denaturing has been at work. It is important to distinguish in Virgil's Latinity between its base, the 'common style', as a recent critic has called it,[23] which relates directly to the medium itself, the dactylic hexameter,[24] and what is specific and original to Virgil himself: his *callidae iuncturae*[25] and his management of the verse-period.[26] Virgil's penchant for 'coining . . . expressive original phrases out of extremely elementary words',[27] as seen in lines like

sensit laeta dolis et formae conscia coniunx (*Aen.*, VIII. 393)

(his consort felt, and, smiling at her ruse, knew that she was fair)[28]

is something more than a trick of style; it is part and parcel of the allusive, ambiguous and allegorical mode in which the *Aeneid* was composed. Ovid's diction (as will be illustrated below) is on the whole no more and no less plain than Virgil's; his use of it is infinitely more straightforward, because that straightforwardness was what the mode in which he was writing called for. Bömer's careful and perceptive analysis of this problem[29] perhaps fails to do full justice to its complexity when it speaks of the *debasement* of Virgil's diction by Ovid.[30] It would be more proper to say that Ovid restored to common currency what Virgil had temporarily taken out of general circulation. When however Bömer speaks of Ovid's 'profaning' his original[31] the term may be accepted if it is understood in the sense of making generally available. Ovid's adaptations of Virgilian diction and phraseology (which are of course not confined to the *Metamorphoses*) are best seen as a deliberate *vulgarisation* (in the strict French sense) by a poet who was himself a master-craftsman. His contribution to the subsequent development of Latin poetry may be described as the perfection of a poetic *koine*, a stylistic instrument which was freely manageable by writers of lesser genius. The Ovidian manner, as generations of clever English schoolboys have discovered, is imitable; Virgil's is not.[32]

Similar considerations apply to the management of the verse-period. The average length of Ovid's periods in the *Metamorphoses*, mechanically measured, probably does not differ significantly from that of Virgil's.[33] However, the important considerations here too are not quantitative but qualitative. Worstbrock's analyses have shown that the Virgilian sentence and period look forward to a concluding 'Schwerpunkt'.[34] The total effect is not thereby discontinuous, for Virgil always provides the necessary insurance against loss of momentum;[35] but it is (allowing for many designed variations in tempo) on the whole deliberate and measured. Ovid achieves his continuity and a markedly higher overall speed by a more even distribution of emphasis over his sentences; his periods less commonly build up in the Virgilian manner. Whereas, for instance, Virgil's 'golden' lines always have a clearly observable climactic function, oc-curing at pauses in the action or exposition,[36] Ovid's are more usually in the nature of casual decoration.[37] His method may perhaps be described as one of reliance on a succession of small surprises and detours: the main thread of the narrative or argument is never lost sight of, but the reader is constantly enter-tained by unexpected changes of subject, parentheses, adversa-tives, antitheses, all illuminated and sustained by a verbal wit that from time to time broadens into a full-scale *tour de force*.[38]

II

Virgil's vocabulary in the *Aeneid* has been exhaustively analysed by
Cordier,[39] and whatever reservations may be necessary about
particular features of his discussion, it clearly emerges from it
that the poet set himself to follow a *via media* between ordinary
speech and cultivated literary diction.[40] Such innovations as were
made by Ovid on the stock of epic diction inherited from his
great predecessor were in the main unobtrusive, but appear to
be designed to adapt it to the purposes of the 'modern' epic, as
I have described it, that the *Metamorphoses* was intended to be.
Archaisms, of which Virgil himself had made extremely sparing
use,[41] had little or no place in this type of poetry, and genuine
archaisms, as distinct from poeticisms – i.e. old words that had
won acceptance as part of the stock poetical vocabulary[42] – are
very rare in the *Metamorphoses*. It is not always easy to decide how
to classify certain isolated words or, what is more important,
how to assess their intended effect. Ovid uses the word *actutum*
(quickly) twice only, at *Her.*, XII. 207: *quos equidem actutum . . .*
(in aposiopesis), and *Met.*, III. 557, there in conjunction with two
elisions, both unusual:

> quem quidem ego actutum . . . cogam . . . fateri

(whom I myself at once . . . shall force to confess.)

As a glance at *T.L.L.* will show, *actutum* is an old word, frequent
in Comedy and occurring also in the fragments of Republican
Tragedy; it is used once by Virgil (*Aen.*, IX. 255). If, as is at least
possible, Ovid's treatment of the Pentheus story owes something
to Pacuvius,[43] *actutum* may have been intended as *color tragicus*
quite as much as *color epicus*. It is difficult to guess how much
impression such a single word can have made even on an alert
reader, but this would not be the only instance in Ovid of such
an allusion.[44] What is clear is that his use of 'poeticisms' is
extremely restrained: using as a convenient basis Cordier's
catalogue of what he (somewhat loosely)[45] classifies as Virgilian
archaisms we find:

(1) Some obviously useful and not obtrusively 'poetic' words
avoided by Ovid for no very clear reason: examples are *celero* (6
times[46] in the *Aeneid*), *fluentum* (3), *loquella**,[47] *pauperies*.[48]

(2) Some more obviously 'poetic' words not used by him: *cernuus, flictus, illuuies, intempestus, obnubo, pernix.*

(3) Some 'poetic' words used once only in *Aeneid* and *Metamorphoses* by both authors: *dius,*[49] *incanus, properus, sentus, suboles, tremebundus*; cf. *uirago* (once in *Aeneid,* twice in *Metamorphoses*).

These are no more than straws in the wind. A clearer picture of Ovid's policy as regards specifically poetic or epic diction can be obtained from studying his use of compound adjectives. That this class of word was recognized as posing a particular problem in Latin is evident from the well-known discussion of Quintilian (*Inst. Or.,* I. 5. 65–70). If Cordier's lists are again taken as a basis[50] we find:

(4) Some compounds used by both poets in *Aeneid* and *Metamorphoses*: *aeripes,*[51] *alipes* (2, 3)*, *armiger* (6, 5), *arquitenens* (1, 2), *bicolor* (2, 3), *bicornis* (1, 3)†[52]*, *biforis**, *biformis* (2, 5)*, *biiugus* (8,[53] 1), *bimembris* (1, 2)*, *caelicola* (8, 2), *corniger* (1, 6)*, *fatidicus* (3, 2)*, *fatifer* (2, 2)*, *grandaeuus* (1, 3)†*, *horrifer* (1, 3), *indigena* (2, 7)*, *laniger* (4, 4)†*, *letifer* (2, 5)*, *longaeuus* (14, 1)*, *magnanimus* (12, 4)†*, *naufragus, nubigena* (2, 2), *odorifer, pacifer, pestifer* (1, 5)*, *quadriiugus* (2,[54] 1)†*, *quadrupedans* (2, 1), *saetiger* (3, 3)*, *sagittifer, semianimis* (5, 4)*, *semifer* (2, 2), *semihomo, seminex* (5, 1)*, *semiuir* (2, 1)*, *septemplex* (1, 2)*, *somnifer* (1, 2), *soporifer, terrificus* (3, 1), *trisulcus*†*, *uulnificus* (1, 2).

(5) Some compounds used by Virgil in *Aeneid* but not by Ovid in *Metamorphoses*: *aequaeuus* (2), *aliger* (2),[55] *Appenninicola, armipotens* (5)*, *armisonus, auricomus, bellipotens, bifrons* (2), *bilinguis, bilix, bipatens* (2), *biremis* (2), *biuius,*[56] *caelifer, centumgeminus, caprigenus, conifer, cornipes* (2)*, *fumifer* (2), *Graiugena* (2), *horrificus* (3), *horrisonus* (2), *ignipotens* (7), *legifer**, *luctificus, malesuadus, malifer, mortifer**, *noctiuagus, oliuifer**, *omnigenus, omniparens, Phoebigena,*[57] *pinifer* (2)*, *primaeuus* (3), *quadrifidus*†, *regificus, septemgeminus, siluicola**, *sonipes* (3), *tergeminus* (2)*, *tricorpor, trifaux, trilix* (3), *Troiugena* (3), *turicremus**, *turriger* (2)*, *ueliuolus**, *uersicolor**, *uitisator, umbrifer, unanimus* (3).

(6) Some compounds used by Ovid in *Metamorphoses* but not by Virgil in *Aeneid* (except where otherwise noted these appear for the first time in Ovid):[58] *amnicola*‡,[59] *anguicomus, anguifer* (Propertius), *anguigena*‡, *anguipes, Appenninigena, armifer* (2)*, *aurigena, bifidus, bifurcus* (Livy), *bimaris* (4)* (Horace), *bimater, binominis** (Plautus?), *bipennifer* (2)*‡, *bisulcus* (2) (Lucretius, al.),

caducifer (2)*‡, *centimanus** (Horace), *Chimaerifer*‡, *circumfluus* (3), *circumsonus*, *clauiger* (3)*,[60] *colubrifer*, *falcifer** (Lucretius), *faticinus* (2)‡, *Faunigena*, *flammifer* (4)* (Ennius), *flexipes*‡, *florilegus*‡, *frugifer** (Ennius, Cicero, Livy), *frugilegus*‡, *fumificus* (Plautus), *gemellipara**‡, *glandifer* (Lucretius, Cicero), *granifer**‡, *herbifer**‡, *Ianigena*‡, *ignifer* (2)[61] (Lucretius), *ignigena*‡, *imbrifer* (Virgil†), *Iunonigena*‡, *laborifer* (2), *lanificus** (Tibullus), *Latonigena*‡, *Lemnicola*‡, *lentiscifer*‡, *liniger**, *luctisonus*‡, *magniloquus*, *mellifer*, *monticola*‡, *multicauus*‡, *multifidus* (2), *multiforus*, *nubifer**, *opifer* (2), *palmifer** (Propertius), *papyrifer**‡, *penatiger*‡, *pinniger** (Lucretius), *portentificus*, *puerperus* (adj.), *racemifer* (2)*‡, *ruricola* (4)*, *rurigena*‡, *sacrificus* (3)*, *salutifer* (3)*, *saxificus**, *securifer*‡,[62] *semicaper**‡, *semicremus*‡, *semideus* (subst.) (2)‡,[63] *semilacer*‡, *semimas* (2)* (Varro), *septemfluus* (2)‡, *serpentiger*‡, *sexangulus*, *spumiger*[64] (Lucretius), *squamiger* (Lucretius, Cicero), *terrigena* (4)* (Lucretius), *triceps* (Cicero), *tricuspis*‡, *tridentifer*‡, *tridentiger*‡,[65] *trifidus*, *triformis* (3) (Horace), *uaticinus* (Livy), *uelifer* (Propertius), *uenefica* (adj.) (?),[66] *uenenifer*.

It has seemed worthwhile to reproduce these lists, since, though mildly repellent in appearance, they provide the material for some simple but enlightening deductions of general relevance to Ovid's lexical choices in the *Metamorphoses*. The proportion of identifiably 'poetic' or 'epic' words in his vocabulary does not seem to differ substantially from that in Virgil's. He does not go out of his way to avoid compounds already used in the *Aeneid* and therefore, so to say, sanctified, but he also innovates on his own account with moderate freedom. His innovations are in the main themselves traditional in so far as they conform to types already well established in poetic usage, with a predominance of verbal suffixes in *-cola*, *-gena*, *-ficus*, *-fer*, *-ger*, etc. and numerical prefixes in *bi-*, *tri-*, *centi-*, *multi-*, *semi-*, etc. Formations on the model of *anguicomus*, *anguipes*, *flexipes*, etc. are in a small minority.[67] In a poem of some 12,000 verses this relatively small number of poeticisms cannot impart any very marked coloration, and (especially if one takes into account other features of Ovid's vocabulary, discussed below) it is probable that their metrical convenience was at least as important to him as their expressive value. Both prefixes and suffixes were a valuable source of short syllables and helped in the unobtrusive production of dactyls. Strategically placed, the longer compounds also contribute to the smoothness, fluency and speed that was necessary to Ovid's narrative. Thus those of the metrical form ∪ – ∪ ∪ occur after a 'weak' (trochaic) caesura in the fourth foot, yielding a rapid rhythm affected by Ovid much more than by Virgil,[68] or, when used in oblique cases, after a trochaic caesura in the first foot, so filling out the first half of the verse and creating 'tension', i.e. the expectation of a noun in agreement to follow, and hence again contributing rapidity.

These metrical considerations are relevant to another class of compound words in the formation of which Ovid exercised some freedom, that of verbs and participles (or words of participial form).[69] For instance, the compound *defrenatus*‡ was clearly coined by Ovid to fit the verse in the scene in which Neptune unleashes the rivers to flood the earth:

> fontibus ora relaxant
> et defrenato uoluuntur in aequora cursu   (I. 281–2)

(they take the curbs from their mouths and in unbridled course roll down to the sea.)

Here however there are other factors at work besides the purely metrical: the development of an image of racing horses begun at l. 280 (*totas inmittite habenas*) and expressiveness in the spondees of *defrenato*, suggesting a pause while the mass of waters builds up before sweeping resistlessly on to the sea in the following dactyls. Even more remarkable are the double compounds, of which one perhaps deserves particular notice. Into his account of the metamorphosis of Ceyx and Alcyone, one of the most poignant passages of the poem, Ovid inserts a short *ecphrasis*, skilfully positioned so as to offer the least possible obstruction to the current of the narrative:[70]

> adiacet undis
> facta manu moles, quae primas aequoris iras[71]
> frangit et incursus quae praedelassat aquarum   (XI. 728–30)

(Right by the waves was a man-made breakwater, which took the first shock of the angry sea and wore out beforehand the oncoming waters.)

The unique *praedelasso*‡[72] is finely descriptive in itself and also contributes to the idyllic atmosphere of calm after storm in which the sufferings of the tormented pair find release:

> tum iacet unda maris: uentos custodit et arcet
> Aeolus egressu praestatque nepotibus aequor (747–8)

(Then [sc. during the 'halcyon days'] the waves are at rest,
for Aeolus keeps the winds close, forbidding them to emerge,
and provides for his descendants a level ocean.)

The rarity of such formations in Latin (for so far as I am aware this possibility was not much exploited by later poets) must have enhanced their effect on the Roman ear.

An especially rich category of Ovidian coinages and *hapax legomena* is that of participles compounded with the negative prefix *in-*.[73] Like many of the other compound words discussed these are often long, but they do not merely serve to fill up the line: they can be used with widely differing effect. One may contrast the contributions made to the movement of the verse by *inobseruatus** and *indeuitatus*‡ in the same story. The first occurs in a piece of fast-moving, relatively colourless 'linking' narrative:

> pulchrior in tota quam Larisaea Coronis
> non fuit Haemonia: placuit tibi, Delphice, certe,
> dum uel casta fuit uel inobseruata, sed ales
> sensit adulterium Phoebeius *eqs.* (II. 542–5)

(In the whole of Thessaly no girl was more beautiful than
Coronis of Larissa: you certainly, Apollo, thought so, as long
as she was faithful – or unwatched. But the bird of Phoebus
discovered her infidelity . . .)

There is enjambment between ll. 542–3, 544–5, and only the lightest of pauses at the end of l. 543 (since *certe*, though pointed, is not strongly emphatic); and the placing of *inobseruata* (ᵕ – – – ᵕ) in the penultimate position in the line is managed so as to convey a characteristically Ovidian point while not impeding the movement of the verses. That point depends for its effect, not only on the sense, but on the greater length of the word that complements *casta*; but the word itself, like the diction of the whole passage (at least as far as l. 549) is colourless, as its function in the context requires it to be. Clearly Ovid coined *inobseruatus* to perform a specific function in this passage, which it does with extreme efficiency. The second word occurs in a narrative sequence which is also fast-moving, but in this case 'pathetic', with a more colourful vocabulary affectively deployed:

> laurea delapsa est audito crimine amantis,
> et pariter uultusque deo plectrumque colorque
> excidit, utque animus tumida feruebat ab ira,
> arma adsueta rapit[74] flexumque a cornibus arcum
> tendit et illa suo totiens cum pectore iuncta
> indeuitato traiecit pectora telo. (II. 600–5)

(His laurel wreath slipped from the god's head as he heard of his beloved's offence,[75] and in one moment his expression changed, he dropped his plectrum, and his face went white. His heart swelling with rage, he snatched up his familiar weapon, strung his bow, and into the breast that so often had been pressed to his he sent deep the arrow that cannot miss.)

Ovid sketches in the god's reaction to the news by focusing attention on externals: and his consternation is neatly conveyed in a favourite figure, syllepsis.[76] There is enjambment between ll. 601–2, 603–4 (note the position of the verbs *excidit, tendit*), 604–5; and the single subordinate clause in l. 602 retards the narrative just enough, and no more, to emphasize that Apollo's consternation is instantly succeeded by a new emotion, anger. This swift period, packed with emotion and incident, is suddenly slowed down and, so to say, stopped in its tracks by the four-word[77] last verse with its enclosing word-order (cf. I. 282 quoted above):

> *indeuitato* traiecit pectora *telo*.

Apollo's precipitate action, which he is immediately to regret (612, *paenitet heu! sero poenae crudelis amantem*), is finished and irrevocable. Again, if Ovid had been content to use existing epic diction, the phrase *non euitabile telum*, which he does in fact use later in the poem (VI. 234), or some similar variant (cf. III. 301, *ineuitabile fulmen*), lay ready to hand on the model of Virgil's *ineluctabile tempus* (*Aen.*, II. 324) or *inexorabile fatum* (*G.*, II. 491).[78]

Instead he chose to coin the strong and majestic *indeuitatus* for the particular effect that he wanted.

Other features of Ovid's diction may be reviewed more briefly. In general it may be said that they were all directed to extending, within the limits of linguistic and literary propriety (i.e. without substantially trenching on either the colloquial or the archaic or the hyperpoetic resources of Latin) the poetical *koine* that in his amatory works he had already gone a long way towards establishing as what might be called a standard literary dialect of Latin.[79] Most of his predilections are obviously dictated by the desire to make his verse more smooth and dactylic: e.g. adjectives in *-ilis*, neuter nouns in *-men*,[80] and above all Greek proper names. As a source of new poetical vocabulary borrowings from Greek had been ruled out by the common consent of the Augustan poets (Horace's remarks on the subject are sufficiently well known), and in the *Metamorphoses* Ovid shows himself predictably restrained.[81] With proper names, in contrast, he is extremely lavish. This, in a poem which takes a wide sweep through Greek mythology, was of course to be expected; and Ovid was as sensitive as any of his predecessors or successors to the emotive or purely musical effects of names.[82] What particularly deserves remark is the way in which, as with the compounds already discussed, his diction is engineered to smooth and accelerate the verse. Thus his evident preference for adjectival forms in *-is*, *-idis/os* over the alternatives available must be largely due to the metrical utility of the endings *-idă*, *-idĭs/ŏs*, *-idĕ*, *-idĕs*, *-idăs*.[83] More striking than this are the variations in adjectival forms of the same name that occur purely as suits the metre: *quid Achaica dextera posset* (XII. 70), *per Achaiadas urbes* (III. 511, al.); *Acheloides unde* (V. 552), *Acheloiadumque relinquit* (XIV. 87); *Cephisidas undas* (I. 369), *Cephisias ora Procrusten* (VII. 438); *Cytherea laboras* (XV. 816, al.), *Cythereia poenam* (IV. 190), *Cythereiadasque columbas* (XV. 386), *diua Cythereide natum* (IV. 288), *Cytheriaca . . . myrto* (*Fast.*, IV. 15); *Dryopeius illa* (VIII. 751), *Dryopeida tradit* (VIII. 872);[84] *Therses Ismenius oris* (XIII. 682), *Ismenides aras* (III. 733, al.); *Latonia si non* (I. 696), *Latoides aras* (VIII. 278), *Latous harundine uictum* (VI. 384), *Latoius adstitit aruis* (XI. 196)[85] (cf. *Latonigena*, above);[86] *Maeoniaeque . . . Arachnes* (VI. 5), *Maeonis elusam* (VI. 103); *rapta Minoide Diam* (VIII. 174), *ne forte parum Minoia credar* (*Her.*, IV. 61); *Alcithoe Minyeias* (IV. 1), *Minyeides intus* (IV. 32, al.), *Minyeia proles* (IV. 389); *Nyseides antris* (III. 314), *Nysiadas nymphas* (*Fast.*, III. 769); *Pallantius heros* (*Fast.*, V. 647), *Pallantias annos* (IX. 421), *Pallantidos ortu* (XV. 700); *cum Parrhasio Ancaeo* (VIII. 315), *Parrhasis erubuit* (II. 460); *Pelias hasta* (XIII. 109), *Peliacae . . . cuspidis ictu* (XII. 74); *Pelopeia Pittheus* (VIII. 622), *Pelopeiadesque Mycenae* (VI. 414), *Pelopeidas undas* (*Fast.*, IV. 285); *post Phaethonteos . . . ignes* (IV. 246), *Phaethontida uersum* (XII. 581); *Phinea cecidere manu* (V. 109), *Phineia mensis* (*Fast.*, VI. 131); *Schoeneia dictis* (X. 660), *Schoeneida dicam* (*Am.*, I. 7. 13); *Sidōnius hospes* (III. 129), *Sidōniae comites* (IV. 543), *Sidōnida nomine dicunt* (II. 840), *Sidōnis inque pyra* (XIV. 80);[87] *Teuthranteusque Caicus* (II. 243), *Teuthrantia turba sorores* (*Her.*, IX. 51); *Titania mota est* (I. 395, al.), *Titanidos atria Circes* (XIII. 968, al.), *Titaniacis ablata draconibus* (VII. 398); *Zanclaea classis harena* (XIII. 729), *Zancleia saxa* (XIV. 47).

In spite of this apparent profusion of forms it becomes clear when the manner of their employment is considered (which must be the justification for quoting and not merely referring to the foregoing instances) that a principle something like that of formulaic economy is here at work. The same principle can be detected in Ovid's employment of some common nouns and adjectives. Thus his favoured formations in *-men*, previously referred to, are used for choice in the ablative singular and accusative plural, where they provide a dactyl ending in an open vowel.[88] Similarly his abstract fourth declension substantive formations in *-us*, of which he is a fancier in a small way,[89] occur mostly in the dative and ablative plural, providing a dactyl ending in *-s*.[90] When variant forms of the same word are employed we have in effect a composite declension: *conamine* but *conatibus*, *hortamine* but *hortatibus*.

Such devices as these for enlarging the compass of the poet's linguistic resources were not invented by Ovid or practised only by him; what is new and peculiar to him is the unobtrusive efficiency[91] with which he applied them to the creation of the copious and limpid style – a transmitting rather than, as with Virgil, a refracting medium – which he saw as appropriate for the *Metamorphoses*. In his exploitation of these possibilities he resembles (though he is more restrained) Lucretius more closely than any of his other predecessors. This is perhaps not surprising, for Ovid, intelligent and impatient of the obscure, was temperamentally equipped to respond to the magnificent and unequivocal clarity of the Lucretian message,[92] to appreciate the masterful handling of the language which made that clarity possible, and to adapt the lessons learned from Lucretius to his own purposes.

III

It may have been J. P. Postgate (for I cannot now trace the reference) who somewhere referred to Ovid as a 'chartered libertine' in matters of syntax. This summary judgment may be allowed to stand if by syntax be chiefly understood the ordering of words in the sentence. Ovid does not seem to me to strain the Latin language as, in their different ways, do Virgil or Propertius or Lucan: his case-usage, for instance, though flexible and versatile, cannot be called either difficult or markedly licentious.[93] So too his use of 'poetic' singulars and plurals, given that the latter especially offer an easily available source of extra short syllables, rarely amounts to abuse;[94] where it may seem to verge on doing so, the motive is plain, to assist rapidity. So within the space of three verses Hyacinthus' wound is now plural, now singular (x. 187–9). That most readers of the *Metamorphoses*, unless they happen to be grammatical lepidopterists, with net and killing-bottle at the ready as they read, do not notice such things is the best possible index of Ovid's linguistic mastery. The same is for the most part true of the dislocations of 'natural' word-order identified by grammarians as *hyperbaton*.[95] Ovid particularly affects this device, as has more than once been noted. His most striking instances, amounting to abuse, occur in the elegiac works;[96] those which are found in the *Metamorphoses* are not usually disturbing 'provided', as Postgate remarks, 'that the words are read and not simply surveyed'; indeed a reader who is moderately well accomplished in Latin is unlikely to notice, unless halted and admonished by (superfluous) editorial commas, that he is confronted with hyperbaton in

> non mihi quae duri colerent pater arua iuuenci
> lanigerosue greges, non ulla armenta reliquit   (iii. 584–5)

(My father left me no land to be tilled by patient oxen, no sheep, no cattle.)

The commentators, displaying it may be unusual tact, in fact
offer no remarks on the word-order, which is in a sense a compliment to the poet; but in a discussion such as this it does
deserve remark for its unobtrusive functional efficiency. In their
context, in which of course they must be read, the verses emphasize that the family's only resource was fishing: this is done
by using the familiar technique of negative enumeration. What
comes of this technique when it is used heavy-handedly can be
seen in Lucan;[97] here the touch is as light as is consistent with
making the point. Grammatically the sentence is articulated
by the repeated *non* (anaphora = copula), and the combined
effect of the word-order and the metre is that the two cola,
though disparate in length, are equivalent in weight. The rapid
dactyls of ll. 584-5[a] carry the reader on to the slow spondees
of l. 585[b], and the first *non, pater* and *arua* all look forward to the
verb *reliquit* which completes both syntax and utterance. Conversely, *ulla* is felt as qualifying the first *non* ἀπὸ κοινοῦ (see below).
Dissected in this laborious way, the structure sounds complicated
and difficult; but read as a single syntactical grouping[98] it offers
no impediment to understanding because the relationship of
the syntactical elements, which is independent of the order in
which they occur, cannot be in doubt. Occasionally in the
Metamorphoses we may encounter a hyperbaton seemingly of the
forced 'elegiac' type, such as becomes habitual to Martial:

> nam graue respiciens inter duo lumina ferrum
> qua naris fronti committitur accipis imae   (XII. 314-15)

(for as you look back you receive a heavy spearpoint between
the eyes, where nose and forehead join)

or (if my interpretation is correct):

> hac agit ut pastor per deuia rura capellas
> dum uenit abductas et structis cantat auenis   (I. 676-7)

(With this [i.e. the *caduceus*], disguised as a shepherd, he
drove through unfrequented ways the goats which he stole
as, playing on his reed pipe, he came along.)

The editor who prints these passages with commas around
accipis and *abductas* is no doubt doing his duty as a grammarian,
but the signpost that he thinks to offer the traveller is more

apt to behave as stumbling-block or stile:[99] ancient readers did not need it, nor should a modern reader who is conscious that Latin is not English or French or German and who has trained himself to go on until *the poet* tells him, by providing the awaited syntactical/rhetorical dénouement, that he may stop:

> qua naris *fronti* committitur accipis *imae*;
> dum *uenit* abductas *et* STRVCTIS *cantat* AVENIS.

But are these two instances in fact as purely 'elegiac' as they seem? It is at least worth asking the question whether the positioning of *accipis* and *abductas* is deliberate, to emphasize that the spear struck *in the middle* of the face, that the thefts were accomplished *all the while* the god strolled and played. It does not do to underrate Ovid or any other *doctus poeta* in even the smallest points of technique, and if all he had wanted was to make his verses scan he could have done so in numerous other ways.

Mention has been made of the so-called ἀπὸ κοινοῦ word-order, in which part of the second member of an utterance modifies the first member as well.[100] It becomes unnecessary to embark on an elaborate classification of this usage once it is grasped that it is essentially a special type of ellipse, the figure in which part of an utterance is suppressed for the sake of economy and effect, being readily 'understood' from the context. Not only words but cases may be treated in this way:

> per iuga chrysolithi positaeque ex ordine gemmae (II. 109)

(along the yoke chrysolites and jewels set in fair array
(F. J. Miller), i.e. 'per iuga ex ordine positi chrysolithi et
(aliae) gemmae')

or

> ut limbus totumque appareat aurum (II. 734)

(so that the whole of the golden border shall be seen, i.e. 'ut totus appareat limbus totumque aurum', or rather, since hendiadys too is at work, 'ut totus appareat aureus limbus'.)[101]

The principles that sentences should be read as wholes and that each word should be understood in relation to the entire context is fundamental to a correct reading of Latin poetry and a good deal of Latin prose. In their light even Ovid's more apparently wilful games with syntax ought not to impede comprehension:

> fluminaque obliquis cinxit decliuia ripis　　　　　　　(I. 39)

(and confined the rivers within sloping banks and made them flow down [sc. to the sea].)

As has been pointed out by Bömer,[102] the attributes proper to rivers and their banks have changed places. Double enallage, as this is termed, was already known to Ovid's readers from Virgil and earlier poets,[103] and both words were familiar enough in their proper senses for an accomplished reader to grasp and relish what Ovid was up to. But, once again, is this pure play? May there not be a deliberate stroke of wit, a hint of the chaos from which order was emerging and a suggestion of a period during which the rivers were still learning their place in the new order of things and in which, for the moment, stream and banks were as yet not clearly distinguished? It is at least a piquant thought. The main point to be made, however, is that identification and classification of the various syntactical figures to be found in Ovid's Latinity, though an entirely praiseworthy occupation, is not essential to intelligent comprehension of his poetry; indeed there is a danger that such exercises may encourage the disposition to see an abnormality, deserving defence or at least palliation, in what is really the acquisition by Latin of a flexibility which, compared with Greek, it lacked in its rude and inartificial state.[104]

IV

We may now turn from grammar to rhetoric, from this necessarily partial and fragmentary review of Ovid's linguistic resources and expedients to consider how he employed them in action, i.e. in the continuous utterance of the poem. That Ovid's style is 'rhetorical' his critics all agree; not all trouble to define adequately what they mean by the term. Most good Latin poetry is rhetorical in the sense that it is engineered to produce a particular effect on the reader; the artistic success of the result depends principally on whether the poet observes a due proportion between ends and means. For Ovid, writing the sort of poem that the *Metamorphoses* was intended to be, two principal ends had to be kept in

view if the reader's attention was not to flag: the need to keep
the poem moving continuously, and the need to vary the tone
and tempo according to the character of the episodes themselves.
It is the first of these needs that dictated a fundamental characteristic of his style, the contrast between the elegiac (as one might
term it) brevity and terseness of individual members (clauses,
cola) and the flowing amplitude of the sentences as a whole.
Professor Nims, I think, puts his finger on this point when he
remarks that 'Ovid . . . has been found long-winded, even if
musically so, but the general effect of his writing is one of
conciseness'.[105] One of the devices by which he achieves this
effect is not peculiar to him, the so-called 'theme and variation'.[106]
Sometimes, it is true, this amounts to little more than saying the
same thing twice:

> sed te decor iste, quod optas,
> esse uetat, uotoque tuo tua forma repugnat   (I. 488–9)

(but that beauty of yours prevents you from being what you
want to be [sc. a virgin], and your prayer is thwarted by your
loveliness)

differs essentially very little from

> nequitiam fugio, fugientem forma reducit;
> auersor morum crimina, corpus amo   (*Am.*, III. 11. 37–8)

(I flee from your infidelity, but as I flee your beauty brings
me back; I hate your character, I love your body.)

These are indeed 'the hexameters of an elegist'; yet the emphasis
on Daphne's beauty as the cause of her undoing is after all at the
centre of the story. More clearly disciplined and functional is the
creation of Man:

> pronaque cum spectent animalia cetera terram,
> os homini sublime dedit caelumque uidere
> iussit et erectos ad sidera tollere uultus   (I. 84–6)

(and whereas the rest of the animal creation go on all fours
and look down at the earth, to man he gave an uplifted face
and bade him gaze on the heavens and raise his eyes aloft to
the stars.)

The contrast between man and the other animals (a commonplace of ancient thought, as Bömer's note shows) is pressed home by the tricolon structure and the progressive amplifications *sublime > caelum > sidera*: the divine element in man's composition is *en rapport* with the stars, themselves divine. The triple structure of ll. 85–6 responds to that of the opening verses of the paragraph:

> sanctius his animal mentisque capacius altae
> deerat adhuc et quod dominari in cetera posset   (76–7)

(There was as yet no animal more godlike than these, more capable of receiving lofty intelligence,[107] and such as might rule over the rest.)

A pathetic effect is evident in

> sternuntur segetes et deplorata coloni
> uota iacent, longique perit labor irritus anni   (I. 272–3)

(The crops are laid flat, the farmer's prayers lie given over for dead, and the long year's toil has gone for nothing.)

Here variation combines with imagery, diction (the effect of the stately *deplorata*) and interlocking word-order (l. 273: aBbA) to emphasize the peasants' despair. Grandeur is the note struck in

> sed regina tamen || sed opaci maxima mundi ||
> sed tamen inferni pollens matrona tyranni   (V. 507–8)

(but yet she [Proserpine] is a queen, the greatest in that dark world, powerful wife of the lord of the underworld.)

Here the tricolon structure is formally articulated and spaced by the repeated *sed*, and the splendour of Proserpine's position emphasized by the 'golden' line 508 (abBA). This technique can also be effective in narrative:

> Lydia tota fremit, Phrygiaeque per oppida facti
> rumor it et magnum sermonibus occupat orbem (VI. 146–7)

(All Lydia is in turmoil, the news of the deed goes through the towns of Phrygia and fills the whole world with rumour.)

Here variation is accompanied by extension: the words connoting rumour, *fremit*, *rumor*, *sermonibus*, act as a sort of semantic anaphora articulating the account of the spread of the news from

Lydia through Phrygia and out into the wide world. The dactyls
of l. 146 and the enjambment *facti/rumor* add speed, and the
enclosing word-order *magnum . . . orbem* rounds off the picture
and emphasizes how completely the news filled the world, vast
as it is. In the same way, on a slightly larger scale, the different
phases of an action are brought out both pictorially and con-
ceptually in

> his, ut quaeque pia est, hortatibus impia prima est
> et, ne sit scelerata, facit scelus; haud tamen ictus
> ulla suos spectare potest, oculosque reflectunt
> caecaque dant saeuis auersae uulnera dextris   (VII. 339–42)

([Pelias is murdered by his daughters at the instigation of
Medea.] At her bidding each daughter, the more she loved
her father, the more eagerly she struck, and to avoid the
reproach of wickedness did a wicked deed. Yet none could
bear to look at the blows she dealt, all averted their eyes and
turning away inflicted with cruel hand wounds they could not
see.)

This is a fine example of Ovid's extreme verbal dexterity in the
exploitation of paradox, conveyed through a sort of double
theme and variation. The idea of the first occurs more than once
in the poem, varied with Ovid's habitual ease:

> incipit esse tamen melior germana parente
> et consanguineas ut sanguine leniat umbras,
> impietate pia est   (VIII. 475–7)

(However the feelings of a sister began to prevail [in Althaea]
over those of a mother, and to placate with blood the ghost
of a blood-relation,[108] she is undutifully dutiful)

and, more succinctly,

> ultusque parente parentem
> natus erit facto pius et sceleratus eodem   (IX. 407–8)

([Themis on the killing of Eriphyle by Alcmaeon to avenge
the death of Amphiaraus] . . . and his son, avenging parent on
parent, shall be by the same deed dutiful and wicked.)

This idea is then exploited in the second theme and variation by
being, so to say, translated into action; as in other cases the period

is completed by a verse with interlocking word-order (ab A B; but for the position of the verb a golden line). There is a tendency here towards what in later poetry, especially in Juvenal, becomes a mannerism, the rounding off of a train of thought with a self-contained and quotable *sententia*. So in

nec tam

turpe fuit uinci quam contendisse decorum est,
magnaque dat nobis tantus solacia uictor.   (IX. 5–7)

(It was less shameful to be beaten than it is honourable to have fought, and it is a great consolation to have succumbed to so mighty a victor [Achelous on his wrestling defeat by Hercules].)

There is in fact a concealed tricolon structure here, for l. 6 falls into two portions of unequal length, linked and contrasted by the two pairs of verbs in different tenses, whereas the interlocking word-order of l. 7 welds it into a single whole:

turpe *fuit* VINCI ‖ quam CONTENDISSE decorum *est*,

magnaque dat nobis tantus solacia uictor.

The quality of Ovid's technical achievement in the *Metamorphoses* is not fully grasped unless the reader has trained himself to be consciously aware of the enormous range of variations which the poet imparts to these basic poetic structures. It is because of this variety that he is not monotonous as, say, Lucan is monotonous. Lucan provides an instructive contrast precisely because, though his techniques are in many respects essentially Ovidian, he lacks Ovid's versatility and flexibility in applying them.

V

It is convenient to use the device of 'theme and variation' to illustrate the application of Ovid's techniques on a small scale. To extend these illustrations and this style of analysis on a larger scale would involve the discussion of whole books and episodes, which space does not allow and which is perhaps rather the province of the commentator.[109] I shall therefore conclude the chapter by reviewing a number of slightly longer passages which seem to me to exemplify certain other aspects of Ovid's art, without pretending to completeness or even system. In a poem of such immense variety and of a richness sometimes verging on indiscipline (though never anarchy) random, or perhaps more accurately capricious, sampling is perhaps as good an approach as any. All my examples (and the same, I suspect, would be true of any others that might be preferred) are in fact essentially making the same point: they all illustrate the (on the whole, barring certain isolated *tours de force*) unobtrusive efficiency (I have used this phrase before, but make no apology for the repetition) with which Ovid keeps his poem moving and holds continuously the attention of his readers.

I have said that Ovid is never monotonous as, for instance, Lucan is monotonous. He was aware of the need for continual slight variations in tone and tempo in such a long poem. So in the account of Jason and the fire-breathing bulls:

> postera depulerat stellas Aurora micantes;   100
> conueniunt populi sacrum Mauortis in aruum
> consistuntque iugis; medio rex ipse resedit
> agmine purpureus sceptroque insignis eburno.
> ecce adamanteis Vulcanum naribus efflant
> aeripedes tauri, tactaeque uaporibus herbae   105
> ardent; utque solent pleni resonare camini
> aut ubi terrena silices fornace soluti
> concipiunt ignem liquidarum adspergine aquarum,
> pectora sic intus clausas uoluentia flammas
> gutturaque usta sonant. tamen illis Aesone natus   110
> obuius it; uertere truces uenientis ad ora
> terribiles uultus praefixaque cornua ferro
> puluereumque solum pede pulsauere bisulco
> fumificisque locum mugitibus impleuerunt.
> deriguere metu Minyae; subit ille nec ignes   115
> sentit anhelatos (tantum medicamina possunt)
> pendulaque audaci mulcet palearia dextra
> suppositosque iugo pondus graue cogit aratri
> ducere et insuetum ferro proscindere campum   (VII. 100–19)

(As soon as next day's dawn had banished the bright stars, the people assembled at the sacred field of Mars and took their stand on the surrounding hills. In their midst sat the king, purple-clad and resplendent with his ivory sceptre. Now,

breathing fire from their adamantine nostrils came the
brazen-footed bulls, and the grass shrivelled as their breath
touched it. As a well-stoked furnace roars or as baked lime
burns when slaked with water, so the chests of the bulls
and their fiery throats roared with the flames within.
Nevertheless the son of Aeson went to meet them. They
menacingly swung their fearful heads and iron-tipped horns
to face him as he came, pawed the dusty earth with their
cloven feet, and filled the place with their smoky bellowings.
The Minyans were rigid with terror, but Jason approached
without feeling the fiery breath (so powerful were the charms)
and with daring hand stroked their dewlaps, yoked them, and
constrained them to draw the heavy plough and cleave with
the share the unaccustomed soil.)

Ovid presents the scene, in contrast to his model Apollonius,
as an amphitheatral set-piece,[110] with the bulls in the centre;
for Jason's victory is such a walk-over as scarcely to merit
description. This concentration on a particular moment of the
action and the taking of the rest for granted is of course Alexandrian and characteristic of Ovid's procedure in many episodes
of the poem. Down to l. 112 the narrative moves swiftly, only
ll. 100 and 103 being heavily endstopped, and enjambment
being frequent (102–3, 104–5, 105–6, 107–8, 109–10, 110–11,
111–12). Similarly with ll. 115–19, where enjambment (115–16,
118–19) and parenthesis[111] help to polish off the actual accom-
plishment of the feat in very short order. Between these lively
passages intervenes the description of the bulls: static and so
menacing. Their initial reaction to Jason's appearance is conveyed by the (enjambed) *uertere truces . . . uultus*, but that is the
only movement in the scene. Each of the three succeeding verses
is self-contained: the bulls stand staring, horns at the ready (112),
pawing the ground (113; note the alliteration) and bellowing
(114; note the onomatopoeic and metrical effects – slightly overdone?). All this, as the reader knows perfectly well, is a sham. The
Minyans of course are not in on the secret, but Jason, as Ovid
tells the story, is not called upon (or possibly lacks the wit?) even
to simulate anxiety or effort.[112] This brief static interruption in
the brisk current of the episode (which continues in what follows)
is not an unmotivated descriptive excursus but a subtle stroke of

wit. By pausing to call attention to the appearance and behaviour of the bulls Ovid is reminding us how the whole encounter has been 'set up' by Medea – who is of course the figure that he and we are really interested in. The bulls *look* alarming – to the outsider and those not in the know – but they do not actually *do* anything; they just stand, stare, fume and bellow.

In this passage the variations in tempo are directly connected with the incidence of enjambment (among other things); and we may now recall the criticism mentioned earlier, that Ovid's hexameters are 'under-enjambed'. In the *Aeneid* it has been calculated that Virgil enjambs on an average about forty per cent of his verses, a higher proportion than in any other hexameter poetry.[113] Taking *Metamorphoses* VII as a representative book I have estimated that the corresponding figure for Ovid is in the region of thirty-five per cent: not exactly a low figure when compared even with the *Aeneid*, let alone with the twenty per cent of the *Eclogues*. But just as with Virgil,[114] considerable variations occur, especially in speeches: to look no further than the beginning of Book VII, the proportion of enjambed verses rises sharply towards the end of Medea's soliloquy, at ll. 46–71; for other examples see also ll. 159–62 (swift 'linking' narrative), 188–91 (preliminary to prayer), 406–15 (parenthetic explanation), etc. Nor do the types of enjambment used by Ovid seem to differ appreciably from those of Virgil;[115] the main and substantial difference is in overall frequency of employment.[116] In such matters Ovid's practice seems to represent an instinctive compromise. If enjambment were to exceed the Virgilian figure, more frequent and stronger pauses in the interior of the verse would be necessary to prevent it from accelerating into a breathless gallop, but too many such pauses would unbalance the relationship between hexameter and sentence. Ovid's practice represents what his ear told him suited the general narrative pace that he wished to maintain.

To illustrate the speed at which Ovid can, when he wishes, make his verses move, we may consider the description of Myrrha's sleepless night:

> noctis erat medium, curasque et corpora somnus
> soluerat; at uirgo Cinyreia peruigil igni
> carpitur indomito furiosaque uota retractat   370

et modo desperat, modo uult temptare, pudetque,
et cupit et quid agat non inuenit, utque securi
saucia trabs ingens, ubi plaga nouissima restat,
quo cadat in dubio est omnique a parte timetur:
sic animus uario labefactus uulnere nutat   375
huc leuis atque illuc momentaque sumit utroque.
nec modus et requies nisi mors reperitur amoris;
mors placet; erigitur laqueoque innectere fauces
destinat et zona summo de poste reuincta
'care uale Cinyra causamque intellege mortis'   380
dixit et aptabat pallenti uincula collo   (x. 368–81)

(It was midnight, and all around minds and bodies lay
relaxed in sleep. Only Cinyras' daughter was wakeful, tormented by the flame she could not subdue, as she went over
in her mind again and again her frenzied prayers. Now she
despaired, now she was for the attempt; shame and lust
alternated in her, but she could not tell what to do. As a
great tree, mortally stricken by the axe and awaiting the final
blow, inspires fear on all sides as men wait to see which way
it will fall, so her purpose, undermined by conflicting
assaults, wavered unsteadily now this way and now that and
moved in alternate directions. The only end and rest for her
passion that she could find was death, and death she decided
upon. She rose, determined to hang herself, and tying her
girdle to the lintel and murmuring 'Goodbye, dear Cinyras,
and understand why I die', she was, deathly-pale, in the act
of adjusting the noose about her neck.)

Having already in ix. 454–665 dealt very fully with the rather
similar story of Byblis, Ovid had necessarily to vary his treatment
of Myrrha – and no doubt embraced the opportunity of doing
so.[117] Myrrha is given one, by Ovidian standards relatively brief,
soliloquy (ll. 320–55), and once her state of mind has been established, the translation of her feelings into attempted action (to
be thwarted by the Euripidean figure of the Nurse) is speedily
accomplished in the passage under review. Ovid is here ultimately
indebted, *via* Virgil (*Aen.*, iv. 522ff.), to the famous night-scene
in Apollonius (iii. 744–69), but his treatment is compressed
and summary, representing or rather recalling (for ll. 320–55 are

still in the reader's mind) Myrrha's successive mental states by a rapid succession of verbs. It is redeemed from dryness by the effective simile,[118] which moves almost as fast as the surrounding narrative but yet manages momentarily to arrest attention by concentrating all Myrrha's vacillations into one powerful and original image.[119] Here, it may be remarked, enjambment is well up to the Virgilian norm, with six strong (ll. 368, 369, 372, 378, 379, 380) and three weaker (370, 371, 376) instances in fourteen verses. Its employment is, as already emphasized in other passages, strictly functional.

No writer on the *Metamorphoses* has failed to pay tribute to Ovid's powers of description. 'There is a plastic quality about his work. He catches the significant moment or attitude or gesture and imprints it on our mind.'[120] That there is usually more to this than embellishment for its own sake has been emphasized by recent investigation.[121] Not all Ovid's descriptions, of course, are symbolic, but very few if any are otiose. Wilkinson's pertinent comment can be illustrated best from one or two descriptions of characters in action; for a landscape, after all, is static and, given the care lavished on such technical problems in formal rhetorical instruction and the existence of good models, relatively easy to depict competently in its salient details.[122] Figures in violent motion present a less tractable assignment. Ovid's method is essentially to suggest rather than to describe,[123] as three examples will show. The first is Daphne, running from Apollo:

> plura locuturum timido Peneia cursu
> fugit cumque ipso uerba imperfecta reliquit,
> tum quoque uisa decens: nudabant corpora uenti
> obuiaque aduersas uibrabant flamina uestes
> et leuis impulsos retro dabat aura capillos,
> auctaque forma fuga est.   (I. 525–30)

(He would have continued, but the daughter of Peneus fled in alarm leaving the god alone with his unfinished speech, beautiful also in her flight. The wind bared her body, her clothes and hair streamed behind her in the breeze, and running enhanced her loveliness.)

Ovid describes the girl as she appeared in the eyes of her pursuer, with her graceful body made to seem even more desirable by her flight; his method is impressionistic, concentrating on the effects

of the wind on her hair and clothes and using theme (*uenti* . . .
flamina . . . *aura*) and variation with two golden lines of identical
'shape' (528–9 = abAB) to fix the moving picture for a short
moment. If, as their construction seems to suggest they should
be, these two verses are read as a combined whole, the reader
receives a compound impression: the girl's clothes were partly
pressed against her body (*obuia* . . . *aduersas*), partly waved and
streamed in the breeze (*uibrabant* . . . *retro dabat*), as also did her
hair. Ovid takes care to end his description in the middle of a
verse so as to preserve narrative continuity, and to make it last
for just so long a time as may allow the god to recover from his
surprise (note the witty *fugit* ‖ *cumque ipso* eqs.) and take off in
pursuit. The same focusing on similar details (of which Ovid
was fond: see Bömer *ad loc.*) is seen in the depiction of Europa:

> pauet haec litusque ablata relictum
> respicit et dextra cornum tenet, altera dorso
> imposita est; tremulae sinuantur flamine uestes   (II. 873–5)

(In terror she looked back at the shore from which she
was being carried off, holding a horn with her right hand
and resting the other on the bull's back; her clothes
fluttered and waved in the breeze.)

The pose is a classic one, often represented in ancient art and a
favourite with poets.[124] Ovid has exercised great restraint in
his depiction, singling out three features only, the turned-back
head and body (implied by *respicit*), the position of the hands, and
the robe fluttering in the breeze.[125] Moschus (*Europa*, 125–30)
is much more elaborate and, though extremely pretty, not more
effective.

The description of Europa just quoted occupies the concluding
lines of Book II. When Book III opens the rape has been accomplished and the ravisher's identity disclosed. The technique is
reminiscent of the cinema: a fade-out on a carefully posed shot,
followed by a complete change of tempo and mood in the next
scene. This 'cinematic' characteristic of Ovid's descriptive
technique (which is not peculiar to him) has been acutely remarked by Mlle Viarre[126] and deserves study. A striking instance
is that of Phaethon in the chariot of the Sun:

> tum uero Phaethon cunctis e partibus orbem
> adspicit accensum nec tantos sustinet aestus

feruentesque auras uelut e fornace profunda
ore trahit currusque suos candescere sentit   230
et neque iam cineres eiectatamque fauillam
ferre potest calidoque inuoluitur undique fumo
quoque eat aut ubi sit picea caligine tectus
nescit et arbitrio uolucrum raptatur equorum   (II. 227–34)

(And now Phaethon saw the world on fire everywhere, and
the heat was more than he could bear. He breathed in air hot
as the blast of a great furnace far below and felt the chariot
growing white-hot. Now he was overcome by the shower of
cinders and glowing ash and found himself enveloped in hot
smoke. Shrouded in pitch-black darkness he could not see
which way he was going or where he was, and he was swept
along at the will of the swift horses.)

As with Daphne, the description is presented from the point of
view of a protagonist – in this case *the* protagonist. The impression
of overwhelming heat is conveyed by a succession of key words:
*accensum, aestus, feruentes, fornace, candescere, cineres, fauillam, fumo,
caligine* (a remarkable display of Ovidian *ubertas* and *copia uerborum*),
with the emphasis gradually shifting from heat, *via* cinders and
ash, to smoke and obscurity, as Phaethon finally loses, not only
control of, but all touch with his situation. His increasing helplessness is conveyed by the verbs which provide the syntactical
articulation of the picture: *adspicit, nec . . . sustinet, ore trahit,
neque . . . ferre potest, inuoluitur, nescit* and finally *raptatur* (I do not
think that the frequentative form is purely *metri gratia*). There is
in fact very little actual description in the way of pictorial epithets
and the like, and much is left to the reader's imagination to supply;
but the stimulus is adroitly applied, as, for instance, in *profunda*,
with its hint of the great gulfs below.[127] The effect is that of a
series of shots of the flames and smoke alternating with close-ups
of Phaethon's face as it registers horror, bewilderment and
despair. The syntactical structure enforces rapidity of reading:
even editors who habitually over-punctuate are sparing with
commas in this passage, but it seems to me that Ovid's Latin here
requires no punctuation at all, and I have so printed it.

A special class of descriptive problem is posed by the metamorphoses themselves. As with the transitions, variety was of

the essence, especially in the numerous cases of persons who were changed into birds. Clearly it gave Ovid pleasure to rise to this technical challenge, and he delighted to lavish on these descriptions all that cleverness which has so much annoyed some of his critics.[128] On occasions they constitute what might be called set-pieces of *enargeia*. Are they anything more? In this sort of writing Ovid has been praised by Addison and blamed by Adam Smith;[129] and in this remarkable disagreement I find myself siding with the great economist's apparently prosaic objection that these descriptions 'are so very much out of the common course of nature as to shock us by their incredibility'. However far-fetched the premisses of Ovid's *ethopoeia*, he never parts company completely with the fundamental humanity of his characters: into whatever excesses of speech and behaviour their passions may carry them, the reader is never quite out of touch with the real world, and the Callimachean rule of poetical credibility, 'so to lie as to persuade one's hearer',[130] is not broken. With what might be termed the *ethopoeia* of material phenomena Ovid is less successful. For him, this was essentially an extension of the rhetorical exercise 'Imagine the words of so-and-so in such-and-such a situation' ($\tau i \nu a\varsigma\ \ddot{a}\nu\ \epsilon\ddot{i}\pi o\iota\ \lambda\acute{o}\gamma o\upsilon\varsigma\ \acute{o}\ \delta\epsilon\ddot{i}\nu a;$). He handles such themes like the great rhetorical artificer that he was, and it is impossible not to admire the versatility with which he varies the 'basic' transformations into birds, trees, rocks, etc.[131] An especially elaborate example is the metamorphosis of Cyane into a spring:

at Cyane raptamque deam contemptaque fontis   425
iura sui maerens inconsolabile uulnus
mente gerit tacita lacrimisque absumitur omnis
et quarum fuerat magnum modo numen, in illas
extenuatur aquas: molliri membra uideres,
ossa pati flexus, ungues posuisse rigorem,   430
primaque de tota tenuissima quaeque liquescunt,
caerulei crines digitique et crura pedesque
(nam breuis in gelidas membris exilibus undas
transitus est), post haec umeri tergusque latusque
pectoraque in tenues abeunt euanida riuos,   435
denique pro uiuo uitiatas sanguine uenas
lympha subit, restatque nihil quod prendere possis (v. 425–37)

(But Cyane, as she mourned the rape of the goddess and the
insult to the rights of her spring, cherishing deep in her heart
a wound that could not be assuaged, dissolved away in
tears and was rarefied into the very waters whose great
godhead she had lately been. One could have seen her limbs
softening, her bones becoming limp, her nails losing their
hardness. First it was the thinnest parts of her that
liquified, her blue-green hair, her fingers, toes, feet and legs
(for the thinner members are easily changed into cool
water); next her shoulders and back, flanks and breast
melted away into liquid streams. Finally into her softened
veins instead of living blood clear water flowed, and there
was nothing left of her that one could grasp.)

From the purely technical aspect this is first-rate writing, able to
give much intellectual pleasure to a sophisticated reader.[132] It
obeys the principles of *enargeia*. The reader is invited to witness
the transformation (429 *uideres*) and to test it for himself when it is
complete (437 *quod prendere possis*). The introductory passage is
heavily enjambed and moves fast; the start of the description
proper is signalled by the molossus *molliri* (429), with alliterative
reinforcement. First come theme and variation to convey the
notion of softening; then the graduated list of parts of the body
in order of their susceptibility and disappearance; finally the inner
structures and the blood within. The articulation of the description is clear, with a hint of pedantry that is made explicit in
the sly parenthesis[133] in which the order of events is explained.
The whole is rounded off by antithetical responsion with chias-
mus: 428–9 *magnum modo numen . . . aquas* ∼ 437 *lympha . . . nihil*.
All very efficient; but we cannot suspend our disbelief so as to
share emotionally in Cyane's experience in the sense that we can
share the experiences of Byblis or Phaethon. The reader cannot
feel sympathy with her. In the metamorphoses the method of
leaving things to the reader's imagination, so effective in descriptions of the real world and of familiar phenomena, does not
come off: for the imagination has nothing to work upon, nothing
that it recognizes and can use as a starting-point.

We may perhaps discern in the arch semi-pedantry of this
particular description the hint of a realization of this fact on the
poet's part, an implicit acknowledgment that the reader's pleasure

must here be, as has been said, intellectual rather than emotional. Perhaps this should be seen as in some sense a confession of failure. By that I mean that the pleasure felt by the reader of a poetical description, if it is to amount to anything at all, must be essentially emotional and sympathetic; and that by using the suggestive and impressionistic methods appropriate to real descriptions in the composition of unreal or fantastic scenes such as few, if any, sane readers could envisage, Ovid can be seen failing to relate his stylistic means successfully to his ends.[134] The distinction that I have in mind between what it is and is not reasonable to expect from a reader of poetry may emerge more clearly if we consider Ovid's great allegorical set-piece descriptions of Hunger, the Cave of Sleep, etc.;[135] there is grotesque detail and to spare in these, but the best of them succeed because what is enlarged or diminished or distorted remains fundamentally recognizable and part of human experience. It is the difference, perhaps, between Dürer and Hieronymus Bosch. If there is anything in these criticisms of Ovid's transformation-scenes, it should not be allowed to weigh heavily when set against the stylistic excellences that I have tried to illustrate and, partially, to account for. In the *Metamorphoses* descriptions of the act of metamorphosis could hardly be lacking, but unlike some recent interpreters of the poem, I do not believe that for Ovid this element had more than a formal importance. It posed a technical problem which he solved adroitly, on occasions brilliantly; but the scenes of metamorphosis are not what linger in the reader's mind. It was in the depiction of *human* actions and emotions – and what could be more human than the gods of the *Metamorphoses*? – that Ovid displayed the full range of his poetic powers.

Notes

1 J. W. Mackail, *The Aeneid edited with Introduction and Commentary* (1930), p. lxxvii. Mackail's brief but trenchant discussion of Virgil's hexameter fails to receive due acknowledgment from F. J. Worstbrock, *Elemente einer Poetik der Aeneis* (1963), who does not even cite its title correctly.
2 P. Green, *Essays in Antiquity* (1960), 130.
3 Cf. *ibid.*, 129.
4 T. R. Glover, *Greek Byways* (1932), 191.
5 L. P. Wilkinson, *Ovid Recalled* (1955), 150.
6 Now conveniently accessible, together with many other such verdicts.

in the useful and entertaining compilation of W. Stroh, *Ovid im Urteil der Nachwelt. Eine Testimoniesammlung* (1969).

7 Cf. Wilkinson's comparison of Virg. *G.*, IV. 463–9 with *Met.*, X. 11–16 and his pertinent comment: 'Virgil is concerned to create atmosphere by his rhythm, Ovid to get on with the story' (*Golden Latin Artistry* [1963], 131–2).

8 M. von Albrecht, 'Zum Metamorphosenproem Ovids', *Rheinisches Museum*, 104 (1961), 269–78.

9 H. Herter, 'Ovids Kunstprinzip in den Metamorphosen', *American Journal of Philology*, 69 (1948), 129–48 (= *Ovid*, ed. M. von Albrecht and E. Zinn [1968], 340–61). Cf. B. Otis, *Ovid as an Epic Poet*, 2nd ed. (1970), 332–4.

10 *P. Ovidius Naso Metamorphosen*, ed. M. Haupt, 10. *Auflage*, ed. M. von Albrecht, i (1966), p. 486.

11 D. Little, 'Richard Heinz: Ovids elegische Erzählung', in E. Zinn (ed.), *Ovids Ars Amatoria und Remedia Amoris. Untersuchungen zum Aufbau (Der altspr. Unterricht*, Reihe XIII, Beiheft 2, 1970), 72. Little may have somewhat underrated the fundamental unity of the *Metamorphoses*, but he is right to insist (69 n. 6) that the style of the poem is dictated by a 'difference of intent'.

12 R. G. G. Coleman, 'Structure and intention in the *Metamorphoses*', *Classical Quarterly*, N.S., 21 (1971), 461–77.

13 E. J. Bernbeck, *Beobachtungen zur Darstellungsart in Ovids Metamorphosen* (1967), 130: 'spielerische Abwandlung des Epos'. Bernbeck stresses (130–1) that the poem is a unity.

14 Otis, *op. cit.*, 1st ed. (1966), 334, 345; but see the new concluding ch. of 2nd ed. (1970), interpreting the poem as a blend of 'anti-epic' and 'un-epic', of 'iconoclasm and human sympathy' (374).

15 C. P. Segal, *Landscape in Ovid's Metamorphoses. A study in the transformations of a literary symbol (Hermes Einzelschriften*, 23 [1969]), 93: 'one may wonder if it is not rather an epic of rape. Its very subject, metamorphosis, implies violence.' This of course raises the question whether or in what sense metamorphosis *is* the subject of the poem; cf. my review of S. Viarre, *L'image et la pensée dans les 'Métamorphoses' d'Ovide* (1964), *Classical Review*, N.S., 17 (1967), 51–2, and see below, *sub fin.*

16 *C.R.* N.S., 18 (1968), 58.

17 Little, *op. cit.*, 71.

18 Wilkinson, *op. cit.* (n. 7), 202.

19 Quint., *Inst. Or.*, IV. 1. 77; Wilkinson, 'The world of the Metamorphoses', in *Ovidiana* (1958), 231–44; J. M. Frécaut, 'Les transitions dans les Métamorphoses d'Ovide', *R.E.L.*, 47 (1968), 247–63.

20 Cf. G. E. Duckworth, *Vergil and Classical Hexameter Poetry* (1969), 73, on the 'Greekness' of Ovid's metre compared with Virgil's.

21 Lucan's challenge was to this extent on Virgil's own ground, that the *Bellum Civile* best makes sense if read as in some measure an answer to the *Aeneid*, an 'anti-*Aeneid*' in fact.

22 A. R. Zingerle, *Ovidus und sein Verhältniss zu den Vorgängern und gleich zeitigen römischen Dichtern* (1869–71), *passim*.

23 See K. Quinn, *Virgil's Aeneid. A Critical Description* (1968), 375–84.

24 Cf. Worstbrock, *op. cit.*, 148: 'Die Syntax der Poesie ist eine metrische Syntax.' The remark can of course be extended to cover diction.

25 See Quinn, *op. cit.*, 384–91; Wilkinson, 'The language of Virgil and Horace', *Classical Quarterly*, N.S., 9 (1959), 181–92.

26 See Worstbrock, *op. cit.*, ch. III, 'Vers und Syntax', 122–67.

27 W. A. Camps, *An Introduction to Virgil's Aeneid* (1969), 63; cf. Quinn, *op. cit.*, 385.

28 J. Jackson (1908).

29 F. Bömer, 'Ovid und die Sprache Vergils', *Gymn.*, 66 (1959), 268–88 (= *Ovid*, 173–202).

30 'So schnell sind innerhalb einer Generation die Worte der hohen Dichtersprache abgenutzt, abgesunken' (*op. cit.*, 277 = 185).

31 *Op. cit.*, 279 = 188–9.

32 G. B. Pighi, 'La poesia delle "Metamorfosi" ', *Atti del convegno internaz. Ovidiano*, i (1959), 16: 'tutta la dizione epica latina, dopo l'inimitabile Virgilio e l'imitabile Ovidio, è più ovidiana che virgiliana.' Cf. E. V. Marmorale, *Persio*, 2nd ed. (1956), 199.

33 Worstbrock, *op. cit.*, 131, gives three verses as the average in Virgil's narrative, three to four verses elsewhere. My own rather crude count of *Met.*, III (using the text of G. M. Edwards and simply counting the lines between the editor's full stops) gives an average of about 3.5 verses for the Ovidian period.

34 *Op. cit.*, 147, 150.

35 *Ibid.*, 147–8.

36 *Ibid.*, 162.

37 This is not invariably the case, as some of the examples discussed below demonstrate. In Book I the golden lines at ll. 100, 112 are both obviously functional, but by Virgilian standards this is overdoing it. Cf. 1. 528, 529, discussed in the text; also 147 (not at the end of its period), 165, 265, 484, etc.

38 A good summary characterization at Bernbeck, *op. cit.*, 78.

39 A. Cordier, *Études sur le vocabulaire épique dans l' 'Énéide'* (1939).

40 Cf. Wilkinson, *op. cit.* (n. 25), 185–6.

41 Quint, *Inst. Or.*, VIII. 3. 24.

42 Such as, for instance, *extemplo*, used by Ovid ten times, only in *Met.*, and thus marginally more strictly than by Virgil, who uses the word once in the *Georgics* as well as fourteen times in the *Aeneid* (cf. R. G. Austin on *Aen.*, I. 92). Contrast Livy, with 370+ instances.

43 See G. D'Anna, 'La tragedia latina arcaica nelle "Metamorfosi" ', *Atti*, ii. 220–6; Otis, *op. cit.*, 400–1.

44 See, e.g., H. Jacobson, *Phoenix*, 22 (1968), 299–303; D. G. White, *Harvard Studies in Classical Philology*, 74 (1970), 187–91 (Ennius); *Ovid Metamorphoses Book VIII*, ed. A. S. Hollis (1970), p. xxiv (Accius).

45 F. H. Sandbach, *Classical Review*, liv (1940), 198.

46 Where no figure is given in these lists, the word occurs once only.

47 * = occurs in Ovidian corpus outside *Met.*

48 *paupertas* is not used by Virgil, three times (one in *Met.*) by Ovid.

49 Accepting Heinsius' conjecture at *Met.*, IV. 537.

50 For this purpose I have conflated the two lists at 40–1 ('archaisms') and 46 ('coinages'). Defects in Cordier's classification (Sandbach, *loc. cit.*) are of no moment for our present purpose.

51 At Ov., *Her.*, VI. 32 certainly and at XII. 93 probably read, with Heinsius, *aenipedes*.

52 † = occurs in Virgilian corpus outside *Aen.* Comparison of the respective incidence of † and * (above, n. 47), when due allowance is made for the difference in bulk, offers some guide to the 'purity' of the two poets' attitude to epic diction.

53 Including *biiugis* at XII. 355; the variation in declension can only be ascribed to the demands of euphony.

54 Including *quadriiugis* at X. 571; see preceding n.

55 *aliger* v. l. at *Fast.* IV. 562 (*alifer*); cf. below (6) under *armifer*.

56 In the phrase *in biuio* also at *Aen.*, IX. 238; Ov., *Rem.*, 486.

57 Ovid affects *Phoebeius* (4), not used by Virgil. On his predilection for proper adjj. ending in *-ius* and *-eius* cf. E. Linse, *De P. Ovidio Nasone vocabulorum inventore* (1891), 23–4; so far as those in *-eius* are concerned, metrical considerations were clearly paramount.

58 Cf. Linse, *op. cit.*, 39–40, 42–7; A. Draeger, *Ovid als Sprachbildner* (1888), 4–16.

59 ‡ = *hapax legomenon* or occurring only in Ovid, as indicated by the context.

60 In *Met.* = 'club-bearing'; at *Fast.* I. 228 (of Janus) = 'key-bearing'.

61 But at II. 392 it is possible that editors are wrong to prefer *igniferum* to *ignipedum* in the face of Stat., *Theb.*, I. 27 (*ignipedum frenator equorum*). Statius often echoes Ovid in his choice of rare compound epithets.

62 *securiger* at *Her.*, IV. 117 and in later poets.

63 *semideus* (adj.)* and in later poets.

64 v. l. *spumifer*; cf. Stat., *Achill.*, I. 59.

65 v. l. *tridentifer*.

66 v. l. at XIV. 365; *preces . . . precantia*, though predictably swallowed by modern editors, cannot possibly be right. The adjectival use of *uenefica* is analogous to that of *puerpera* above.

67 In this respect he does not follow the example set by his admired Lucretius, who compounded with great freedom (*T. Lucreti Cari De Rerum Natura Libri Sex*, ed. C. Bailey, i [1947], pp. 133–4), but shows himself as an Augustan of the Augustans. Cf. R. G. Austin on Virg., *Aen.*, I. 224.

68 See *P. Ovidi Nasonis Metamorphoseon Liber I*, ed. A. G. Lee (1953), p. 36; and cf. *Met.*, II. 642, XV. 744 *salutifer*; VI. 337, IX. 313, X. 511 *puerpera*; VII. 316 *uenefica*; VIII. 391 *bipennifer*; VIII. 596 *tridentifer*; XIV. 609 *binominis*.

69 Cf. Linse, *op. cit.*, 48–51, 52–6.

70 It is worth pausing to point out how this result is achieved: note (*a*) the change of subject at the bucolic diaeresis of l. 728; (*b*) the closeness of the enjambment between ll. 728–9, 729–30; (*c*) the change back to the original subject at the beginning of l. 731; (*d*) the placing of the verbs

ait, adiacet, insilit. Such techniques are fundamental to Ovid's use of parenthesis: see below, n. 111.

71 *iras* recc., Heinsius: *undas* codd. The repetition *undis . . . undas* is quite pointless and cannot be ascribed to Ovid: cf. above, n. 66.

72 *delasso* does not appear to have been an especially 'poetic' word: it was used before Ovid by Plautus and Horace (*Sat.*), after him by Manilius and Martial.

73 Cf. Linse, *op. cit.*, 49–50.

74 *rapit* recc., Heinsius: *capit* codd. The tempo of the narrative imperatively demands the more violent verb.

75 In spite of *amantem* at l. 612 I believe that the older interpreters were right in taking *amantis* here as referring to Coronis and not to Apollo.

76 Ovid's predilection for this figure is notorious: H. Fränkel, *Ovid, A Poet Between Two Worlds* (1945), 197; Haupt–von Albrecht on IX. 135; F. Bömer on I. 750. It is usually wrongly termed zeugma.

77 An effect of which Ovid is fond: S. E. Winbolt, *Latin Hexameter Verse* (1903), 228.

78 Cf. Zingerle, *op. cit.*, part 2, 112; on Ovid's predilection for adjj. in *-ilis* cf. below.

79 See E. Bednara, *De sermone dactylicorum Latinorum quaestiones* (1906), *passim.*

80 Ovid's freedom in coining such words (Linse, *op. cit.*, 31–2) is reminiscent of Lucretius: cf. Bailey, *op. cit.*, 134–5.

81 Of the instances collected by Linse, *op. cit.*, 8–14 (most of which are taken from the *Halieutica*, which is not by Ovid) only a handful merit remark: *canna* (8)* (but cf. *F.P.L.* ed. W. Morel, p. 98; *Adnot. super Lucanum*, p. 184 Endt); *harpe* (v. 69, 176), *vox propria* of Perseus' weapon; *moly* (XIV. 292); and some names of plants and animals such as *morus; ciris, echidna, epops, haliaeetos, hyaena.*

82 See, e.g., Wilkinson, *op. cit.* (n. 5), 235–6, quoting *Met.*, II. 217–26.

83 Cf. the almost 'formulaic' use of *Asis‡* in *Asida terram* (v. 648), *Aside terra* (IX. 448).

84 On these readings see the notes of A. S. Hollis *ad locc.*

85 The whole context deserves quotation: *ultus abit Tmolo liquidumque per aera uectus / angustum citra pontum Nepheleidos Helles / Laomedonteis Latoius adstitit aruis: / dextera Sigei, Rhoetei laeua profundi / ara Panomphaeo uetus est sacrata Tonanti.* On *Tonans = Iuppiter* see Haupt–von Albrecht *ad loc.*

86 Of these variants Λητωΐς, Λητῷος were established in Greek. I have followed the spellings of MSS and editors, but I suspect that Ovid consistently used the Greek spelling, as given by the MSS at VII. 384 *Letoidos* and VIII. 15 *Letoia.*

87 The prosodic variation is Virgilian.

88 The figures for *Met.* (of instances, not of individual words) are: nom. sing. 2, acc. sing. 6, gen. sing. 1, abl. sing. 23 (of which *uelamine* accounts for 2); nom. pl. 5, acc. pl. 26 (*uelamina* 11). Note the variant forms *solacia* (saepius), *temptamenta* (2), *irritamenta, uelamenta*; cf. Hollis on *Met.*, VIII. 729, Austin on *Aen.*, I. 649.

89 Linse, *op. cit.*, 28–9; Lucretius is much less restrained (Bailey, *op. cit.*, 135, J. Perrot, *R.E.L.*, 33 [1955], 333–43).

90 Dat. *conatibus, cruciatibus, narratibus, saltatibus, uenatibus, uictibus* (+ *uictu*); abl. *adflatibus* (+ *adflatu* 3), *hortatibus* (2), *iactatibus, latratibus* (4) (+ *latratu* 3, *latratus* acc.), *suspiratibus, uenatibus* (2) (+ *uenatu* 2), *ululatibus* (5) (+ *ululatu*; and note XI. 17 *Bacchei ululatus*).

91 More material in Linse, *op. cit.*; I hope that the examples quoted here may suffice to make the point.

92 Cf. P. Boyancé, *Lucrèce et l'épicurisme* (1963), 213.

93 Cf. P. Hau, *De casuum usu Ovidiano* (diss. Münster, 1884). His usage is in general bolder in *Met.* than in his other works (Hau, 141–2). Some idea of the respective freedom of the Latin poets can be obtained from comparing entries in the index of the great museum of syntactical specimens, A. J. Bell, *The Latin dual and poetic diction* (1923).

94 Margaret W. Herr, *The additional short syllables in Ovid* (1937), 30: 'the nominative and accusative cases of neuter plural nouns are not the chief source of Ovid's . . . additional short syllables.' However, consideration of a verse such as I. 181 *talibus inde modis ora indignantia soluit* shows that a purely mechanical approach does not reveal anything like the whole truth.

95 H. A. J. Munro on Lucret., III. 843; Postgate, *Classical Review*, 30 (1916), 145; cf. A. E. Housman, *Journal of Philology*, 18 (1890), 7.

96 Two especially distinguished by Postgate, *op. cit.*, 145–6, belong not to Ovid but to the unknown poet of the *Somnium* (*Am.*, III. 5).

97 *Bellum Civile*, II. 350–80; cf. Heitland's remarks in the edition of C. E. Haskins (1887), p. lxxii; J. Marouzeau, *Traité de stylistique latine* (1946), 259–60.

98 Cf. Postgate, *Proc. Brit. Acad.*, 3 (1908), 167.

99 In such cases as I. 458 *qui dare certa ferae, dare uulnera possumus hosti* (copiously illustrated by Housman in his note on Manil., I. 269–70) the anaphora dictates a comma after *ferae*, but a second after *possumus* would simply trip the reader up. With practice the ear is conditioned by the movement of the verse to accept these distributions.

100 The definition adopted by J. B. Hofmann–A. Szantyr, *Lateinische Syntax und Stilistik* (1965), 834. For further discussion see H. M. Eller, *Studies in ἀπὸ κοινοῦ in Ovid* (1938), 1–7. Cf. Kenney, *Classical Quarterly*, N.S., 8 (1958), 55; and add F. Leo, *Ausgew. Kl. Schriften*, i (1960), 77ff.

101 The following further instances have been casually culled from a single book: II. 231 *cineres eiectatamque fauillam*, 406 *fontes et non audentia labi / flumina*, 438 *odio nemus est et conscia silua*, 490 *ante domum quondamque suis errauit in agris* (this last noticed by Bömer *ad loc.*), etc.

102 F. Bömer, *Gymn.*, 74 (1967), 223–6; cf. his notes *ad loc.* and at I. 466, and to the literature cited by him add Bell, *op. cit.*, 317ff. Both adjj. would be felt as predicative in sense.

103 E.g. Lucret., III. 972–3 *anteacta uetustas / temporis aeterni*, exactly equivalent in sense to I. 558 *infinita aetas anteacti temporis omnis*.

104 For further discussion of certain Ovidian figures see my review of

Bömer's commentary on Books I–III, *Classical Review*, N.S., 22 (1972), 38–42.

105 *Ovid's Metamorphoses: the Arthur Golding translation (1567)*, ed. J. F. Nims (1965), p. xxii. The whole of Nims's introduction is excellent value.

106 See J. Henry, *Aeneidea*, i (1873), pp. 206–7, 745–51. For its use by Lucretius see my ed. of Book III (1971), p. 25. It is, as Henry remarked, 'almost inseparable from poetry'.

107 Bömer's suggestion that *mentis capacius altae* stands by enallage for *mentis capax altioris* seems to be mistaken. *mens alta* is an attribute of divinity, of which man was enabled, as the beasts were not, to receive a share (cf. A. G. Lee *ad loc.*).

108 'A forced and almost pointless word-play' is the comment of A. S. Hollis *ad loc.* I am not so sure. Ovid can scarcely have had in mind the old idea that a mother was not related by blood to her offspring (cf. Kenney on Lucret., III. 743). The shedding of blood called for a bloody expiation, and in this case the victim was related to both avenger and avenged: in other words *sanguine* in l. 476 is felt in the context (after '*con*sanguineas'; cf. Kenney on Lucret., III. 261) as = not merely 'blood' but 'kindred blood'. I do not know exactly what Hollis means by calling the oxymoron *impietate pia est* 'not very pleasing'. What are the criteria which an oxymoron must satisfy in order to please?

109 An attractive discussion of XIII. 750–897 (Acis, Galatea and Polyphemus) by D. West, *Individual Voices* (inaugural lecture, University of Newcastle, 1970), 8–14.

110 The bulls appear (104 *ecce*) as if released from the *caueae*; in Apollonius (III. 1288ff.) Jason has to track them down to their murky lair, and Aeetes is not formally enthroned as in Ovid but simply stands by the river (see the ed. of H. Fränkel *ad loc.* for the textual variants).

111 On Ovid's use of parenthesis see M. von Albrecht, *Die Parenthese in Ovids Metamorphosen und ihre dichterische Funktion* (1963), reviewed by me in *Gnomon*, 36 (1964), 374–7. His discussion shows that Ovid employs parenthesis for more than one effect, but one characteristic is constant: it is always so incorporated, beginning and ending with the verses themselves or their main caesuras and unambiguously signposted (cf. above, n. 70), as to interrupt the flow as little as possible. The text printed above is as punctuated by the old editors and some of the moderns; the punctuation of, e.g., Magnus and Ehwald, which begins the parenthesis at *nec*, contravenes the ambiguity principle, which requires that a parenthesis should not be deemed to begin before it has to.

112 In contrast to Apollonius' Jason, who at least braces himself for the encounter and holds a shield in front of himself (III. 1293–6), and actually has to exert himself when it comes to the yoking (1306–8). Did Emily Dickinson have Ovid in mind when she wrote 'Jason – sham – too'? (Reference due to Mr R. G. Mayer.)

113 Worstbrock, *op. cit.*, 156.

114 *Ibid.*, 157.

115 Worstbrock, 159–62.
116 To maintain comparability I have interpreted 'enjambment' in a fairly strict grammatical sense, applied to lines whose syntax is completed by what follows. Ovid makes much use of what might be called 'quasi-' or 'semi-enjambment': that is, a structure which, while it does not disallow, certainly discourages a pause at the end of the line in reading. So, for instance, in (e = strict, q = quasi-enjambment):

o cui debere salutem	(e)
confiteor, coniunx, quamquam mihi cuncta dedisti	(q)
excussit*que* fidem meritorum summa tuorum . . .	(VII. 164–6);

or

constitit adueniens citra limenque foresque	(q)
et tantum caelo tegitur refugitque uiriles	(e)
contactus statuitque aras e caespite binas,	(q)
dexteriore Hecates, at laeua parte Iuuentae	(VII. 238–41).

The close connexion is very often achieved by *et* or *-que*; but other devices are used, as in the second quotation, where the unemphatic *binas* does not invite the reader to pause (as the order *binas . . . aras* would have done) and is at once picked up by *dexteriore*, which in turn looks forward to its complement in *laeua*. Examples could be multiplied; the upshot is that the overall speed of the verse is greater than the figures quoted for enjambment proper would lead one to suppose.

117 The Byblis episode contains little narrative and is mostly taken up with the soliloquies (in which her letter must be included) in which the heroine's warring states of mind are analysed. Cf. H. Tränkle, 'Elegisches in Ovids Metamorphosen', *Hermes*, 91 (1963), 459–76, stressing the similarities with the *Heroides* (but see also Otis, *op. cit.*, 221–2). With the passage quoted above compare IX. 523–8.

118 A treatment of Ovid's similes in *Met.* is outside the scope of this chapter: see J. A. Washietl, *De similitudinibus imaginibusque Ovidianis* (1883); T. F. Brunner, *Classical Journal*, 61 (1966), 354–63; E. G. Wilkins, *Classical Weekly*, 25 (1932), 73–8, 81–6; S. G. Owen, *Classical Review*, 45 (1931), 97–106.

119 The idea goes back to Homer: Sarpedon goes down like a felled tree (*Il.*, XVI. 482–4). In spite of the usual descriptive elaboration of the tree the application of the image is very simple. Virgil enlarges its scope and grandeur enormously when he compares the fall of Troy to that of a great tree (*Aen.*, II. 626–31; cf. R. G. Austin *ad loc.*). Ovid applies it differently again, to the psychology of the situation: Myrrha is not compared to the tree; it is the painful moments, that seem to last for hours, while the tree totters, that resemble her plight, always on the verge of making up her mind but not quite able to do so. But just as the tree must fall once it is cut through (cf. the wound image of l. 375), so must she decide.

120 Wilkinson, *op. cit.* (n. 5), 172. Cf. H. Stephanus, in the Preface to his *Poetae Graeci Principes* (1566): 'Poetis autem penicillum quum tribuo,

cum ad alios multos multorum poetarum locos, tum ad complures Ovidianarum metamorphoseων locos respicio.' See also the literature cited by Stroh, *op. cit.*, 159.

121 Segal, *op. cit.*

122 A good example is Virgil's description of the Trojan landfall in Africa (*Aen.*, I. 159–69), which, unlike its Homeric prototypes (on which see G. Williams, *Tradition and Originality in Roman Poetry* [1968], 637–44), is clearly organized by the poet so as to lead the mind's eye of the reader from point to point in a certain order. It is also, however, organized so as to bring out the symbolism of the landscape (cf. V. Pöschl, *Die Dichtkunst Virgils* [1950], 231–5), which prefigures both the repose and the subsequent danger that the Trojans will find in Africa – and in the cave of the nymphs (l. 168) are we not intended to sense that other, more fateful cave?

123 'Un trait seul, un grand trait, abandonnez le reste à mon imagination; voilà le vrai goût, voilà le grand goût. Ovide l'a quelquefois' (Diderot, quoted by Stroh, *op. cit.*, 85).

124 See Haupt–von Albrecht *ad loc.* An especially charming instance is a Coptic bronze of the 5th–6th century A.D. (in private possession), in which the pose and the girl's robe have been reduced to a design of hieratic simplicity (D. G. Mitten and S. F. Doeringer, *Master bronzes from the classical world*, no. 316).

125 So too at *Fast.*, V. 607–9, but there the effect is more crisp than decorative.

126 Viarre, *op. cit.*, 99–100.

127 The comparison itself, as Bömer observes *ad loc.*, is conventional; it is the choice of epithet that lifts it out of the ruck.

128 'Sometimes Ovid is indeed too clever. He was told so in his own time, and his ghost has been hearing it ever since' (Nims, *op. cit.*, xxvii).

129 *Spectator*, no. 417 (28 June 1712); *Lectures on Rhetoric and Belles Lettres*, ed. M. Lothian (1963), 61–2 (both passages quoted by Stroh, *op. cit.*, 71, 86).

130 *Hymns*, I. 65 Ψευδοίμην ἀίοντος ἅ κεν πεπίθοιεν ἀκουήν.

131 See G. Lafaye, *Les Métamorphoses d'Ovide et leurs modèles grecs* (1904), ed. M. von Albrecht (1971), 245–9; W. Quirin, *Die Kunst Ovids in der Darstellung des Verwandlungsaktes* (diss., Giessen 1930), esp. 118–19 on Ovidian *variatio*.

132 It is the first transformation into water that we encounter in *Met.*, and by far the most elaborate: cf. Quirin, *op. cit.*, 106–8.

133 Editors do not usually print *nam breuis . . . transitus est* as such, but this is obviously what Ovid intended: so, rightly, von Albrecht, *op. cit.* (n. 111), 52.

134 The poem has a rich iconographical tradition, but artists have on the whole preferred not to illustrate the actual moment of metamorphosis: cf. *Classical Review*, N.S., 17 (1967), 52.

135 Inuidia: II. 760–82; Fames: VIII. 788–808; Somnus: XI. 592–623; Fama: XII. 39–63.

V

The Tristia: *Poetry in Exile*

R. J. Dickinson

Quod quicumque leget (si quis leget) aestimet ante,
   compositum quo sit tempore quoque loco.
aequus erit scriptis, quorum cognoverit esse
   exilium tempus barbariamque locum.

(Tr., III. 14. 27–30)

(Let anyone who reads this (if anyone does) first take into
   account its time and place of composition.
He will be fair to writings which he knows were composed
   in time of exile and in a foreign place.)

The catastrophe in Ovid's life occurred towards the end of the
year A.D. 8 when he was fifty. From the island of Elba,[1] where
he was accompanying his friend M. Aurelius Cotta Maximus,
he was summoned to Rome,[2] tried (if that is the right word)
by Augustus himself in private,[3] and banished to Tomis, a town
situated on the edge of the Empire, on the Black Sea a little to
the South of the Danube, on the coast of the recently established
province of Moesia.

   There were degrees of banishment. Although Ovid both in
the quotation above and elsewhere talks of *exilium*, and describes
himself as *exul*,[4] he uses these words for their strong emotive
quality and not in a strictly legal sense. What he in fact endured
was not *exilium* but *relegatio*, as he himself makes clear:

quippe relegatus,[5] non exul, dicor in illo [sc. edicto].

(Tr., II. 137)

(For I am called 'relegated', not exile, in your edict.)

A 'relegated' person, unlike an exile, retained his property and his civic rights; on the other hand he was usually assigned a place of residence, whereas the exile could live anywhere beyond a prescribed distance from the capital. In Ovid's case the ostensibly milder form of banishment was very severe indeed, because he was sent to live in an outlandish spot from which he was never recalled.

At the time of his banishment, he was the most popular living poet in Rome, a public figure. What wrong had he done to deserve this punishment? He himself is very eager to tell us – half the story:

> perdiderint cum me duo crimina, carmen et error,[6]
> alterius facti culpa silenda mihi.   (*Tr.*, II. 207–8)

(Though ruined by two offences, a poem and a mistake, about one of my misdeeds I must remain silent.)

About the poem he is explicit: it was his *Ars Amatoria*,[7] the popular and celebrated guide to seduction, published in about A.D. 1 or 2. This fact raises questions. If the *Ars* was a direct cause of his exile, why did Augustus wait for several years before condemning the culprit, and if one of the two offences was really a poem, why did Augustus allow Ovid to continue publishing poetry both during those intervening years and after his removal from Rome? Or was the poem a pretext, an extra weight thrown into the pan? There is no certainty. But it is the poet's refusal to reveal his '*error*' that has drawn more attention: certain vague comments in the poems about its nature, together with categorical statements[8] that he cannot reveal it, have provoked the curiosity of scholars for centuries.[9] A host of solutions has been offered. *Quot editores tot 'errores'*. The question is insoluble. If I declare (and this is a popular theory) that Ovid was implicated in the immoral behaviour of Julia, Augustus' granddaughter, and actually saw her perform a strip-tease at a drunken orgy, this explanation would fit tolerably well the hints which one finds in the *Tristia*, and would be no worse – and no better – than any other explanation.

But what *is* worse, the riddle[10] has diverted the attention and energies of scholars away from the poetry itself. Of published work on Ovid in the last two generations, relatively little has been devoted to the poems of exile, and most of *that* has been biographical, that is, concerned with the reasons for his exile and with the nature of his *error*.[11] In consequence, the poems themselves have too often been dismissed as inferior stuff. Critics have pointed to the poet's 'slavish fawning', or 'the language of an abject and pusillanimous flatterer', and have complained of 'monotony in the constant complaints, a sense of lack of dignity and fortitude'; and even L. P. Wilkinson,[12] that sensitive critic, is disappointed by their collective 'monotony of subject', and because, not surprisingly, he finds in them neither the same wit that seasoned the earlier poetry[13] nor the ethnological observations of a trained scientist.

Others may pursue that elusive phantom, the *error*; more important is the poetry and the effect of exile on the poet. First we must meet Ovid squarely and form some impression of his poetic *persona*, and then we must face up to the poems, without demanding either of the man or of his poetry qualities which they could not possibly possess.

Ovid was not by temperament a 'noble Roman': certain Republican virtues were lacking, such as fortitude, physical endurance, and a high moral sense. But, to compensate for this, other no less important virtues were prominent: Cicero, who was never reluctant to enumerate a man's qualities, might have described Ovid as a man endowed with *comitas, facilitas, humanitas*. The words are not easy to translate, but mean roughly affability, good-nature (and fluency), and the kindly-disposed and outward-going refinement of a highly cultivated man. These virtues emerge from his poetry, and are detectable in his mildness of manner, his wit, his respect for all fellow poets, and above all in his awareness of the blessings of civilized society. What he has to say in the following celebrated passage has the ring of personal conviction;[14] it was, of course, written before exile:

> simplicitas rudis ante fuit; nunc aurea Roma est
> et domiti magnas possidet orbis opes.
> aspice, quae nunc sunt, Capitolia, quaeque fuerunt:
> alterius dices illa fuisse Iovis.
> Curia consilio nunc est dignissima tanto,
> de stipula Tatio regna tenente fuit;
> quae nunc sub Phoebo ducibusque Palatia fulgent,
> quid nisi araturis pascua bubus erant?

prisca iuvent alios, ego me nunc denique natum
    gratulor: haec aetas moribus apta meis,
non quia nunc terrae lentum subducitur aurum
    lectaque diverso litore concha venit,
nec quia decrescunt effosso marmore montes,
    nec quia caeruleae mole fugantur aquae,
sed quia cultus adest nec nostros mansit in annos
    rusticitas priscis illa superstes avis.

(A.A., III. 113–28)

(Crude plainness is a thing of the past; now Rome is paved
    with gold
and possesses the great wealth of the conquered world.
Look at the Capitol as it is now and as it was:
    you will say that it formerly belonged to a different Jupiter.
The Senate House is now most worthy of so great an assembly:
    when Tatius was on the throne it was roofed with thatch.
Where now the Palatine gleams under Apollo and our leaders –
    what was there but pasture-land for plough-oxen?
Let antiquity delight others; as for me, I pat myself on the
    back,
    for having been born now: this age suits my personality,
not because nowadays pliable gold is mined from the earth,
    and the pearl, gathered on a distant shore, is imported here,
nor because whole mountains shrink as their marble is quarried
    out,
    nor because the blue seas are driven back by the breakwater,
but because civilization has arrived, and there has not lingered
    on into our own age
    that rusticity of life as a survival from our forebears of old.)

Tomis[15] was a shock: for Ovid, crude plainness became a thing
of the present. His world was turned upside-down, and the
damage to his temperament was very real. Imagine the effect on
Byron of deportation to Australia, or on Oscar Wilde of exile
to the far north of Canada. Ovid was faced with the prospect of
spending the rest of his life in an uncivilized town, surrounded
by barbarian and alien peoples and having to endure a harsh and
bleak climate. It is astonishing that he continued to write; but
then his very despair drove him to compose, and that composition

was an anodyne he tells us more than once, particularly in the impressive opening poem of *Tristia*, IV:

> nos quoque delectant, quamvis nocuere, libelli,
>   quodque mihi telum vulnera fecit, amo.
> forsitan hoc studium possit furor esse videri,
>   sed quiddam furor hic utilitatis habet.
> semper in obtutu mentem vetat esse malorum,
>   praesentis casus immemoremque facit.
>
> (*Tr.*, IV. 1.35–40)[16]

(I too find pleasure in my books, although they have harmed me,
  and the weapon that has dealt wounds on me I love.
Perhaps this preoccupation may appear to be madness,
  yet this madness has a certain usefulness.
It stops my mind from constantly contemplating my troubles,
  and makes it forget my present predicament.)

The exile poems themselves indicate the change in Ovid's fortunes. For besides being unique in classical literature as poems of exile, they possess a quality which is unusual in Roman elegiac poetry: the utterance of the author is directly referable to his own experience and he emerges from the poems in his own person.[17] This authentic tone ought to be attractive to modern readers, who have been nurtured on traditions of personal poetry, for the *Tristia* is personal poetry of a high order, despite the fact that the poet was addressing the emperor, the Roman world, and posterity. Indeed the reality and vividness of Ovid's portrayal of himself is one of the most important aspects of the whole body of exile poems.

In consequence, a clear line can be drawn between tradition and originality, mainly because literary tradition had not sufficiently catered for the expression of such a tragic personal experience. But the case for originality can be overstated: E. J. Kenney[18] has claimed that, 'for the type of poetry that Ovid was now called upon to write there was no precedent and no model. It is necessary, therefore, to regard the *Tristia* and the *Epistulae ex Ponto* in the light of a series of poetic experiments, in which Ovid was feeling his way towards a type of poetry that should be appropriate to his feelings and his situation. Viewed thus the poems can lay claim, as Mr A. G. Lee[19] has pointed out, to considerable originality: "an Ovidian invention, without parallel in Greek or Latin Literature." ' It would be juster to say that in these late poems Ovid was doing what Kenney a little earlier in the same article ascribes to him as a normal practice: he was using and developing existing models, in this case, models from his own poetry. He adopted the form of the book of elegiac poems from the *Amores* and from earlier poetic tradition (Propertius, Tibullus, Gallus and beyond), and the form of the epistle from his own *Heroides*. Furthermore, most of his late poems resemble poems of the *Heroides* in mood; they are, it is true, devoid of sexual frustration, but are not devoid of longing, a longing which is not now the mood adopted in a poetical exercise, but which instead is deeply and actually experienced. There is much to be said for the view that Ovid was enabled to write his exile poems largely because he was the author of those other poetical epistles. Apart from the extended *suasoria* of *Tristia*, II (which *is* remarkable in form), two-thirds of the remainder of the *Tristia* are clearly epistolary, as are all the *Epistulae ex Ponto*. Moreover, in the *Tristia* the tendency to address poems to particular (usually unnamed) persons increases as Ovid proceeds to the later books: thus, less than half of the poems of Book I, half or more of the poems of Books III and IV, and nearly all of the poems of Book V are so addressed. In summary, the form of the exile poems is a development of previous Ovidian models, whilst their unique quality resides in their status as poems of exile which are a crystallization of personal experience.

Ovid left Rome for Tomis in November or December[20] A.D. 8 and reached his destination probably in the summer of the following year. Biographically-minded scholars have sought to establish his route and rate of progress.[21] Those are minor matters; it is more important that he wrote the first book of the *Tristia*[22] or *Poems of Sadness* on the journey, as the epilogue poem indicates:

> Littera quaecumque est toto tibi lecta libello,
>   est mihi sollicito tempore facta viae. (*Tr.*, I. II. 1–2)

(Every written symbol that you have read in the whole of my
  book
was formed by me during the troubled time of my journey.)

On arrival at Tomis he completed four more books of *Tristia* before the end of A.D. 12.[23] The whole work contains fifty-one elegies and the long poem which forms the second book; and the total number of lines, just over 3,500, falls not far short of Propertius' whole output. On average, Ovid composed an elegy per month, which is not fast writing. He tells us, however, that he burnt much that he wrote.[24]

Some scholars[25] distinguish Books I and II from the rest on the grounds that the former offers greater variety than the rest and the latter is unusual in being a full-length apologia. Furthermore, L. P. Wilkinson groups *Tristia*, III–V with all the *Epistulae ex Ponto* as seven books which 'may be treated as an entity, for they are all too homogeneous'. Such opinions are unwarranted and misleading, for not only does each of Books III–V contain a considerable amount of good poetry (each, in my view, is superior to Book II), but in addition each was constructed as a separate entity by the poet himself. Ovid planned his work carefully: with the obvious exception of Book II, the poems of each book of the *Tristia* are arranged symmetrically in a pattern which both offers variety between contiguous poems and reveals the basic motifs of the book, as I hope to show in more detail.[26] In this respect the *Tristia* differs from the *Epistulae ex Ponto*, in which no such arrangement is detectable. Ovid refers to this peculiarity of the *Epistulae* in the epilogue to the first three books, which were published as one unit:

> nec liber ut fieret, sed uti sua cuique daretur
> littera, propositum curaque nostra fuit.
> postmodo collectas utcumque sine ordine iunxi:
> hoc opus electum ne mihi forte putes.   (*E.P.*, III. 9. 51–4)

> (Not to construct a book, but to send to each
> his letter, has been my purpose and concern.
> Later I gathered them in a random and unordered collection –
> in case you might think that this was a select work of mine.)

The words *utcumque sine ordine* do not refer 'primarily if not exclusively to chronological order',[27] but to symmetrical arrangement, which is plain to see in the four relevant books of the *Tristia*, but is not a feature of the *Epistulae*.[28] In the latter, as Ovid clearly says, the letters were separate and individual; when they were subsequently published together, they were simply assembled at random. Chronological order concerned Ovid neither in the *Tristia* nor the *Epistulae*. There are other differences also between these works: for example, in the *Tristia* the identity of the addressees is almost always suppressed; the reverse is true in the *Epistulae*.

In the former work, as with books, so with elegies: each was thoughtfully constructed, often in a quite intricate pattern. I propose to examine each book in order, to discuss it as a whole, and to choose from it one or two elegies for examination in greater detail.

Book 1, written on the way to Tomis, contains 738 lines in eleven elegies, which are arranged as follows:

A   1   (128) Address to his book – imagery of storm and hardship.

B   2   (110) Storm at sea.
     3   (102) Ovid's last night in Rome.
     4   (28) Storm at sea.

C   5   (84) To a faithful friend – Ovid's woes: Odysseus image.

D   6   (36) To his wife – her loyalty: Penelope image.

C   7   (40) To a close friend – The Metamorphoses.
     8   (50) To a treacherous friend – imagery of the reversal of nature.
     9   (66) To a loyal friend – The Ars Amatoria.

B   10   (50) Ovid's route – storm imagery absent.

A   11   (44) Epilogue – description of hardship and storm.

Elegies 3 and 8 have a part to play in the chiastic pattern, since each provides a strong contrast with its immediate neighbours: in the sequence 2–4 the main contrast is topographical, and in 7–9 it is one of mood. In the whole book, apart from the linked prologue and epilogue, two themes are evident, the poet's stormy journey, and his relationship to his friends. In the central position, an important place, is the elegy to his wife; but it is short, and the wife motif is not prominent elsewhere in the book, except in elegy 3. The poet devotes roughly the same amount of space to his themes:

Prologue and epilogue   : 172 lines
Travel and storm (2, 4, 10): 188
Friendship (5, 7, 9)   : 190
(The remainder (3, 6, 8)   : 188)

The poetry provides good examples of Ovid's usual technique

in, for example, the widespread use of imagery from Greek mythology (cf. 1. 2. 5–10), and swift accumulation of image upon image in rhetorical fashion (cf. 1. 6. 5–16; 1. 9. 7–14), and the frequent employment of names to add colour to the verse (the tenth poem is a notable instance of this). But now there is a new vividness, which is consequent upon the fact that this whole book is an ordering of recent personal experience; and occasionally Ovid brings that experience into the present, and pretends to describe it as it is happening: the following utterance breaks in upon a prayer to the gods of sea and sky:

> verba miser frustra non proficientia perdo.
>> ipsa graves spargunt ora loquentis aquae,
> terribilisque Notus iactat mea dicta, precesque
>> ad quos mittuntur, non sinit ire deos. (*Tr.*, 1. 2. 13–16)

(Poor wretch! I am wasting words vainly, they are useless.
  The heavy waves splash my very lips as I speak,
the terrifying Southerly snatches my pleas and forbids
  my prayers to go to the gods to whom they are offered.)

There follows a 'running commentary' on the storm as it occurs, and a similar technique is used in elegies 4 and 11; at the end of the latter, which is also the end of the book, Ovid is still at sea, and the water is splashing his manuscript as he writes:

> iactor in indomito brumali luce profundo
>> ipsaque caeruleis charta feritur aquis. (*Tr.*, 1. 11. 39–40)

(I am being tossed on a winter's day on the unconquerable deep
  and my very page is being dashed by the dark sea water.)

Of a similar couplet earlier in the same poem, in which Ovid describes himself as having doggedly composed while his boat was awash (11. 17–18), L. P. Wilkinson remarks,[29] 'Granted that he may have made phrases in his head, and even jotted them down, in such conditions, we should take this claim with a drop of salt water.' Wilkinson misses the point, just as he may be misleading us in his statement earlier on the same page of his book, that 'the events of the voyage are told in the First Book of the *Tristia*'. Ovid was writing not a factual memoir of his voyage, but a book of poetry, and poetical truth does not necessarily coincide with historical fact. Within the context of the poem,

Ovid's page *was* splashed by the waves, and whether or not the poet actually had these experiences is unknowable and quite irrelevant. We are dealing with a powerful image: storms in this book are a symbol of the danger and uncertainty of Ovid's fate, and when the waves splash the page as he writes and the gale snatches away his poetic prayer he is telling the reader of his poem about the effect on him of exile and about the threat to his poetic psyche.

A suitable elegy to examine first is the third: we begin in Rome, for Ovid writes about his last night in the capital. This is one of the best of all the *Tristia*, and one of the finest poems of its length in his output. It is not only 'a sincere and vivid record of a poignant personal experience',[30] but also a carefully constructed work of haunting poetry:

> Cum subit illius tristissima noctis imago,
> > qua mihi supremum tempus in urbe fuit,
> cum repeto noctem, qua tot mihi cara reliqui,
> > labitur ex oculis nunc quoque gutta meis. (*Tr.*, 1. 3. 1–4)

(When there looms the sad, sad vision of that night,
  on which I spent my last hours in the capital,
when I recall the night when I left so many things dear to me,
  there falls even now a tear from my eyes.)

This preface is an indication of what is to follow: in line 1 the repeated 'i' sounds have a wailing quality, and the language has ghoulish overtones – *imago* means 'ghost', as well as 'memory-image'; *noctis . . . noctem* enhance this notion, as well as informing the reader that a night scene is about to be described, and *mihi . . . mihi . . . meis* together with the first-person verbs emphasize Ovid's personal involvement.

Four main sections, of roughly the same length, make up the rest of the poem: they recount, in turn, Ovid's predicament, his prayer, his acceptance of his fate, and the anguish of his wife. The final couplet is an epilogue, containing a prayer for her future welfare and support:

> vivat, et absentem, quoniam sic fata tulerunt,
> > vivat ut auxilio sublevet usque suo.   (*Tr.*, 1. 3. 101–2)

(May she live on, and in my absence (since fate has so willed)
  may she live on to lighten my load with constant help.)

The boundaries of the four main sections are in most cases marked by references to the passing of time: 5–6, 27–8, 47–8 (71–2 does not perform this function). The first section, quoted and translated by Wilkinson (pp. 312–13), describes the reaction of Ovid, his family and his friends, to the sentence of exile; a couplet is devoted to the poet's wife:

> uxor amans flentem flens acrius ipsa tenebat,
>   imbre per indignas usque cadente genas. (17–18)

(My loving wife held me weeping, weeping louder herself;
    tears streamed constantly down her innocent cheeks.)

Note the juxtaposition of *flentem flens*,[31] the continuation of the imagery of weeping from line 4, and the reference to someone who is going to be an important character in this drama. In the section as a whole the poet emphasizes the sadness with images of violent death and of his own funeral (11–12, 15, 21–6: in the last passage the words *luctus, gemitus, funeris, funere maerent, lacrimas* appear within four lines). Meanwhile the section moves outwards from Ovid himself, to his friends and members of his family, and then more widely to a description of the appearance of the whole house, at the end of which (25–6) the picture of Troy on the night of her capture widens the vista still further.

The twenty lines which form the second section (27–46) contain Ovid's prayer to the gods. The atmosphere is heightened, and the time link (27–8) reinforces the ghostliness of the prologue:

> iamque quiescebant voces hominumque canumque,
>   Lunaque nocturnos alta regebat equos.

(Now were hushed the cries of men and dogs,
    and the moon was driving high her nocturnal team.)

The mention of dogs (albeit silent) and the moon in this night scene provides overtones which suggest, if not Cerberus, the dog of Hades, then at least Hecate, who had been a moon goddess in early mythology, and who as a witch goddess was traditionally accompanied by hounds.[32] The prayer is introduced, and in it Ovid, hoping against hope, requests the ancient gods of the Capitol to intercede with the god Augustus (who, incidentally, dwelt on the Palatine). In the six lines which follow the prayer Ovid gives a now fuller and more dramatic description of his wife's anguish; he is preparing the reader for the last part of his

poem. So this whole section is a speech of ten lines preceded by
a double preface and followed by the six lines devoted to the
poet's wife.

The following section (47–78) is basically of very similar
pattern, but is complicated by the intrusion of two passages
(51–60, 75–6) which appear to break up the pattern. In thought,
too, this is a complicated section: the poet describes how he
solves a dilemma in the process of coming to terms with his
banishment. Already in the prayer to the gods of the Capitol the
tension in his mind has been evident: in part he accepts his fate
(their temples are never to be seen again; they are gods whom he
must leave), yet in part also he hopes that these same gods may
instruct Augustus to lay aside his hatred and be appeased. Now
this conflict of mind is described at greater length: Ovid must
leave Rome, yet Rome draws him back:

> iamque morae spatium nox praecipitata negabat,
>   versaque ab axe suo Parrhasis Arctos erat.
> quid facerem? blando patriae retinebar amore:
>   ultima sed iussae nox erat illa fugae. (47–50)

(Now hurrying night denied me time for delay,
    and the Great Bear had revolved upon its axis.
What should I do? I was held by the enthralling love of my
        country,
    yet that was the last night before my decreed exile.)

The time link (47–8) which begins this section contains a note of
urgency, and also mentions the Parrhasian (i.e. Arcadian) or Great
Bear, a constellation which frequently appears in the *Tristia*.
The statement of the dilemma in lines 49–50 is followed by a group
of ten lines which are highly rhetorical in tone – a combination of
passionate, yet balanced, utterance. In this group of lines, which
seems to stand on a higher plane than that of the rest of the section,
the dilemma is acted out; the opening words of each couplet
give some indication of the inner structure of this short passage:

51 a! quotiens . . .
53 a! quotiens . . .
55 ter limen tetigi, ter sum revocatus . . .
57 saepe . . .
59 saepe . . .

Here lies the central crisis, and in a sense the central point of the poem. The resolution follows immediately, as Ovid faces facts at last:

> denique 'quid propero? Scythia est, quo mittimur', inquam,
>   'Roma relinquenda est. utraque iusta mora est . . .
> dum licet, amplectar: numquam fortasse licebit
>   amplius. in lucro est quae datur hora mihi.'
> nec mora . . . (61–2, 67–9)

(Finally I said, 'why hurry? It is Scythia to which I am sent;
   Rome I must leave. Both facts justify my delay . . .
Whilst I may, I'll embrace you [my friends]: perhaps I'll be allowed to
   never again. I count as gain the brief hour granted to me.'
I delayed no longer . . .)

At this point, Ovid departs from his practice of using the time link to mark the boundary between sections. That which now occurs is situated within the third section, a second note of urgency. Day is just over the horizon:

> dum loquor et flemus, caelo nitidissimus alto,
>   stella gravis nobis, Lucifer ortus erat. (71–2)

(Whilst I spoke and we wept, very bright in the well of the sky
   a star of doom for me, the Light-bringer, had arisen.)

Ovid's inner conflict wells up again; he feels as if he is being torn apart, and in 75–6 employs the simile of Mettus, a general in early Roman history, who was torn apart as a punishment for treachery. The image is superfluous. The hint of treachery jars, and the couplet is superimposed harshly upon the basic pattern.[33] Despite this recurrence of anxiety, Ovid has come to terms with his fate; but for his wife no such resolution has been effected. The final part of the poem belongs to her. It begins on line 79, yet is closely bound to what precedes, as can be seen from the repetition of *tum vero* in line 77, in the last couplet of section three, and 79, in the first couplet of section four. The wife cannot be separated from her husband, yet he is firm in his resolve that she must, and so as he departs she breaks down. It is a harrowing scene, and the imagery of death and burial recurs in lines 89–100; for example:

egredior, sive illud erat sine funere ferri,
  squalidus immissis hirta per ora comis. (89–90)

(I set out – no, it was a funeral procession without the funeral –
  unkempt, my hair straggling over my unshaven face.)

What happened to his wife was later told to him (*narratur*, 91),
and the description culminates in the penultimate couplet of the
poem:

et voluisse mori, moriendo ponere sensus,
  respectuque tamen non periisse mei. (99–100)

(and she wanted to die, and by dying to relinquish all feeling,
  and yet through regard for me she did not pass away.)

Ovid seeks to counter the double *mori, moriendo* by the reiterated
vivat . . . vivat of the final couplet, but the final note is not one of
optimism or reassurance. The poem has no sure end, because it
describes the circumstances of exile at its very beginning, and the
poet makes it clear that for his wife and for himself (see lines 3–4)
the anguish of separation can never be mitigated.

This third elegy is framed by storm poems, not simply to provide variety of location and mood, but also to relate as fully as
possible the storm imagery to the distress of exile. The latter of
these two storm elegies, elegy 4, is one of the shortest of the
Tristia and provides good instances of one of Ovid's most
accomplished techniques, one which adds to the remarkable
flexibility of his poetry and renders it anything but static. I refer
to his ability to treat a theme from two standpoints, and to widen
the scope of his poetry and the sensibility of the reader by the
contrast and alternation of these treatments. In this elegy, he
treats his topic now from the point of view of the elements, now
from that of the poet, the ship and the crew which are subject
to those elements. This double effect is visible in the earlier part
of the poem:

Tingitur oceano custos Erymanthidos ursae,
  aequoreasque suo sidere turbat aquas.
nos tamen Ionium non nostra findimus aequor
  sponte, sed audaces cogimur esse metu.   (*Tr.*, 1. 4. 1–4)

(Dipped in the Ocean is the guardian of the Great Bear,[34]
  and with his stars he rolls the sea waters.

Yet I am cleaving the Ionian sea not of my own
   will, but am compelled to act bravely through fear.)

There is in the first line the possibility that Ovid is giving us an
actual date, 26 May A.D. 9. That should satisfy the biographically
minded! The guardian of the Great Bear, Arctophylax (also called
Boötes) experienced its cosmical, or morning, setting at that
point in the year according to Ovid, writing in the *Fasti*.[35] But
it is of more importance for the poem itself to know that the
ancients associated the setting of this constellation with stormy
weather.[36] So this first line is no mere date, but a cue for the
second line; a storm is rising and Ovid looks at it in this couplet
from a cosmic standpoint. In contrast, in the second couplet he
considers his own situation (*nos tamen*), afflicted by compulsion
and fear in a dangerous situation. This process of contrasted
viewpoints is continued: lines 5–8 (apart from *me miserum*!)
vividly describe the effect of the storm on the ship, and lines
9–12 describe the reactions of the ship to that assault – it creaks
and groans (*sonant . . . ingemit*) – and how the sailor gives way to
fear and the demands of the tempest:

> navita confessus gelidum pallore timorem,
>   iam sequitur victus, non regit arte ratem. (11–12)

(The sailor admitting cold fear in his pallor,
   now defeated lets the boat go, with no skill to steer her.)

From this last line is developed the fullest image of the poem,
a simile of the rider who has lost control of his horse. This
simile drives home the picture of the powerless helmsman, and
occupies together with that picture four lines exactly in the centre
of the poem:

> utque parum validus non proficientia rector
>   cervicis rigidae frena remittit equo,
> sic non quo voluit, sed quo rapit impetus undae,
>   aurigam video vela dedisse rati. (13–16)

(and as a weak rider lets the useless reins
   fall on the neck of a horse of stubborn pride,
so it is not where he intended, but where the wave's surge plunges
      him,
   that my 'charioteer' I see has given the ship full rein.)

In the final line Ovid boldly converts the simile into a meta-phor, by using the word *auriga*, which means 'charioteer', as if it could mean 'helmsman'. There is a clever touch, too: *vela dare* (to spread one's sails) is often used metaphorically in Latin to mean 'give way to', 'give rein to', and what Ovid is doing is using a nautical phrase in a nautical context in a metaphorical sense. Oddly, this double irregularity within one line succeeds in the Latin, whereas in English it is safer to avoid it; the translation concentrates on the image of chariot driving.

The last part of the elegy is concerned with Ovid's plight, the storm, and two prayers: the danger of being driven back to Italy, the forbidden land (17-20), evokes the prayer that the wind may turn and obey the great god Augustus (21-2); the reply of the storm, which continues to rage (23-4), evokes the prayer that the gods of the sea shall not add their anger to that of Jupiter (i.e. Augustus) (25-8). Note the two instances of imperial flattery in these final lines. Hence the basic structure is as follows:

$$2 + 2. \mid 4 + 4 \mid [4] \mid 6 + 6$$
$$4 + 2 \qquad 2 + 4$$

Before leaving Book 1, I should like to refer briefly to elegy 6, the central poem. E. J. Kenney has discussed this poem and with most of his views I am in agreement.[37] However, in one respect he finds the poem wanting, or, to be more accurate, superfluous: he finds lines 23-8 a problem, a passage which artistically is worse than irrelevant, one which is disastrous; the poem is better off without it. Now this poem, like the rest of the *Tristia*, is carefully constructed. Does the pattern of the elegy demonstrate that this passage is an excrescence? I shall try to show briefly that it does not. But first, although the whole poem is in praise of Ovid's wife, these six lines are largely flattery of the empress Livia. Now flattery is not 'British', but a Roman habit it was – we tend to overlook it in Virgil and Horace and castigate it in Ovid, Martial and the Silver Age generally, where it is usually no more intense. Kenney partly dislikes these lines because of the flattery, yet the flattery is no greater than that of the Emperor in the fourth poem, just discussed. Kenney remarks, 'the implication of v. 28, that the great archetype of marital fidelity, Penelope herself, was a less dutiful wife than Livia, besides being adulation of an almost

Martialian sort, destroys the whole basis of Ovid's panegyric'.[38] Well, if that implication resides in line 28, it is so remote that it can only be read into the line by dragging in an unrelated impossibility from three couplets before, where Ovid tells his wife that if she had married Homer she would have been more famous than Penelope (21-2). Here are 27-8 (part of a sentence):

> . . . adsimilemque sui longa adsuetudine fecit,
> grandia si parvis adsimulare licet.

Ovid is considering the possibility that Livia has '. . . made [his wife] like herself by long acquaintance, if one may consider great things as being like small ones'. The pentameter is really quite discreet, a recognition that empresses are greater than ordinary women. Ovid is probably more concerned with the play between *adsimilemque* and *adsimulare*; Penelope is out of the picture. Moreover, to suggest, as Kenney does in some detail on the same page, that Ovid inserted lines 23-8 at a later date and left loose ends of thought development and even of syntax is unrealistic. Examination of the structure reveals that the poem is a doublet: certain features of 1-18 recur in the same order in 19-36, and this structure establishes 23-8 as authentic:

- 1-4 Homage to wife by double mythological reference.
- 19-22 Homage to wife by triple mythological reference.
- 5-8 The loyalty of his wife has rescued Ovid.
- 23-8 The origin of her loyalty – two possible sources considered.

(Lines 23-8 are a natural development both from 5-8 and 19-22.)

- 9-18 Nature of wife's achievement: the threat to Ovid removed by his wife and others.
- 29-36 Ovid's near helplessness: he lacks the ability to give his wife due praise, yet will attempt to do so, to the limit of his powers.

(These last two parts of the poem are mainly a contrast between the strength of the wife and the weakness of the husband, but in the final couplet of the poem Ovid tries to show the courage which he ascribes to her in line 15.)

The single poem which forms the second book of the *Tristia* is mainly an elaborate defence against one of the two grounds for the poet's exile. Ovid cannot reply in detail to the charge

concerning his *error*, and in fact accepts his guilt in that matter;
but to the other charge, the *carmen*, he is ready and eager to reply:

> perdiderint cum me duo crimina, carmen et error,
>   alterius facti culpa silenda mihi:
> nam non sum tanti, renovem ut tua vulnera, Caesar,
>   quem nimio plus est indoluisse semel.
> altera pars superest, qua turpi carmine factus
>   arguor obsceni doctor adulterii.   (*Tr*. II. 207–12)

(Though my ruin stems from two offences, a poem and a mistake,
    about my guilt in one of them I must remain silent:
For I do not deserve to reopen your wounds, Caesar;
    it is too much that you have been hurt once.
The other part remains, the charge that by an unseemly poem
    I became the teacher of foul adultery.)

The language of the last couplet, with the words *turpi . . .
obsceni . . . adulterii*, reflects Ovid's feelings on this charge, and
reveals the deep motivation, springing from professional pride
and probably also a basic sense of injustice, for the elaborate and
sustained defence which follows in the rest of the poem.

But Ovid is shackled: one of the charges he must accept without
complaint, and so he must plead not for pardon but for a lighter
sentence, a safer place of exile;[39] all his indignation is reserved
for the defence of his Muse, but when that defence is examined,
it hardly rings true, and clever though it is as a piece of forensic
oratory in elegiacs, it would be unlikely to persuade a *princeps*
who had seen his moral reforms fail, had seen adultery within his
own family (twice), and nevertheless seemed determined in his
declining years to combat the permissiveness of the capital.

By its very nature Ovid's defence could not be cogent. He had
to plead a negative case: he could not insist that he had wrought
good with his *Ars Amatoria*, but only that he had not wrought
evil;[40] he could not insist that the content of the poem was pure,
but must needs incriminate the world, that is, take refuge in the
claim that there were many examples of corruption in Roman
society and that others in great numbers had produced the
same kind of literature;[41] he could not insist that the poem was
morally good, but had to argue instead that he at least was so[42] –
dangerous ground, for if the poet is morally good, what is the
source of his immoral poetry? These are the three main grounds

of his defence against the charge of having published an immoral poem.

The whole plea is constructed in the form of a speech to be delivered in court, as others have noted:[43]

exordium (1–26) to conciliate the court (that is, Augustus).
propositio (27–8) in which the pleader states his object.
tractatio (29–578) in which he develops his case:
    29–154 (probatio) proof of his case by the evidence available.
    155–206 (epilogus I) conclusion, pleading for mercy.
    207–572 (refutatio) rebuttal of the charge against him.
    573–8   (epilogus II) second conclusion, pleading for mercy.

The opening lines of the *refutatio*, quoted above, show that Ovid defends himself in detail against only one of his charges. Those opening lines are also an important boundary between all that precedes and virtually all that follows. In the first 210 lines the poet is meek and repentant: awe of Augustus' power and large slices of flattery are mingled with firm legal arguments in the *probatio*, some of the salient points of which are as follows: Augustus has shown mercy to enemies of the state, but Ovid, who has been loyal to the régime, has been punished (51–76); Ovid, since the publication of his poem, has continued to be acknowledged as an *eques* (89–92, and also 539–42), and as a respectable judicial officer and party in private suits (93–6).

But a change occurs at 211. Beginning with the impassioned couplet 211–12, Ovid's plea becomes more vigorous as he strives to refute the charge of immorality in the necessarily negative manner outlined above; and the consequence of his spirited yet negative rhetoric is a desperation and wildness and overelaboration which critics have frequently noticed and which makes this poem the weakest of the *Tristia*. Yet there is a kind of order in the *refutatio*, as Ovid rings the changes on the main arguments for defence:

213–52 The work is beneath Augustus' notice. It broke no existing law. The reader is warned about its contents (and to illustrate this last point Ovid quotes four lines from *Ars Amatoria*, Book 1 at lines 247–50 of this poem).

253–76 Defence A: poetry, like all else, may be injurious, but only to the sinful; it does not harm those of upright mind.

277–306 Defence B: there are many other instances of vice and temptation elsewhere in Roman society.

307–12 Defence A: to the upright erotic verse is not harmful.

313–42 Interlude: Ovid is not suited to epic verse and the praise thereby of Augustus.

343–60 Defence C: Ovid's hands are clean and his intentions pure.

361–546 Defence B: many instances of vice elsewhere in literature, and in other pursuits such as dice and other games.

547–72 Defence C: Ovid's aims are honourable and his intentions pure.

There is a certain imbalance, nevertheless: Ovid was striving for a total effect, and paid relative disregard to proportion. Moreover, he exaggerates, and so distorts and weakens his case: the noble generalization

> omnia perversas possunt corrumpere mentes (301)

> (All things can corrupt perverted minds)

is immediately preceded by a passage in which the poet oddly maintains that the very temples of Rome may remind one of the erotic associations and immoral loves of the deities to whom they are dedicated, and so may have an immoral influence; and the line is followed by the equally curious remark that the *Ars Amatoria* was written for prostitutes only. Again, in the near exhaustive (and exhausting) review of Graeco-Roman 'love' poetry, the *Iliad* and *Odyssey* are, by a simplification of an extreme kind, described as poems of adulterous love; and the passage about dice playing, ball games, swimming and so forth (471–92) is a weak inclusion, even though the treatment of dice playing has been defended on the grounds that Augustus was himself, so it is believed, addicted to it.

How one reacts to this book of the *Tristia* may well depend on one's reaction to the *Ars Amatoria*. He who believes, like Owen,[44] that 'the *Ars Amatoria* is voluptuous and almost brutal in its coarseness, and is a dangerous work because it sets up the pursuit of selfish pleasure as the standard of life', may not be distressed at Ovid's failure to defend it adequately. Owen himself finds that 'Ovid's defence of the *Ars Amatoria* is not entirely convincing'.[44] On the other hand, he who, as Lord Macaulay did, thinks highly of the *Ars*, will look with more sympathy upon the defence of it and will deeply regret that Ovid at certain points in his apologia allowed himself to be carried away by his own enthusiasm.

When precisely the second book was composed is not known; Wilkinson thinks that it may have been composed on the way to Tomis and sent to Rome immediately upon arrival there.[45] However, lines 187–200, in which Ovid emphasizes the remoteness of Tomis from Rome, suggest that the poem was at least partly written and completed at Tomis:

longius hac nihil est . . . (195)
hactenus Euxini pars est Romana sinistri. (197)
haec est Ausonio sub iure novissima . . . terra. (199–200)

(nothing is further than this land . . .
This is the limit of Rome's domain on the ill-omened Euxine.
This is the furthest land under Roman rule.)

It is reasonable to suppose that, whereas Ovid may have been forming the main lines of his defence ever since exile had been pronounced upon him, he completed his apologia on arrival at Tomis, and sent it to Rome after putting the final touches to it. At all events it is not surprising that this book-length poem should stand at this point in the *Tristia*: it is probable that in order to complete this large-scale work Ovid needed to be free from the distractions of travel in order to devote all his attention to it; and that completion he rated as a matter of high priority.

Book III, 788 lines long, not surprisingly is very much concerned with Tomis itself. Of the three main themes of the book, two are devoted to the hardship of exile, and to descriptions of the place of exile; the third theme concerns Ovid's friends, and his separation from them. There is also a prologue and a balancing epilogue, and a centrally placed[46] elegy devoted to Perilla, probably his stepdaughter. She is the only person in the *Tristia*, apart from Augustus, to be addressed by name. These last three poems are all literary in tone and therefore stand together, and thus provide a fourth theme for the book. The poems are in the main carefully arranged:

A	1	(82)	Prologue – Ovid's book arrives in Rome.
B	2	(30)	Hardship of exile – Ovid prefers death.
	3	(88)	To his wife – death in exile contemplated –
C			Ovid's epitaph.
	4a	(46)	To a true friend – advice to live humbly.
B	4b	(32)	To friends – Ovid cut off in a harsh country far from Rome.
	5	(56)	To a true friend – Ovid hopes for mercy: his *error*.
C	6	(38)	To an old friend – Ovid's *error*: a plea for intercession.
A	7	(54)	To Perilla.
B	8	(42)	The prayer of the exile – release from Tomis by death or Augustus.
	9	(34)	Origin of the name Tomis – an aetiological poem.
D	10	(78)	Description of Tomis – harsh and inhospitable place.
B	11	(74)	To an enemy – Ovid cut off in a harsh country.
	12	(54)	Spring comes to Tomis – games and festivals – Italy.
D	13	(28)	Birthday at Tomis – a cruel experience for Ovid.
A	14	(52)	Dedication of book to a friend – epilogue – Tomis theme.[47]

The four main themes occupy roughly the same amount of space in the book:

A	(1, 7, 14)	: 188 lines
B	(2, 4b, 8, 11):	178
C	(3, 4a, 5, 6)	: 228
D	(9, 10, 12, 13):	194

Certain of these elegies have attracted the attention of scholars in the recent past;[48] I shall examine the seventh and tenth.

Like the poem to Ovid's wife in Book 1, the centrally placed seventh elegy to Perilla is made notable both by position and addressee. Despite the remark in line 1 that it is a 'quickly written letter' (*subito perarata . . . littera*), it is a finely constructed poem. Ovid's theme is the relationship between physical death and the

immortality which poetic fame brings, and he skilfully varies his
treatment by approaching the topic from the two main standpoints or poles which it presents. There is a further basis for
contrast and alternation: Ovid includes himself and Perilla as
personae who have an important role to play in the pattern of the
elegy. The result is a poem which derives power from the care
and complexity of its construction. The inspiration was perhaps
largely drawn from the fact of exile itself: it was a commonplace
that a poet was a special mortal, whose genius and fame were
protected by the heavenly Muses; but in this instance the poet was
in exile, a harsh exile, a situation which made him aware of his
own life and death. This conflict between death and immortality
is already hinted at in lines 7-10 (1-6 are an introduction) in which
Ovid tells his letter what message he wishes it to deliver to
Perilla:

> vivere me dices, sed sic, ut vivere nolim,
>   nec mala tam longa nostra levata mora:
> et tamen ad Musas, quamvis nocuere, reverti,
>   aptaque in alternos cogere verba pedes.
>
> (*Tr.*, III. 7. 7-10)

(Say I live, but in such a manner that I do not wish to live,
    and that my woes have not been lightened by so long a time;
Yet I am returning to the Muses, although they have harmed me,
    and forcing words to fit alternate measures.)

Another source of inspiration, and possibly of consolation, for
the exiled poet, was his belief that his poetic fame, his key to
immortality, could not be affected by the anger of Augustus,
however much he might punish his victim (see 47-52). No doubt
Ovid was also inspired by his concern for Perilla; a double concern for her both as a mortal woman (33-42) and as a poetess
who might achieve immortality through her own poetry (11-20).

After line 10 the poem is divided into two parts of equal length,
each concluded by a couplet which points a lesson for Perilla
and urges her to a course of action; the elegy is not without a
didactic element. The earlier part (11-32) deals with poetry,
firstly with Perilla's muse (11-20) and then the fear that Ovid's
fate and his absence may have been harmful to her poetic inspiration (21-30). In the injunction which concludes this part of

the poem, Ovid urges her to continue writing, and he refers to
the occupation as a fine art, and a holy one too. He particularly
offers encouragement in the address *doctissima*; *doctus* in Latin
was often used to describe a true poet:[49]

> ergo desidiae remove, doctissima, causas,
> inque bonas artes et tua sacra redi. (31-2)

(Therefore dispel the causes of sloth, most talented girl,
  and return to the fine art and the holy rites that are yours.)

The latter of the two main parts of the poem is devoted to
considerations of mortality: Ovid hints at human mortality by
powerfully describing the process of ageing which Perilla herself
must one day undergo, and by alluding to human frailty and to
the changes of fortune which life can bring (33-42). The next
couplet contains the message of the whole poem:

> singula ne referam, nil non mortale tenemus
> pectoris exceptis ingeniique bonis. (43-4)

(To be brief, we possess nothing that is not mortal
  except for the blessings of our heart and mind.)

These two lines introduce the passage in which Ovid considers
his own case (43-52): he is a good instance of the sentiment just
quoted, for he has lost virtually everything, and yet is assured of
immortality as a writer, an immortality which no one, not even
Augustus, could take from him. The injunction which concludes
the whole poem bids Perilla follow suit and cheat death by
acquiring some literary fame:

> tu quoque, quam studii maneat felicior usus,
> effuge venturos, qua potes, usque rogos! (53-4)

(May you too – and let a happier use of your art await you –
  escape the coming pyre by whatever means you can.)

The following scheme may illustrate the structure:

6	4	22	22
intro-duction	life, death and the muses	poetry: 10 Perilla's muse 10 Ovid and the threat to Perilla's muse 2 exhortation to write	mortality: 10 Perilla's mortality 10 Ovid's immortality 2 exhortation to acquire immortality

The tenth elegy is very different: it describes the discomforts of Tomis. It follows an elegy on the origin of the name of the place and is to be succeeded by two or three others in this same book dealing with the place itself. In this poem Ovid describes two main discomforts, the cold and inhospitable climate, and the insecurity of the region, that is, the continued threat of violence and warfare. My purpose is not to give an account of the details which Ovid vividly brings before the reader – these may best be found by reading the poem itself or the works of such critics as have concentrated on such matters[50] – but to draw attention to it as another example of competent composition. Like the elegy to Perilla, this poem opens with a formal introduction (in this case of four lines), and then in the next eight states the two main themes, which are so described that it is clear that Ovid regards them as closely interdependent: the cold of winter increases the threat of invasion:

> Sauromatae cingunt, fera gens, Bessique Getaeque,
>   quam non ingenio nomina digna meo!
> dum tamen aura tepet, medio defendimur Histro:
>   ille suis liquidis bella repellit aquis.
> at cum tristis hiems squalentia protulit ora,
>   terraque marmoreo est candida facta gelu,
> dum prohibet Boreas et nix habitare sub Arcto,
>   tum patet has gentes axe tremente premi.
> nix iacet . . . (*Tr.*, III. 10. 5–13)

(The Sauromatae, a cruel tribe, beset me, and the Bessi and Getae.
    How unworthy of my talent the names are!
Yet while the breeze blows warm, we are protected by the
    Danube's barrier;
    he wards off warfare with his flowing waters.
But when harsh winter thrusts forth his grisly face,
    and the ground grows marble-white with frost,
while the North Wind and snow prevent life beneath the Great
    Bear,
    then it is clear that these tribes are hard pressed by the shivering
    pole.
The snow lies . . .)

Nix at the beginning of line 13 picks up the *nix* of line 11, and guides the reader into a supplementary passage of twelve lines (13–24) which contains details of the winter cold and the measures taken by these Northern inhabitants to keep it at bay. The main part of the poem, fifty-two lines long, begins at line 25, and in it the two themes of cold and insecurity are treated much more fully, not haphazardly, but with careful attention given to balance of material:

25–30 (6 lines) Frozen rivers – the frozen Danube.⎫
31–4   (4) Sarmatians invade across the ice.   ⎬
35–50 (16) Frozen sea (*vidimus* at 37 and 49 helps to hold this passage together).
51–66 (16) Invading enemy, from the standpoint both of invaders and invaded.
67–70 (4) Fear of the enemy even in peacetime leads⎫
           to neglect of the land.   ⎬
71–6   (6) The consequent desolation of the land. ⎭

Such is the somewhat chiastic structure of the main part of the poem; the central passages of sixteen lines are also each constructed with care and repay close study. Awareness of the structure of a poem brings with it a mental 'map' of the whole, and consequently, I believe, a clearer understanding. The final couplet is a formal conclusion:

> ergo tam late pateat cum maximus orbis,
>   haec est in poenam terra reperta meam. (77–8)

(So despite the vast extent of the immense world,
    this is the land that has been discovered for my punishment.)

Book III belongs to A.D. 9 or 10; Book IV was completed about a year later. It is shorter than average, though not as short as Book II, and contains ten elegies amounting to some 678 lines. The themes of the Book do not present anything really new: life at Tomis did not provide a significant variety of personal experiences ripe for transmutation into poetry; the life of an exile drags. So the two main themes are already familiar, the hardship of exile, and friends at home (including the poet's wife). There is also a prologue and balancing epilogue, addressed to the reader (see the first couplet of the prologue, and the last couplet of the epilogue); these two poems deal with the life and poetry of Ovid himself, and with the solace which the Muses bring. There is no central elegy, but instead two panels of elegies are juxtaposed and present a contrast of mood:

2–5 mainly optimistic in mood, with themes of flattery prominent.
5–9 mainly pessimistic, with the motif of time prominent.

The following is the arrangement of the poems:

A   1   (106) Prologue – contains some autobiography about his exile.
B   2   (74) Joyful triumph in Rome, but Ovid cut off in exile.
C   3   (84) To his wife: virtue and renown in adversity.
C   4   (88) To a noble friend: the justice of Augustus.
C   5   (34) To a loyal friend: best wishes to one who may help Ovid.
B   6   (50) Time the healer is no healer for Ovid: his desire of death.
C   7   (26) To a lapsed friend: a reproachful letter.
B   8   (52) Ovid in exile, and at his time of life: divine wrath.
B   9   (32) Threat to an imaginary enemy: rage and wrath.
A 10 (132) Ovid's autobiography up to the time of his exile.

A (prologue and epilogue)   : 238 lines
B (exile poems, and address to enemy): 208
C (friendship poems)   : 232

The tenth elegy is unique in classical literature, for it is an autobiography in verse. Its presence at the end of this book suggests that Ovid intended to produce these four books of the *Tristia* only, and intended this poem to be the epilogue to the whole work. The poet's own autobiography would not be inappropriate as the final poem in a work which was to an unusual degree based upon personal experience. But he also wrote a fifth book, and in the opening poem of that book his tone is almost apologetic; he feels it necessary to defend his continued writing of poetry. In the opening couplet of the poem he seems to be alluding to the four previous books as a single group:

Hunc quoque de Getico, nostri studiose, libellum
    litore praemissis quattuor adde meis. (*Tr.*, v. 1. 1–2)

(Add this book also, my devoted friend,
    to my four already sent from the Getic shore.)

Moreover, that whole poem is one of the most important of the
Tristia, for it is a detailed defence of the writing of poetry in
exile, and in it Ovid rebuts objections which might be (and perhaps *were*) raised by readers.

Elegy IV. 10 itself has attracted the attention of readers precisely
because of its autobiographical content. From this source is
obtained much of the information which is known about Ovid's
life.[51] Yet some critics are not satisfied with this, and in their
thirst for biographical detail they regret the fact that the poem had
to be written in verse (which is so fettering), and are suspicious
of its omissions of fact (for example, there is no reference in it
to most of the poetry which Ovid wrote before exile). The truth
is that even in this poem Ovid was presenting not an exhaustive
account, but an artistic construction. As such it deserves close
study, but is rather too complex to discuss in detail here, save
that between the introduction (1–2) and the conclusion (129–32),
the main body of the poem is divided into some six sections,
which display an internal pattern and a variety of thematic
material as the poet moves easily to and fro between details of
his personal life and of his life as a poet. There are also digressions,
one on Ovid's contemporary poets (41–56) and also a prayer for
his parents (85–90); these are situated with precision within the
main body of the poem. In short, although Ovid was informing
the reader of his own life, and was specifically addressing posterity
(2), he was nevertheless constructing a poem and was not aware of
the demands which modern scholars are prepared to make in
their search for biographical material.

The second poem of this same book is also constructed with
considerable subtlety. The main theme is a triumph over the
Germans which Rome may be celebrating in the capital, and the
relationship of the exiled poet to that celebration (he has already
alluded to this possible triumph at III. 12. 45–8). In the course of
the poem he describes the ritual of a triumph, and so vivid is
his description that he might almost be present in person at the
event. He was aware of this himself, I think, for in this same poem

he tells of the freedom which he still has as a poet, the freedom of
imagination (57–64). On the other hand he cannot be physically
present, and when the news of the event reaches him it will no
longer be news, but history (67–71). In addition to this conflict
between the unchained imagination and the physical restraint
upon the poet, there is a contrast between the joyful people in
Rome and the sad exile at Tomis, though in the last three lines
of the poem (72–4) we are told that even the stale news of the
triumph will be able to lift his gloom.

The first fifty-six lines are a sustained account of the ritual of
a triumph, describing its events in the order in which they would
occur, starting with the preparations and initial sacrifices, proceeding to the procession of the captives and the floats illustrating
the victories won, and culminating in the ride of the Caesar to the
Capitol and the final rites in the temple of Jupiter (55–6). One
couplet (17–18) does not belong to this picture, but glances at
the exiled Ovid and anticipates the last eighteen lines of the poem:

> nos procul expulsos communia gaudia fallunt,
>> famaque tam longe non nisi parva venit. (17–18)

> (But I, the remote exile, miss the common rejoicing,
>> and only a faint rumour penetrates so far.)

The couplet is flanked on both sides by references to the rejoicing
of the loyal subjects of Augustus at the triumph (15–16, 19f.).
The reverse occurs in the last eighteen lines of the poem, which
deal with Ovid himself: a single couplet in the passage takes the
reader back to the citizens, the triumph and its joyful spectacle:

> vera tamen capiet populus spectacula felix,
>> laetaque erit praesens cum duce turba suo. (65–6)

> (But the real spectacle will be enjoyed by the happy people,
>> and the crowd will rejoice in the presence of their leader.)

When these two couplets (17–18, 65–6) are compared, the contrasts are clear between Ovid, the remote exile missing the
celebration, and the crowd at Rome taking part in it with their
leader, or, to be more precise, between *fama* and *vera . . . spectacula*,
between *fallunt* and *capiet*, and between *nos procul expulsos* and
praesens cum duce turba suo.

These remarks by no means exhaust all that can be said about
the poem: for example, a detailed study of the structure is worth

making, and will reveal how the movement ascends to the central passage 27–46, made more vivid by use of direct speech, and in turn descends from it in the final section of the poem. Where it is tempting to see only flattery and self-pity, there really exists a powerful poetic mind at work.

The last book of the *Tristia* is longer, with some 750 lines and what are in the editions fourteen poems, but in actual fact fifteen, since the second elegy is really two separate, though closely connected, elegies.[52] This is a complex book, containing four main themes: poems to the poet's wife, four in all, distributed with care throughout the book; two kinds of poem to friends, bright poems to his true friends and pleas to those in power, and sad poems to others, together with a poem to an enemy at the centre of the book; and also two further poems descriptive of the harshness of life at Tomis. The prologue poem, already referred to earlier, is largely concerned with literary matters, but lacks the same kind of balancing epilogue found in earlier books; however, in the last elegy, addressed to Ovid's wife, certain literary remarks do in fact remind one of the opening elegy, but the tone is quite different: gone is the submissive apologia of the prologue, and instead the poet proudly tells his wife of the immortality she has achieved in his poetry (1–14).

The poems of Book v are distributed as follows:

A   1   (80) Prologue: apologia for his continued writing.

B   2a (44) To wife: his troubles.
     2b (34) Suppliant's prayer, to Augustus.
C   3   (58) Prayer to Bacchus.
     4   (50) To a true friend: an appeal.
B   5   (64) His wife's birthday: greetings from the land of the Getae.

D   6   (46) To an angered friend.
E   7   (68) To a friend: description of life among the barbarians.
F   8   (38) To an enemy.
C   9   (38) To a true friend.
E   10 (52) Tomis: to his friends: a description of its evils.

B	11	(30)	To wife: consolation and concern for her.
	12	(68)	To a friend: Ovid's muse dimmed among the
D			barbarians.
	13	(34)	To a lapsed friend.
B	14	(46)	To wife: her fame in his poetry.

As usual, Ovid allots equal weight to his main themes:

wife poems	:	184 lines
pleas and poems to true friends	:	180
sad poems to friends, poem to enemy	:	186
the rest: prologue and Tomis elegies (1, 7, 10)	:	200

Written soon after Book IV, the poems of this book are in no way inferior: each is, as usual, a well-constructed and carefully-thought-out composition. I take as examples the two prayers to Augustus and Bacchus. Poem 2b, addressed to Augustus, has a single introductory couplet and then four equal sections of eight lines, in which the poet skilfully approaches the specific plea which is made in the last of the four sections:

Introduction (2)
⌈ Address and plea in general terms (8)
⌈Augustus' anger has been moderate (8)
⌊Yet even so, Ovid is in dire straits at Tomis (8)
⌊ Plea specified: the place is insecure, and
he begs for removal to some safer spot (8)

He draws upon his ability as an advocate in making this plea, and for good measure presses it home in the final couplet:

> quod petimus, poena est: neque enim miser esse recuso,
>   sed precor ut possim tutius esse miser.

> (What I seek is punishment, for suffering I do not reject,
>   but I pray that I might suffer in greater safety.)

The following prayer, to a second god (see lines 45–6, quoted below), is more detailed: the poet weaves a pattern around three separate *personae*, poets (as a group), Bacchus, and himself. He has already described Augustus as Jupiter in the first couplet of 2b, and now prays that Bacchus may intercede with him:

> sunt dis inter se commercia; flectere tempta
>   Caesareum numen numine, Bacche, tuo. (*Tr.*, v. 3. 45–6)

(Between the gods there are dealings. Seek to prevail
   upon Caesar's divine power with your divine power, Bacchus.)

In the first four lines of the poem, Ovid introduces two of his
three *personae*:

> Illa dies haec est, qua te celebrare poetae,
>   si modo non fallunt tempora, Bacche, solent,
> festaque odoratis innectunt tempora sertis,
>   et dicunt laudes ad tua vina tuas. (1–4)

(This is the day when poets are accustomed to honour you,
   provided I am not confusing the date, Bacchus,
and bind their festive brows with fragrant garlands,
   and utter your praises over the wine that belongs to you.)

In the following eight lines he brings in the remaining character,
himself, a man who is a poet, but who is now in distress. This
leads to the first main section of twenty-two lines (13–34), in
which Ovid in some fine and picturesque poetry stresses the
obligation which a god of poetry owes to a poet in trouble; in
the course of this section the fates of Bacchus and Ovid are
compared and contrasted. In the final section of the poem (35–58)
a sustained plea to Bacchus is succeeded by another of the same
length addressed to Ovid's fellow poets, in which he prays that
they may support his plea to the patron god. We have come full
circle, for the two *personae* present at the opening of the poem are
dominant in the final section. Ovid is present in those final twenty-
four lines, it is true, but his main role is played in lines 5–12 and
13–34. Hence the structure:

Praise of Bacchus by the poets (4)
Ovid's plight in exile (8)
Bacchus' obligation to Ovid (6)
Bacchus' fate (8)
Ovid's fate (4)
Bacchus' obligation to Ovid (4)
Appeal to Bacchus (12)
Appeal to fellow poets for their support (12)

This is the skeleton. The flesh is provided by Ovid's poetical
technique: he had an unsurpassed ability to compose in elegiac
couplets; his imagery is memorable – like that of '*clouded* fate' in

line 14, or the Bear constellation of line 7, which together with stars and lightning (30 and 31), is a recurrent image in the *Tristia*; or consider the wealth of names in this poem, names both mythological and real, on average one name per couplet. These and other features of composition add to the richness of his poetic texture, not only in this poem, but in the *Tristia* as a whole, and elsewhere. In particular he constantly draws upon Greek mythology and literature, up to the end of the *Tristia* (see *Tr.*, v. 14. 35–40) and on into the *Epistulae ex Ponto*.

In the last century and a half it has been common practice to regard the *Tristia* as poor stuff, the long melancholy complaint of a poet whose vitality had flagged when he was exiled, but whose capacity for self-pity had grown proportionately. L. P. Wilkinson[53] questions even the qualified praise of other critics, and claims that the poems 'suffer as a collection, just as the *Heroides* do, from monotony of subject'. There is another manner of approach to this work: Ovid was exiled to a spot where the only possible manner of living was one of *simplicitas rudis*; indeed, Augustus may have sent the poet there precisely because he knew that in that place he would have to live an austere life, whether he wished to or not. In such a place it is amazing that Ovid wrote anything at all, and more so that he wrote anything worth while and that it was preserved for posterity. If poetry written under such conditions frequently reflects the bleakness and monotony of exile, it must not for that reason be rejected, but should be accepted as striking an authentic note, and as intended to do so – for at least part of the time Ovid in the *Tristia* was apparently seeking to convey the monotony of exile by means of the monotony of subject-matter, and was deliberately doing this in order to arouse pity and obtain recall to Rome, or at least transfer to another place.[54] He failed to convey this impression successfully in his lifetime, but more recently has been too successful: his studied monotony has repelled many who in other classical genres, such as Greek tragedy, or epic, do not find harrowing subject-matter a reason for not reading the poetry. Wilkinson, discussing instances of Ovid's wit in these later poems, comments, '. . . the pathos of his situation somehow precludes enjoyment';[55] the poet on such occasions means us to experience the pathos, and not the enjoyment. The *Tristia* is intended to convey suffering. For the more sensitive reader there is a solution:

he may dip into the poems instead of reading whole books of them. The tough-minded reader who is prepared to tackle the whole work, or at least do so book by book, will be rewarded by the experience of reading a moving human document, a record of personal misfortune presented in a near unique manner by an accomplished poet dependent upon no rooted⁰ literary tradition.

So much for monotony of subject. Wilkinson goes further: 'nor is it only the subject, but the treatment also, that is monotonous'. This is unjust. Ovid became an exile, but he remained a poet. He no longer displayed the wit of earlier days (for obvious reasons), but instead a new seriousness and gravity. In imagery, poetic colour, poem and book structure, and in thought too, Ovid displays a variety of treatment which demonstrates that his art had scarcely been impaired by exile. It is to this art in particular, in all its variety, that I have sought to draw attention in this essay.

Ovid knew that the poems of exile were gloomy (hence the title *Tristia* for some of them), and he disliked intensely the circumstances under which he had to compose them. He went so far as to admit that they were bad, meaning, I think, uncongenial to him:

> 'at mala sunt.' fateor. (*Tr.*, v. 1. 69)

> ('But they are bad.' I admit it.)

If he had retained the wit of his earlier poems, he might have completed the couplet differently, and written the sort of reply which years later was to come from the pen of Martial:⁵⁶

> 'ista tamen mala sunt.' quasi nos manifesta negemus.
>   Haec mala sunt, sed tu non meliora facis.

> ('But those poems are bad.' As if I should deny the obvious.
>   These *are* bad, but you do not produce any better!)

Notes

1 *E.P.*, II. 3. 83–4.
2 J. C. Thibault, *The Mystery of Ovid's Exile* (Berkeley, 1964), 5.
3 *Tr.*, II. 133–4.
4 For instance, *Tr.*, I. 1. 3.
5 See also *Tr.*, v. 2. 61; v. II. 21.

6 The words *carmen* and *error* may have appeared in Augustus' formal edict.

7 For instance, *Tr.*, II. 8, 240.

8 For instance, *Tr.*, II. 208 (quoted above); III. 6. 32.

9 For a recent survey of scholarly solutions to the problem, see Thibault, *op. cit.*

10 Another riddle with a similar effect is 'The Homeric Question'.

11 There are laudable exceptions, for example, A. G. Lee, *Greece and Rome*, 18 (1949), 113–20; E. J. Kenney, *Proceedings of the Cambridge Philological Society (P.C.P.S.)*, N.S., 11 (1965), 37–49.

12 L. P. Wilkinson, *Ovid Recalled* (Cambridge, 1955), 359–61.

13 No one was more aware of this than Ovid himself, as the whole of *Tr.*, V. 1 indicates. The poet's own brilliance in the pre-exile poetry tells against him; in a less vivacious poet the exile poetry would have been more readily appreciated for its own sake.

14 See also *Medicamina*, 11ff.

15 L. P. Wilkinson, *op. cit.*, 325–36, has an interesting description of the place. The modern town is Constanza. Ovidiopol (Ovid-town), near Odessa in the South Ukraine and situated on the north bank of the Dniester estuary, gains its name from a geographical error: it is 200 miles north-east of ancient Tomis.

16 The solace of the muse is a major theme in this poem.

17 The hostile comments of Brooks Otis in *Ovid as an Epic Poet* (Cambridge, 1966), 339, on Ovid's character in exile may be dismissed as a rhetorical flourish.

18 *P.C.P.S.*, N.S., 11 (1965), 38–9.

19 *Atti del Convegno Internazionale Ovidiano* (Rome, 1959), 11, 409.

20 *Tr.*, I. 11. 3.

21 For instance, H. Fränkel, *Ovid: A Poet between Two Worlds*, Sather Classical Lectures, 18 (Berkeley, 1945), 117–19, 230–1.

22 For the title see S. G. Owen, *P. Ovidi Nasonis Tristium Libri V* (Oxford, 1889), pp. vii–xii.

23 On the dating of each book see L. P. Wilkinson, *op. cit.*, 324; A. L. Wheeler, Loeb edition of *Tristia* and *Ex Ponto*, p. xxxiv.

24 *Tr.*, IV. 1. 99–104.

25 E. J. Kenney in *Oxford Classical Dictionary*, 2nd edition (1970), 764; L. P. Wilkinson, *op. cit.*, 359 and also in his allocation of material in chapters IX and X.

26 Work on this aspect of the *Tristia* has been done before (see footnote in L. P. Wilkinson, *op. cit.*, 324). The conclusions reached in this essay are based upon entirely independent examination of the four relevant books of poems.

27 A. L. Wheeler, *op. cit.*, p. xxxvii.

28 Except for *E.P.*, I. 1 and III. 9, which are both addressed to Brutus and are respectively prologue and epilogue of the first three books, which were a single unit.

29 *Op. cit.*, 315.

30 Wilkinson, *op. cit.*, 312.

31 See also lines 82, 86 and 99.
32 See Theocritus, Idyll 2, 12–13 and 35–6; Horace, *Satires*, I. 8. 33–5; Virgil, *Aeneid*, VI. 257–9. Ovid mentions dogs in a time link in another ghostly passage, *Fasti*, v. 429ff.
33 F. W. Lenz, *Maia*, 14 (1962), 109–16, actually believes the couplet to be an interpolation.
34 The Great Bear again: *Erymanthis*, like *Parrhasis* (*Tr.*, I. 3. 48), means Arcadian. In Greek mythology Callisto of Arcadia was changed into a bear and placed among the constellations.
35   auferet ex oculis veniens Aurora Boöten. (*Fasti*, v. 733)

    (Approaching dawn will remove Boötes from view.)

Scholars have shown much interest in the chronology of Ovid's journey, and Fränkel (230–1) draws attention to the four separate allusions to constellations at I. 11. 13–16 as evidence for that chronology, making the considerable assumption that they *are* star dates. They might well, together with the similar remark on I. 4. 1, be simply imagery inserted to decorate the storm. Assuming, however, that he is correct in his belief, let us examine his findings: he concludes that the references to the Kids (13) and Pleiades (14) are to their heliacal risings, occurring on 1 and 13 May respectively, and that the reference to the Hyades (16) is to their late or evening (acronychal) rising, occurring on 5 May. Line 15 is another reference to Arctophylax:

    fuscabatque diem custos Atlantidos Ursae

    (and the day was darkened by the guardian of the Great Bear.)

Strangely, Fränkel takes this also as a reference to acronychal rising, interpreting the line thus: 'Arctophylax, when rising, extinguished the day and brought dusk with it.' Not a profound remark, because it could be made of any constellation undergoing acronychal rising. Moreover, the acronychal rising of Arctophylax occurs not in May but about 4 March. *If* Ovid is referring to a date it is more likely that he is alluding to the cosmical setting (26 May), and so also in I. 4. 1; for in that case to say that Arctophylax darkened the day is to suggest that the constellation, setting just before dawn, caused dark storm clouds to appear. The date will agree with the other May dates in those four lines, and more importantly line 15 will have restored to it an association with storms (see n. 36) which those other surrounding lines have – even Auster (16) is a rain-bearing wind.
36 See Plautus, *Rudens*, 70–1; Homer, *Odyssey*, v. 272ff.; *Tr.*, I. 11. 15.
37 *Classical Review*, N.S., 14 (1964), 345; *P.C.P.S.*, N.S., 11 (1965), 39–42.
38 *P.C.P.S.*, N.S., 11 (1965), 41.
39 183–6; 573–8.
40 253–76; 307–12.
41 277–306; 361–546. This kind of defence has been adopted in more recent times by defendants charged with publication of obscene material.
42 343–60; 547–72.

43 For instance, S. G. Owen, *Tristia, Book II* (Oxford, 1924), pp. 48–54.
44 *Tristia, Book II*, p. 55.
45 *Op. cit.*, 302 and 321.
46 The book has fourteen poems in the editions, but as elegy 4 is two poems, the total is really fifteen. A book of poems which in number amount to some multiple of five is common in Augustan poetry.
47 In Book I there is a shift of storm imagery from the penultimate to the final poem to give added weight to the latter and enable it to partake in one of the main themes of the book as well as being an epilogue poem. Much the same occurs here: the evils of Tomis are scarcely described in elegy 13, but are transferred to the final poem, which also acts as an epilogue.
48 Notably the articles by A. G. Lee on elegy 8 (*Greece and Rome*, 18 [1949], 113–20) and by E. J. Kenney on elegy 12 (*P.C.P.S.*, N.S., 11 [1965], 42–4).
49 See, for instance, Catullus, 35. 17; Propertius, I. 7. 11; Ovid, *Amores*, III. 9. 62 and *Tr.*, III. 7. 12.
50 Wilkinson, *op. cit.*, 325ff.; Fränkel, *op. cit.*, 125–6.
51 For a recent discussion of the poem see Guy Lee (= A. G. Lee), *Ovid's Amores* (transl.) (London, Murray, 1968), pp. 195–8.
52 See also n. 46.
53 *Op. cit.*, 359–60, where he is talking about *Tr.*, III–V and *E.P.*, I–IV.
54 See, for instance, *Tr.*, V. 1. 3–6.
55 *Op. cit.*, 361.
56 Martial, II. 8. 7–8.

VI

Ovid in the Middle Ages

Dorothy M. Robathan

Among the poets who flourished in the Golden Age of Latin literature, Virgil and Ovid played an important part in the mediaeval revival of the classics that culminated in the period of the Renaissance. While Virgil's influence predominated in the ninth to eleventh centuries, the *aetas Ovidiana* (a term coined by the German scholar Traube), is usually applied to the period immediately following, which ran through the thirteenth century. In the years that intervened between the Augustan Age and the rebirth of Ovid in mediaeval times there are indications that his poetry continued to be read, for he was imitated by Martial, Lucan and Statius, and was also quoted by both Senecas, the Elder in his rhetorical works, the Younger in the tragedies. His poems were also used in the schools of rhetoric of this period, and Ovidian quotations are found in collections of Latin epigrams as well as in some graffiti at Pompeii.

Not only was Ovid used in the rhetorical schools of the late Empire, but he was also drawn upon in the works of early Christian writers. Fulgentius at the end of the fifth century in his *Mythologiae* quotes from the *Metamorphoses* and *Fasti*, while Prudentius, who has been called 'the Christian Ovid', won this epithet from echoes of the Roman poet in his antipagan monograph *Contra Symmachum*. Interesting parallels have been noted in such passages as his description of the metamorphosis of Lot's wife into a pillar of salt and the description of Niobe who was turned into stone (*Met.*, VI. 285–312). Foreshadowing the use of erotic poems to point a moral was the composition of the sixth-century Venantius Fortunatus, Bishop of Poitiers, depicting a nun's love for Christ. His contemporary, Maximianus, 'a Christian who poses as a pagan', wrote six elegies, which show Ovidian influence along with that of other classical poets.

In the Carolingian Renaissance of the eighth century (with which Alcuin of England was associated) although scholars were mainly concerned with religious literature, some of them read and studied Ovid. As a result their compositions were no longer confined to the conventional themes of the classroom, but became subjective poems of an elegiac nature. Modoin, Bishop of Aubin, wrote elegiac poems so obviously influenced by Ovid that he was accorded the nickname 'Naso'. In his *Rescriptum* addressed to Theodolph, Bishop of Orléans, Modoin reminds him that

> pertulit . . . longos Naso labores
> insons est factus exul ob invidiam.

(Naso endured long hardships, having been exiled because of enmity, although he was innocent.)[1]

Theodolph, 'the Spanish Pindar', not only includes Ovid and Virgil as the only pagan poets in his list of Christian writers of prose and poetry, but he made use of the *Amores* and *Ars Amatoria* in his own compositions. His opinion of their author was circulated in the couplet:

> In quorum dictis quamquam multa sunt frivola
> plurima sunt quae falso tegmine vera latent.

(Although in the words of these poems there are many light-weight observations, there are a great many truths concealed beneath the surface.)[2]

When banished to Angers, Theodolph found the *Tristia* and *Epistulae ex Ponto* relevant to the elegy he composed on his own exile, as did Ermoldus Nigellus, a monk of Aquitaine, when he was forced to live in Strassburg. In his poem Ovid is associated with such Christian martyrs as St John, banished to Patmos, and Sts Peter and Paul in their prison in Rome.

Glosses from Ovid's poetry in some ninth-century manuscripts bear witness to the fact that his poetry had a place in the curricula of the schools of that period. It is interesting to note that a codex which was once in the library of Glastonbury, England, was apparently written by a Welsh scribe, who entered glosses in it in Latin and Welsh. It was, however, chiefly in the Benedictine monasteries of Monte Cassino and St Gall that Ovid's works were studied, along with those of Christian writers, following Charlemagne's death in 814. The increased importance of Ovid among the authors seriously studied is indicated by the expansion of such glosses into a fully-fledged commentary. From the eleventh century it frequently appears as *Accessus* in manuscripts of Ovidian poetry.

In contrast to this kind of anonymous composition there had been developed such aids to learning as the *Ars Lectoria* of Aimeric (1086), who includes Ovid among the pagan writers referred to as 'golden', in contrast to others who were described by baser metals. At the same period Baudry, Bishop of Bourgueil, composed metrical *Epistles* based upon the *Tristia* and *Heroides*, while Hildebert of Lavardin, Archbishop of Tours, found the *Epistulae ex Ponto* and *Tristia* pertinent to his *De Exilio*, as had Theodolph of Orléans and Ermoldus Nigellus some years earlier. The emphasis upon grammar and dialectic in the curricula of the schools, which lasted until the middle of the twelfth century, had reacted unfavourably upon the study of classical poetry. Read primarily for their contribution to the 'modern' educational goals, poets like Ovid were known chiefly from quotations culled from anthologies rather than from complete texts. Among the outspoken critics of this system was John of Garland, who produced a commentary upon the *Metamorphoses* which, in spite of its author's praiseworthy motives, has been described by a modern critic as 'little less than a literary crime'.[3] In 1199 Alexander of Villa Dei espoused the 'new grammar' in his *Doctrinale* and went so far as to take his examples from mediaeval instead of classical authors.

At the end of the following century the status of classical studies in France may be illustrated by the activities of two contemporaries, whose works represent different aspects of the educational system. Arnolph of Orléans, nicknamed 'the redhead', an exponent of the scholastic regimen of the Cathedral School at Chartres, not only lectured on the *Fasti* at Orléans, a centre of humanistic studies, but produced glossaries and detailed commentaries on the *Metamorphoses*, *Ars Amatoria*, *Remedia Amoris* and *Epistulae ex Ponto*. On the other hand, Matthew of Vendôme wrote his own verses (no longer extant) inspired by the tales in the *Metamorphoses*, which he regarded as idylls and not as allegories. In his *Ars Versificatoria*, in contrast to the respect paid to the ancients by some other scholars, he criticized their poetry from the point of view of current prosody, and for an inordinate use of rhetorical figures:

hoc autem modernis non licet.

(Modern poets do not have this licence.)

Both epic and elegiac verses from Ovid were used as examples of things to avoid. In a very different field of French literature Andrew 'the Chaplain' was finding Ovid's poetry invaluable for his own *Flos Amorum* (*Ars Amatoria*), which expounded the rules for courtly love as he had observed them in Poitiers between 1171 and 1174. 'Love is a kind of warfare and every lover is a soldier. Cupid is generalissimo, whose power over men is absolute.'[4]

Not only in France, however, was Ovid's poetry the subject of critical study at this time. The influence of the French schools had spread across the channel, where Joseph of Exeter (d. 1210) made use of the *Metamorphoses* in his epic on the Trojan War, while his fellow-countryman, Walter Map, in the *De Nugis Curialium* transferred some of Ovid's tales to the court of Henry II. In Germany, where, in general, classical studies had waned at this period, Albrecht von Halberstadt's translation of the *Metamorphoses* into his native tongue (c. 1210) is significant. His contemporary, Conrad von Wurzburg, used the *Heroides* as well in his poem on the Trojan War. On the same theme as the *Alexandreis* of Walter of Châtillon (d. 1201) was *El libro de Alexander*, written by an unidentified Spanish poet, who appears to have had direct knowledge of the *Metamorphoses*. It has been described as 'the only case of borrowing from Ovid on the part of a Spanish epic poet'.[5]

Nor was it only in western Europe and the British Isles that scholars were translating Ovid's works and commenting upon them. Excerpts from his amatory poems translated into Greek by a Byzantine scholar have recently been the subject of detailed study. It is now believed that the extracts, in a fourteenth-century codex in Naples, were taken by the compiler from a complete manuscript in Greek, which probably existed much earlier. The suggestion is made that the erudite Byzantine monk Planudes was in some way connected with the commentary. Whether it was a youthful work which he preferred not to acknowledge in his mature years, or whether it was written by one of his students, is the subject of alternate theories.

In the twelfth century too the popularity of the so-called Goliardic poets was at its height. Tradition links these strolling minstrels, who first appeared in the ninth century, with Goliath, the adversary of the shepherd, David. One theory derives their epithet from *gula*, the Latin word for gluttony; *Goliardi* was first applied to thieves and vagabonds and later to wandering clerics. At the end of the twelfth century they sang for their supper either in Latin or in the vernacular, depending upon the patron from whom they hoped to obtain support. Including themes both sacred and profane, in which love and spring were conspicuous, many of their airs were based upon the *Carmina Burana*, a collection of verses in which the erotic themes of Ovid are prominent. Though composed in Bavaria, the *Carmina Burana* are less a reflection of German Goliards than of their French and Italian counterparts. Evidence of the popularity of these themes in England too is attested by the so-called Cambridge Songs. To the mediaeval scholars the combination of profane and religious themes apparently did not seem incongruous. So Ovid could be called *doctor egregius* (distinguished teacher) of the art of love and at the same time 'evangelist' and even 'Pope of Love'. At the University of Paris the professors affirmed: 'God hath spoken in Ovid, even as in Augustine.'[6] Although most of these songs were of anonymous origin, their themes and metres were adopted in the twelfth century by the so-called Archpoet of Cologne (d. 1165). A wandering cleric, he addressed them to an anonymous patron, later the Archbishop of Cologne, in a poem entitled *Confessions of a Goliard*. Their tradition was carried on by the French Troubadours and the German Minnesängers.

Derived from the irreverent Goliardic compositions that had been the repertoire of a 'hobo poets' guild' were the moralizing satiric poems of Walter of Châtillon, which attacked the clergy for avarice and laxity of discipline. Of obvious Ovidian influence is the *alba* (dawn) theme which occurs too in some anonymous verses of this sort. The parting of lovers when the sun rises and

the first song of the bird is heard reminds one of similar strains
in the love poems, as, for example, in *Amores*, I. 13:

> Iam super Oceanum venit a seniore marito
> flava pruinoso quae vehit axe diem . . .
> quo properas, ingrata viris, ingrata puellis?
> roscida purpurea supprime lora manu . . .
> optavi quotiens ne nox tibi cedere vellet,
> ne fugerent vultus sidera suos mota.
> optavi quotiens aut ventus frangeret axem
> aut caderet spissa nube retentus equus. . . .
> iurgia finieram, scire audisse rubebat!
> nec tamen adsueto tardius orta dies.

(1–2; 9–10; 27–30; 46–7)

Guy Lee has rendered this in a lively translation (New York,
1968):

> Here she comes over the sea from her poor old husband,
> frosty axle turning, bringing the yellow day.
> Why hurry? Lovers hate your company.
> Tighten the reins in your rosy fingers.
> If only night would defy you
> and the stars stare you out!
> If only the wind would break your axle
> or frozen cloud give your team a fall!
> She must have heard me – she turned pink!
> But the sun came up on time as usual!

In another field of literature that flourished in the twelfth
century, Ovid's influence is unmistakable. A series of so-called
elegiac comedies, some of which have titles linking them with
ancient comedy, for example the *Aulularia* and *Miles Gloriosus*,
owe more to Ovid than to the plays of Plautus and Terence.
Along with the comedies that can be assigned to such scholars as
Vital de Blois, Guillaume de Blois, and Matthew of Vendôme,
is a longer list of anonymous compositions of this nature. One
of them, the *Pamphilus de Amore*, has been described as 'the first
literary attempt to turn to practical use in scenes of love and in-
trigue the precepts of the *Ars Amatoria*'.[7] The *Pamphilus* is a tale
of seduction, in which to achieve his purpose the lover needs
the explicit tutelage of Venus, as well as the aid of an unscrupu-

lous human go-between. The advice of the goddess is based on Ovid's *Amores*, v. 8. This comedy formed a link between Ovid and Juan Ruiz's important Spanish *El libro de Buen Amor* (1330), which is said to represent 'the highwater mark of borrowing from Ovid in Spanish literature of the Middle Ages'.[8] A recent study of the poem has revealed in it echoes from the *Ars Amatoria*, *Remedia Amoris*, *Heroides* and *Metamorphoses*.

Two other anonymous 'comedies' are reminiscent of the theme of seduction in genuine Ovidian poetry. The *De Nuncio Sagaci* (or *Ovidius Puellarum*), a monologue told in the first person with an inserted dialogue, has been dubbed 'the young ladies' Ovid',[9] while the *De Tribus Puellis* (or *Ovidius Trium Puellarum*) involves a singing contest among three maidens who are vying for Ovid's love, the prize of victory! That such poems were read in the schools is clear from descriptions of them in the curricula and in such explicit comment as that of Hugo of Trimberg (1280) in his *Registrum Multorum Auctorum* (Register of Many Authors), 'to some extent a history of Latin literature for beginners':

> Sequitur Ovidius dictus puellarum
> quam in scolis omnibus non credo fore rarum.

(Next comes 'the girls' ' Ovid, which I believe will be not seldom found in the classrooms.)

A modern critic comments that in comparison with such writings 'the schoolmasters would regard the *Ars* [*Amatoria*] as quite a respectable textbook'.[10]

It is a well-known fact that the twelfth-century Renaissance gave way to a period in which the classical poets declined in popularity. Interest instead was centred upon the study of law, medicine and philosophy at a time when the translation of Aristotle into Latin opened new vistas to scholars. In 1215 the study of the classics was abolished at the University of Paris and formal logic substituted in the curriculum. Under such conditions, however, the *aetas Ovidiana* reached its height! It is more difficult for the modern reader to understand the reasons for Ovid's popularity than that of Virgil in the previous century. How could the creator of light love poems, the narrator of charming myths, possibly supplant in popular appeal the epic poet who was regarded as the Roman Homer? To understand Ovid's appeal to the serious student as well as to the dilettante, to the high dignitary of the church as well as to the worldly man on the street, to the ladies of the court as well as to the cloistered nuns, to the writer on ethics as well as to the salacious-minded lover, it may be helpful to consider certain aspects of thirteenth-century life that resulted in the situation where 'Virgil and Horace were regarded with admiration, Ovid alone was really read'.[11]

In this connection it is important to stress the diverse nature of Ovidian poetry, which appealed to mediaeval scholars of varying interests. To the student of the thirteenth century, *Ovidius Maior* signified the fifteen books of the *Metamorphoses*, which has been characterized by a modern German scholar as the 'Who's Who' (Wer ist Wer) of ancient mythology. References to obscure mythological characters in classical writers could be identified by using the *Ovidius Maior* as an encyclopaedia. The less ponderous part of the Ovidian corpus, the elegiac poems, was to a certain extent used for the same purpose, since some of these love poems contained vignettes of mythological lovers. The amatory compositions that on the surface reflected the sentiments of the gay blades who formed the smart set in Roman society were also read in the cloisters by clergy and nuns who, as we shall see, interpreted them as Christian allegories. Reaction from the strict discipline of monastic classrooms and cathedral schools had resulted in a more liberal attitude toward amatory verse. The development of allegory as a literary device led to the study of all of Ovid's poems, especially the *Metamorphoses* and *Fasti*, and resulted in such elaborate aids to comprehension as the commentaries previously mentioned. Related to allegory as an academic device was interest in parody. Here too Ovidian influence is obvious in the *Speculum Stultorum* (*Mirror of Fools*) of Nigel Wireker, an English scholar from Coventry. This poem, satirizing students and clergy, has as its chief character an ass, named Brunellus, who intends to found a religious order in the modern manner, in which even marriage may be permitted. Wireker's parody has been characterized as 'one of the best satires ever directed against the parade of learning'.[12] In the same spirit of frivolity an anonymous poet has described a court of love, composed only of women and priests, held about 1150 at Remiremont to decide whether a knight or cleric was superior in the *ars amandi*. Precepts were read from the *doctor egregius* ('distinguished teacher'), Ovid. The contestants, Phyllis and Flora, presented the merits of their respective swains. The decision rendered by Cupid was as follows:

> Secundum scientiam et secundum morem
> Ad amorem clericum dicunt aptiorem.

(In view of his learning and his disposition, they declare that the cleric is more suitable.)[13]

In this connection we may note that Jacques d'Amiens and John of Garland had made Ovid's stories available to nuns in an unexpurgated form. 'Here is the mediaeval paradox for us . . . that neither profanity nor obscenity was felt to be so inconsistent with religion as it generally is today.'[14]

It was an easy step from allegory to moralizing, which has been defined as 'a method whereby one could make any author respectable and orthodox, whatever he said'.[15] In France there appeared in the vernacular an anonymous translation of the *Metamorphoses*, complete with commentary, in which *Ovidius Maior* was elucidated from historical, theological, and religious points of view. Consisting of over 70,000 verses, it was for years attributed to Chrétien of Legouais. Inserted into the work is a lengthy tale entitled *Philomena*, based upon the story of Philomela and Procne (*Met.*, VI. 429–647). It was apparently written by Chrétien de Troyes, whose earlier translation of the *Ars Amatoria* is not extant. The comment has been made that 'perhaps only the Middle Ages could have blended elements so diverse as the brittle, cynical, beautiful legend of Ovid and this Christian moralizing'.[16]

Another French writer of somewhat similar interests was Pierre Bersuire, whose *Reductorium Morale* in thirteen books was composed in Avignon in 1335. At a later date it was expanded and Book XV became *Ovidius Moralizatus*. Bersuire's friendship with Petrarch enabled him to copy some passages from the *Africa* which he found useful in his introductory discussion, *De Formis Figurisque Deorum*. A distinguished Petrarch scholar has characterized Bersuire's borrowing as 'the earliest instance in which the influence of any work of Petrarch appears in like work of any other author'.[17]

Also from France comes the anonymous *Roman d'Eneas*, which owes as much to Ovid as it does to Virgil. In a sequel to the love story of Dido and Aeneas, the poet focuses attention upon Lavinia, producing a romantic tale which has been described as a 'contamination' of the two poets, using as it does material from Ovid's *Metamorphoses*, *Amores* and *Ars Amatoria*. This work is important for the influence it had upon later romances which showed only indirect knowledge of genuine Ovidian poetry.

Interesting not only for its content, but for the manner of its composition is the thirteenth-century *Roman de la Rose*, which drew heavily upon the *Metamorphoses*, the *Ars Amatoria*, and the *Remedia Amoris*. The first 4,266 verses were written by Guillaume de Lorris (c. 1225), but it was not completed until nearly fifty years later, when Jean de Meun brought its total to 22,700 verses. Advice to the young maiden, based upon Ovid's precepts, is delivered by an old hag, a character frequently found in classical and mediaeval love poems. A link is thus established between Ovid and Chaucer, who in his youth translated the *Roman de la Rose*. In England too at this time Robert Holkot was producing his *Moralia super Ovidii Metamorphoses*.

In assessing Ovid's influence in the Middle Ages it is perhaps difficult to understand why he was also used to a great extent by writers on scientific subjects. That Lucretius should have been studied in this way is not surprising in view of the scholarly nature of the *De Rerum Natura*, but how could the *praeceptor amoris* have qualified as an authority in such a different field? It was, of course, chiefly as the author of the *Metamorphoses*, but also, to a certain extent, of the elegies too, that he was consulted by writers on natural science. In the major work the poet presented a systematic development of the cosmos, based upon the knowledge available to scholars of the Augustan Age. As he had used the works of Varro and Lucretius, along with Latin translations of Greek philosophers, so later Roman writers, for example Pliny in his *Natural History*, quoted him as an authority on natural science. Of early mediaeval writers Isidore of Seville in the seventh century made use of passages from *Ovidius Maior* in his encyclopaedic work. In the ninth century Rabanus Maurus introduced quotations not only from the *Metamorphoses* but also from the *Fasti* in his encyclopaedic and theological compositions. John of Salisbury in the *Policraticus*, Albertus Magnus in the *Physica*, Michael Scot in the *De Secretis Naturae* and Alexander Neckam in the *De Naturis Rerum* all included nuggets of scientific information found in poetical quotations. The *aetas Ovidiana* coincided with a veritable scientific renaissance.[18] It is interesting to note too that in the realm of medicine the *Remedia Amoris* was used as a text-book for treating the maladies of the lovelorn; it is quoted in this connection by Arnold of Villa Nova at the end of the thirteenth century. For Ovid's contribution to scientific writing, mediaeval authors did not always have resort to the complete works, for many of them knew both the *Metamorphoses* and the elegiac poems only from excerpts in encyclopaedic works such as those of Vincent of Beauvais (c. 1260) and Robert Grosseteste, who in turn had sometimes taken their quotations from one of the collections of epigrams, or *Florilegia*, to which Ovid's poems were a favourite contribution. It is said, for example, that Vincent of Beauvais used such a source for over half of his citations from Ovid, whom he quotes more often than any other Latin poet. This 'scientific' interest in Ovid's poetry is one aspect that made his name respected at a time when the study of classical writers from a purely literary standpoint was frowned upon. Towards the end of the twelfth century and through the one that followed Ovid's poems did not suffer exclusion from the curricula of the schools as had some other ancient poetry which could not be integrated into the popular study of science.

In view of Ovid's popularity in such diverse fields of learning, it is perhaps not surprising that he was often imitated by medi-aeval admirers, some of whom had no scruples in attaching his name to their own compositions. Even as early as the time of Nero there was circulated a poem with the Greek title *Halieutica*, more precisely defined in some eighth/ninth century manuscripts as *Versus Ovidii de piscibus et feris* (*Ovid's Verses on Fish and Wild Beasts*). Although Pliny includes this work in the Ovidian corpus, followed by some twentieth-century scholars, it is probably to be listed as spurious. Also questionable as to its authorship is the *Ibis*, an imitation of the Greek poet Callimachus, which takes its title from the name of a Greek bird. Some other short pseudo-Ovidian poems are concerned with insects and animals. Inspired perhaps by the well-known poem *De Culice* (*The Gnat*), which is included in the Virgilian corpus, a mediaeval admirer of Ovid composed one on the flea (*De Pulice*), with a companion piece on the louse (*De Pediculo*), often preserved in the same manuscripts. Assigned to the twelfth century is a satiric elegiac poem *De*

Lombardo et Lumaca, about a Lombardian farmer who finds a viper in his garden. And of approximately the same vintage is a poem prescribing a remedy for deafness, *De Medicamine Aurium,* the title of which is obviously taken from the poet's genuine *Medicamina Faciei Femineae,* which gives advice to the ladies on how to improve their complexions. Also masquerading under Ovid's name in the thirteenth century was a brief poem *De Ventre,* describing a battle between some other parts of the human body against the stomach of the title. Reflecting the interest of the religious orders in erotic verse is an elegy of forty-four lines *De Distributione Mulierum* or with a more explicit alternate title *De Pulchris Puellis Clero Traditis (On the Lovely Girls given over to the Clergy).* Of a very different character from the preceding is the *De Mirabilibus Mundi (On the Wonders of the World),* ascribed to Ovid in a number of manuscripts dated as early as the eleventh to twelfth centuries and as late as the fifteenth. It consists of metrical inscriptions designed to label works of art such as would be found in the form of frescoes in a mediaeval cloister or banquet hall. The variety represented by the subject-matter of these shorter spurious poems indicates the wide range of topics associated with the poet at this time.

The longest of the pseudo-Ovidian poems, consisting of 2,390 verses divided into three books, was composed in France in the thirteenth century, and on the basis of one ascription in an encyclopaedic work two centuries later has been attributed to the French savant Richard de Fournival. Entitled *De Vetula (The Hag),* it purports to be the tale of Ovid's last love-affair. Duped by the go-between of the title who substituted herself for the maiden with whom 'Ovid' thought he had an assignation, he renounces his profligate ways to devote himself to a concentrated mediaeval programme of study, including astronomy, music, mathematics, philosophy and religion. Having espoused Christianity, the poet ends his metrical autobiography with an invocation to the Virgin Mary. Just as *Ovidius Ethicus* led to the conception of *Ovidius Moralizatus,* so the 'moralized' Ovid was transformed into *Ovidius Christianus.* This process developed from the important place that the poet had occupied in the curricula of the monastic and cathedral schools, where the mythological characters in the *Metamorphoses* were equated with Old Testament characters, for example Noah with Deucalion.

Although the distinguished English scholar Roger Bacon accepted the *Vetula* as genuine in spite of its wealth of mediaeval material, Petrarch says unequivocally that it could not have been written by the Augustan poet. It is interesting to observe that the *Vetula* was used by Juan Ruiz in his *Libro de Buen Amor*, which, as has been noted, also drew upon the anonymous elegiac comedy *Pamphilus*.

The exact date at which the literary activity of the Middle Ages ends and the period of the Renaissance begins is a question on which scholars are not agreed. The difficulty of establishing such a hypothetical boundary-line lies partly in the fact that it would vary in different European countries. In northern Europe the Renaissance developed more slowly than it did in Italy, where Dante, Boccaccio and Petrarch may be designated as early Renaissance rather than as late mediaeval poets. Dante is sometimes called a 'precursor' of the Renaissance, in that he broke with tradition and wrote the *Divina Commedia* in his native tongue instead of in Latin. He himself lists as the great pagan poets Homer, Virgil, Horace, Ovid and Statius, and a study of his use of them has shown that, next to Virgil, Ovid is most frequently cited. Encountered by the poet in Limbo, with Virgil as his guide, are the shades of Homer, Horace, Ovid and Lucan. Direct Ovidian influence is clearly discernible in the composition of certain scenes and in some of his descriptive passages. Dante's praise of the *Metamorphoses* and his suggestion that its allegorical features deserved close study may have influenced Giovanni del Virgilio to undertake this task. Giovanni was a friend of Dante and a teacher in the school at Bologna in 1319. His commentary on *Ovidius Maior* has survived in the Latin version and in a partial translation into Italian. Though not distinguished for its literary merits, it is of interest for the light it throws on certain aspects of the teaching of classical Latin literature in the first half of the fourteenth century. The mediaeval interest in allegory and in Christian literature is echoed in such interpretations as the following: the giants who attacked Jupiter were men who because of their wealth were too haughty to believe in God. Or again: Jupiter gave the infant Bacchus to the nymphs to bring up, indicating that we should always mix water with our wine.[19]

Like those of Dante, Boccaccio's works, both Italian and Latin, bear echoes of the poet from Sulmona. In his early work

L'Amorosa Fiammetta the young lovers Florio and Bianchfiore *saper leggere il santo libro d' Ovidio*, while in his prose composition *De Claris Mulieribus* (*On Famous Women*) the *Heroides* were freely used. A critical study of the *Filocolo* has revealed numerous examples of word-for-word borrowing, chiefly from the two works just mentioned, as well as from other Ovidian poems where the echoes are less obvious. In his later years the Italian poet characterized his Roman predecessor as 'lascivious', but he did not refrain from making extensive use of Ovid in the *De Genealogia Deorum*, where he was surpassed as a source only by Virgil. Boccaccio's change of attitude over the years has been described as follows: 'In his youth Ovid somewhat went to his head, and in his old age was somewhat banished from his heart.'[20]

Petrarch, the last of the 'big three' precursors of the Renaissance in Italy, was also attracted by the poet from Sulmona. The erotic poems which he read in his youth he found a useful source for moralizing in his old age, while many of his mythological examples can be traced not only to the *Metamorphoses* but to the *Heroides*, as well as to the poems from exile. Of the poet to whose *Amores* he was indebted in composing the *Trionfi d'Amore* he wrote:

> puto nullum aequari posse Nasoni poetae.

(I think no poet can equal Naso.)

In a manuscript of Livy which was once in Petrarch's library and is now in the Bibliothèque Nationale in Paris is inscribed a story concerning some travellers who went to Ovid's tomb. One of them suggested that he would like to know which of the poet's verses was the worst one he ever wrote. From the tomb came a voice: 'Jupiter considers that whatever is pleasing is good' (*Her.*, IV. 133). The other traveller wondered which verse the poet considered his best, and again the voice obliged with an answer: 'It is a virtue to abstain from pleasures even when they are lawful' (*Her.*, XVII. 98). By way of thanks the pilgrims proposed saying a prayer for Ovid's soul but before they could begin the poet's voice again proclaimed: 'I don't want your prayers! Be off with you!'[21]

At the risk of straying still further beyond the bounds of the Middle Ages, it is perhaps relevant to mention the distinguished

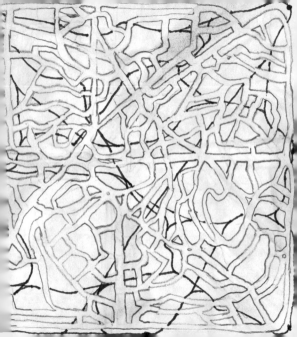

myth

animals

offence to Aug.

vir.

→ (pro- co- calor) - rakes up
memories - dé th + C -
Tiberius?

humanist Coluccio Salutati, a younger contemporary of Petrarch. Not only does he quote Ovid many times in his voluminous correspondence, but his longest and most important work, the *De Laboribus Herculis*, is a prose composition in the same allegorical vein as the French 'moralized' Ovids.

Mention has been made of Chaucer's early acquaintance with Ovid through the Guillaume de Lorris–Jean de Meun *Roman de la Rose*. In introducing the subject of Chaucer's debt to Ovid, a fellow-countryman fancifully suggests that in the fourteenth century 'some seeds from that great blossoming [the Renaissance] floated across into England to start the garden of English verse'[22] and he proceeds to draw parallels between the lives of two poets who were separated chronologically by over one thousand years. In less flowery language attention has been called to the fact that in his first work, *The Book of the Duchess*, Chaucer made use of the legend of Alcyone (*Met.*, XI. 410–78) and that in his complete works he mentions Ovid by name eighteen times. In *The House of Fame* the dwelling was modelled after the description of the Cave of Sleep (*Met.*, XI. 592–615) and it contained statues of Virgil, Ovid, Lucan and Statius, in *The Parlement of Foules* there are echoes of the *Amores* and *Fasti*. As might be expected, the *Heroides* furnished prototypes for Chaucer's deserted heroines in *The Legend of Good Women*, where, for example, in the tale of Theseus and Ariadne, Chaucer is more indebted to Ovid than to the author of the *Roman de la Rose*. *Troilus and Criseyde* too shows many examples of direct use of the *Amores*, *Remedia Amoris* and *Tristia*, as well as the *Heroides*, where Helen was the model for Criseyde. Although the story of Dido and Aeneas might be assumed to have been based on the fourth book of the *Aeneid*, the heroine is portrayed more sympathetically than the hero, and Chaucer himself recommends to his readers not only Virgil but 'the Epistle of Ovide'. In the *Canterbury Tales* too, where use of the *Fasti* has been noted, one of the characters maintains that 'Chaucer has told more tales even than Ovid, then gives a list which reveals with charming irony that Ovid was in fact his chief source'.[23] In another aspect of his poetry Chaucer's name has been associated with Ovid's for his use of the heroic couplet, which first appeared in *The Legend of Good Women*.

In England along with Chaucer mention should be made of Nicholas Trivet, who in commenting on the ten tragedies of

Seneca has a number of direct quotations indicating his acquaintance with the *Metamorphoses*, *Heroides*, *Fasti*, *Tristia*, and *Epistulae ex Ponto*. A recent study has shown that 'Ovid was used chiefly for mythology, religion, and astronomy'. In the preface to this commentary Trivet lists along with Virgil and Lucan 'Ovidius in Transformatis'. Chaucer's contemporary, John Gower, in his *Confessio Amantis* also borrowed a number of Ovid's stories.

This summary of Ovid's posthumous fortune has taken us from the very early Middle Ages to the dawn of the Renaissance, from his native land and its nearest neighbours to the northern islands which would have seemed as remote to him as the planet Mars does to twentieth-century inhabitants of the earth. But no less strange to Sulmo's son would have been the fame that he has acquired in his picturesque birthplace. A modern scholar aptly remarks that 'had it not been for the accident of Ovid's being born there, few people in the outside world would ever have heard of Sulmo'.[24] Just as Mantua honoured Virgil under many guises, so the peasants of his Abruzzi birthplace not only regarded Ovid as the son of Solymus, the legendary Trojan founder of Sulmo, but by the sixteenth century had 'metamorphosed' him into magician, alchemist, merchant, philosopher, priest and saint. In the Museo Civico of Sulmona may still be seen a fourteenth-century statue of Ovid, one of three that are known to have been erected to him there, and the present Corso Ovidio, following the route of the chief thoroughfare in Roman times, reminds those who traverse it of Sulmona's most famous citizen. With the genius of the poet undoubtedly approving, in 1958 a gathering of internationally distinguished scholars met in Sulmona, where the letters S.M.P.E. conspicuously displayed (*Sulmo Mihi Patria Est*) (Sulmona is my Native Country) reminded them of the famous citizen in whose honour the symposium was being held.[25] The wide range of subjects in the volumes containing the learned papers presented at that time bears witness to the many facets of the poet's genius, as well as to his influence over the centuries.

The generalization concerning the *aetas Ovidiana* in contrast to the preceding 'ages' of Horace and Virgil has sometimes given the impression that Ovid's poetry suddenly burst upon the mediaeval world in the late twelfth century. It is to be hoped that the abbreviated sketch in the preceding pages has shown that at no time from the date of his death through the Middle Ages was Ovid not known and admired, although not always by all segments of society. Although the earliest manuscripts of the complete poems date from the tenth and eleventh centuries, quotations in the *Florilegia* and in the school-books of the Carolingian period are evidence that his works were read and excerpted at this time. 'The black sheep of Augustus became the white-headed boy of the schoolmaster.'[26] Though the period of his greatest popularity coincided more or less with the end of the thirteenth century, his influence was felt for centuries later in lands remote from his birthplace. Shakespeare's tale of Pyramus and Thisbe may be traced by a tortuous route back to the version of the 'ill-starred lovers' in the *Metamorphoses*. 'Ovid lives still two thousand years after his birth in the Italian homeland as well as in the rest of the world.'[27] In the poet's own words quoted by Petrarch at his coronation on the Roman Capitol:

iamque opus exegi quod nec Iovis ira nec ignis
nec potest ferrum nec edax abolere vetustas (*Met.*, xv. 871–2)

(I have composed a work which neither the anger of Jupiter, nor fire, nor the sword nor the ravages of time will be able to destroy.)

Notes

1 G. Brugnoli, 'Ovidio e gli esiliati Carolingi', *Atti del Convegno Internazionale Ovidiano* (Rome, 1959), II, 215.
2 Joseph de Ghellinck, *L'Essor de la Littérature Latine au XIIe Siècle* (Brussels, 1946), II, 60.
3 E. H. Alton and D. E. W. Wormell, 'Ovid in the Mediaeval Schoolroom', *Hermathena*, 94 (1960), 21–38; 95 (1961), 67–82 (p. 35).
4 Andreas Capellanus, *The Art of Courtly Love*, trans. with intr. by J. J. Parry, Columbia University Records of Civilisation, Sources and Studies (New York, 1941), 6.
5 Rudolph Schevill, *Ovid and the Renascence in Spain*, University of California Publications in Modern Philology, vol. 4, no. 1 (Berkeley, 1913), 19.
6 Helen Waddell, *The Wandering Scholars* (London, 1927), 84.
7 Schevill, *op. cit.*, 28.
8 *Ibid*.
9 Frederic James Edward Raby, *A History of Secular Latin Poetry in the Middle Ages* (Oxford, 1957), II, 67.
10 *Hermathena*, 94 (1960), 33.
11 Frederick Adam Wright, *Three Roman Poets: Plautus, Catullus, Ovid* (London, 1938), 246.

12 Edward Kennard Rand, *Ovid and his Influence* (London, 1926), 122.
13 Helen Waddell, *op. cit.*, 199–200.
14 L. P. Wilkinson, *Ovid Recalled* (Cambridge, 1955), 381.
15 *Hermathena*, 95 (1961), 69.
16 Gilbert Highet, *The Classical Tradition* (Oxford, 1949), 62.
17 Ernest Hatch Wilkins, *The Life of Petrarch* (Chicago, 1961), 19.
18 See on this subject Simone Viarre, *La Survie d'Ovide dans la littérature scientifique des XIIe et XIIIe Siècles*, Publications du Centre d'Études Supérieures de Civilisation Médiévale, 4 (Poitiers, 1966).
19 Philip H. Wicksteed, *Dante and Giovanni del Virgilio* (London, 1902), 318.
20 E. K. Rand, *op. cit.*, 152.
21 Pierre de Nolhac, *Petrarque et l'humanisme* (Paris, 1907), II. 17, n. 1.
22 F. A. Wright, *op. cit.*, 247.
23 L. P. Wilkinson, *op. cit.*, 393.
24 E. T. Salmon, 'S.M.P.E.', *Ovidiana*, ed. N. I. Herescu (Paris, 1958), 3.
25 *Atti del Convegno Internazionale Ovidiano*, 2 vols (Rome, 1959).
26 *Hermathena*, 94 (1960), 26.
27 E. H. Wilkins, *Studies in the Life and Works of Petrarch*, Medieval Academy of America Publication No. 63 (Cambridge, Mass., 1964), 307.

In addition to the works referred to in notes 1–27, the following select bibliography may be found useful:

Karl Bartsch, *Albrecht von Halberstadt und Ovid im Mittelalter* (Amsterdam, 1965, reprint of 1861 ed.).
C. Besana, 'La traduzione greca medioevale dei *carmina amatoria* di Ovidio', *Aevum*, 41 (1967), 91–113.
Cornelis de Boer, *Ovide Moralisé* (Amsterdam, 1920).
Robert Ralph Bolgar, *The Classical Heritage and its Beneficiaries* (Cambridge, 1954).
L. Born, 'Ovid and Allegory', *Speculum*, 9 (1934), 362–79.
Karl Breul, *The Cambridge Songs – a Goliard's Songbook of the XIth Century* (Cambridge, 1915).
Ernest Robert Curtius, *European Literature and the Latin Middle Ages*, trans. Willard Trask, Bollingen Series XXXVI (New York, 1953).
D. Engels, 'Berchoriana', *Vivarium*, 2 (1964), 62–124.
Edmond Faral, *Les Arts poétiques du XIIe et du XIIIe siècle* (Paris, 1962).
Hermann Fränkel, *Ovid: A Poet between Two Worlds* (Berkeley, 1945).
Fausto Ghisalberti, 'Arnolfo d'Orléans, un cultore di Ovidio nel secolo XII', *Memorie Istituto Lombardo Classe di Lettere*, 24 (1932) and J. de Garlandia (ed.), *Integumenta Ovidii* (Milan, 1933).
E. J. Kenney, 'A Byzantine Version of Ovid', *Hermes*, 91 (1963), 213–27.
Paul Lehmann, *Pseudoantike Literatur des Mittelalters* (Berlin, 1927); *Die Parodie im Mittelalter* (Munich, 1922).
F. W. Lenz, 'Der Pseudo-Ovidische Gedicht *De Pediculo*', *Eranos*, 53 (1955), 61–117; 'De Lombardo et Lumaca', *Maia*, 9 (1957), 204–22; 'De

Ventre', *Maia*, 11 (1959), 169–211; 'Der Frauenfeindliche', *Orpheus* (1960), 107–17.

F. Munari, *Ovid im Mittelalter* (Zurich, Stuttgart, 1960).

J. Rico, 'Sobre el Origen de la Autobiografía en el Libro de Buen Amor', *Annuario de Estudios Medievales* (Barcelona, 1967), 301–25.

Edgar Finley Shannon, *Chaucer and the Roman Poets*, Harvard Studies in Comparative Literature, vol. 7 (Cambridge, Mass., 1929; reprinted New York, 1964).

VII

Ovid in the Sixteenth Century

Caroline Jameson

The limitations of space and capability which I shall have to impose on this immense subject are, of necessity, considerable. My own knowledge will limit it primarily to a study of Ovid in England with only passing reference to his influence abroad, and even to mention the writers who show his influence would make this an unwieldy catalogue. I will attempt, however, to give some impression of the historical development and extent of his influence, the aspects of his work which were taken up, and the directions in which they led.

The attitude to Ovid seen in editions of his work just prior to and during this period shows a marked trend away from mediaeval allegorizing and towards a concern for style and Latinity.[1] The ages of faith which produced the vast *Ovid Moralized* used his work, especially the *Metamorphoses*, for tropological and moral ends, disregarding historical perspective and ambiguity to see, for instance, Pyramus and Actaeon as both typifying Christ and symbolizing disobedience and lust. Several Italian editions in the fifteenth century, such as Bonsignori's *Metamorphosoes Volgare* of 1497, illustrate this approach. Because of the resemblance between Ovid's and the Biblical accounts of Creation and the Flood, Ovid was even seen by some as having the same divinely-given insight as was attributed to Virgil for the Messianic Eclogue. In 1492, however, Raphael Regius produced his edition of the *Metamorphoses*[2] as a printed text with annotations. He attempted to correct misreadings, elucidate difficult passages and give a glossary and notes on philological problems, history and genealogy, but without allegory or moral comment. Its importance was in this purely literary emphasis and it was both widely used and widely influential, running into at least thirty editions before 1586. Thus the edition most in use during the sixteenth century was primarily an informative classical dictionary. In England Thomas Thomas's edition was the fullest, with marginal notes, glosses and classification of fables and tropes. Georgius Sabinus' edition of 1554 was mainly grammatical and rhetorical in emphasis. He entirely abandoned theological allegory but cited reasonable examples among the stories demonstrating a general divine plan rewarding virtue and punishing vice. He commented that the transformation of men into beasts stood for the men who, though human, behaved monstrously. His work, especially the preface and commentary, was widely used in English editions, and further encouraged this trend in interpretation. Thus during the sixteenth century the view of Ovid as a theological allegory more or less disappeared, the moralizing was confined to certain obvious *exempla*, what had been seen as divine revelation was considered historically, and interest centred above all on rhetorical analysis, appreciation of style and the rich mythological content.[3]

For subject matter alone Ovid had already been well explored by the storytellers. Chaucer, sharing Ovid's skill and delight in narrative, fairly pillaged the storehouse of Ovid's works for material, from his exquisite retelling of the tale of Ceyx and Alcyone in *The Book of the Duchess* to his adoption of Ovid's story of Apollo and the crow as a complete tale for the Manciple in the *Canterbury Tales*. *The House of Fame*, its Cave of Sleep and pairs of lovers all originate in Ovid's works, all but one of the heroines of *The Legend of Good Women* are from Ovid, and many smaller cameos in the *Canterbury Tales* are drawn from his poetry. Gower in his *Confessio Amantis* of 1390 draws heavily on the *Metamorphoses* and *Heroides* and even on the *Fasti* and *Tristia* for his stories. Through these writers alone the matter of many of Ovid's tales would have become widely current by the sixteenth century, but it is the assimilation of his style and tone which distinguishes this century as the great Ovidian age.

> For the elegancy, facility, and golden cadence of poesy . . .
> Ovidius Naso was the man . . . for smelling out the
> odoriferous flowers of fancy, the jerks of invention.[4]

This testimony to Ovid in the mouth of Shakespeare's schoolmaster Holofernes provides a clue to the heart of Ovid's greatness in sixteenth-century England. It commends him for the style and grace to which the writers of this century responded, but its context, being used as a touchstone for English poetry by a schoolmaster, shows how Ovid permeated English literary culture at 'grass-roots' level. A quotation from a writer on England under Elizabeth describes the education system thus:

> Besides these universities, also there are great number of Gramar schooles through out the realme, and those verie liberallie indued, for the better reliefe of poore scholers, so that there are not manie corporat townes now under the queenes dominion, that hain not one Gramar schoole at the least, with a sufficient living for a maister and usher appointed to the same . . . from whence, after (the scholers) have beene well entered in the knowledge of the Latine and Greeke toongs and rules of versifieing . . . (they are sent to University).[5]

The 'rules of versifieing', letter writing and the higher exercises of rhetoric were taught primarily out of Ovid. The *Heroides*, recommended by Erasmus as an aid to letter writing, and the works in general for senior rhetoric, were in use at Eton by 1528. Ipswich School, on Wolsey's instructions, added the *Metamorphoses* and *Fasti* to the curriculum by 1529. In his book *The Governor* (1531) Sir Thomas Elyot also recommended these two, even though his personal preference was for Horace. Bury St Edmunds School and Eton used the *Tristia* as a model for versification, and in 1530 Winchester boys were learning twelve lines of the *Metamorphoses* by heart every week. These schools set the pattern for the general national system of education. Scholars probably began with an anthology such as Mirandula's *Flores Poetarum* (1559) which contains innumerable passages, extensive and brief, from Ovid's works. It opens with a long quotation from the *Amores* in praise of poetry (concluding, incidentally, with the lines Shakespeare prefixed to *Venus and Adonis*) and includes the Pythagorean description of the ages of man, references to Titania and Autolycus, and aphorisms on age, beauty, sleep and other popular subjects for poetry out of Ovid's works.

T. W. Baldwin in his great study of Elizabethan education, *William Shakspere's Small Latine and Lesse Greeke* (Urbana, 1944), demonstrates in detail how the Ovid of the classroom saturates the work of one distinguished pupil but he also emphasizes that the position of Ovid in the field of poetry was peerless. Brinsley's statement in his *Ludus Literarius* of 1627 cannot be taken as evidence of common sixteenth-century practice, but his basic method may well be similar to that of schoolmasters of the period when he writes: 'In this matter of versifying as in all the former exercises, I take this Imitation of the most excellent patternes to be the surest rule . . . and therefore I would have the chiefest labour to make these purest Authors our owne, as *Tully* for prose, so *Ovid* and *Virgil* for verse, so to speake and write in Latine for the phrase, as they did.'[6] The use of translations, especially versified ones was not frowned on for school use as it has been since, as the knowledge of Latin was a practical skill rather than an intellectual exercise, so it is quite possible that major translations such as Golding's, Turberville's and Churchyard's became interwoven with the original in the pupil's mind. Much of these exercises in imitation, encouraging scholars to translate and compose as closely as possible to the Ovidian model must have resulted in the style, tone and habits of thought of Ovid's poetry becoming assimilated into the English writers' and readers' minds and must have formed the taste as well as the literary productions of subsequent years.

With this interest in the ascendant, translations soon began to appear; the first was Thomas Howell's close translation, in 1560, of *The fable of Ovid treting of Narcissus* (*Met.*, III. 342–510), a verse translation in couplets with lines of six and seven feet alternately (to which he added a very long moralizing passage on Narcissus as an *exemplum* of pride). After 1565 translations both multiplied and became detached from extensive moralization. In 1565 Thomas Peend produced *The Pleasant fable of Hermaphroditus and Salmacis* from the *Metamorphoses* and Golding produced the first instalment of his great and profoundly important translation of the *Metamorphoses* which he rendered in rhymed 'fourteeners'. His translation was expansive but unalloyed, and selected moral *exempla* were merely attached in his dedicatory epistle. In 1567 Turberville produced the *Heroycall Epistles*, a complete translation of the *Heroides* in various metres. In 1569 William Hubbard translated *The Tragicall and lamentable historie of Ceyx . . . and Alcione* (from *Met.*, XI); Underdown translated *Ibis* and in 1572,

Thomas Churchyard, a poet of some note, translated the first three books of the *Tristia*. Later, in 1597, one of the greatest poets of the age, Christopher Marlowe, translated three books of the *Amores* which he called *Elegies* (issued with Epigrams from Sir John Davies) and which he had probably completed in his student days, between 1581-7 and circulated widely in manuscript. Brown produced the *Remedia Amoris* in 1599 but the *Fasti* were never translated in this period (nor at all until John Gower produced a translation in 1640). Of these works three at least are of considerable importance to the development of English literature.

Turberville was already a notable translator, having produced versions of Mantuan's *Eclogues* and tales from Boccaccio and Bandello, but the *Heroycall Epistles* were by far his most important contribution; the *Heroides* was already a work of some 4,000 lines but his English rendering almost doubles this number. He favoured shorter lines than Golding, four-line stanzas in ballad metres, and for six of the epistles he used blank verse. His verse tends to jog-trot and the lines are well sprinkled with archaic and colloquial diction; this at times gives them vigour, but they are more often bathetic and incongruous. For example, his rendering of one of Ovid's most sensitive passages, Hermione's complaint (*Her.*, VIII. 89-96), is marred by inappropriate colloquialism:

> My dame I was bereft in youth,
>   my father waged warre:
> And though they both did live, yet I
>   from them was kept afarre.
> Not I to thee in tender yeares,
>   nor cradell clowtes did crye
> Deare mother mine: nor from my lippes
>   the lisping wordes did flie.
> Ne did I with my pliant armes,
>   thy seemely neck enfolde:
> Nor thou upon thy loving lap
>   thy babling Brat didst holde.
> No carke of clothing me, ne care
>   did pierce thy pensive breast.

However, when he is rendering passages which depend less on balance and compression, some lyrical grace does break through, as, for example, in Leander's letter to Hero (*Her.*, XVIII. 125–54):

> Oh Gods, why should the surge
>   two lincked harts devide.
> Why they that are of greeing mindes
>   one hostage are denied . . .
> Why doe I cease to swim
>   for raging waters yre?
> Or why the roving winde (a slen-
>   der cause) makes me retyre? . . .
> Leander makes no coumpt
>   of any of their light:
> No not of hir whom Perseus chose
>   or Bacchus, for delight.
> Another starre I have
>   surmounting all the rest
> That will not see my earnest love
>   with darcksome clowde opprest.

The *Heroycall Epistles* seem to have been popular and went through four editions by 1600, no doubt helping to make the legendary heroines and their stories much more familiar. One of Turberville's traits is to incorporate into his translations anachronistic English touches (as, for example, when he has Leander playing tennis) and this is a notable feature of the *Epillia*, which often draw heavily on the *Heroides*; this probably assisted Ovid's assimilation into the more popular literature. Their success also may have inspired the much more popular English imitation by Drayton, *England's Heroicall Epistles* (1597), in which famous couples from English history exchange letters.

The first four books of Golding's *Metamorphoses* came out in 1565 with a short prose dedication to the Earl of Leicester which urged the work's 'pithie instructions and wholesome examples'. The complete edition added an expanded epistle in which Golding alluded to the natural philosophy of, and resemblance between, Ovid's and the Bible's first books, and cited a moral example from each of the fifteen books, but did not otherwise expand the moral significance at length. This was followed by a preface of over 200 lines in a similar defensive moralizing vein, explaining the common significance of the deities but acknowledging that they had a multiple significance which he left to the interpretation of the reader. Having thus disposed of the moral justification he leaves the entire translation unmoralized. His metre, the long 'fourteener', tempted Golding all too often to fill it out with repetition, additional adjectives, padding and tags. Terseness, the essence of Ovid's wit and art, is totally lost on him. Winter, in the palace of the Sun, of whom Ovid merely says 'et glacialis Hiems canos hirsuta capillos' (*Met.*, II. 30) is expanded in Golding to four full lines:

And lastly quaking for the colde, stood Winter all forlorne,
With rugged heade as white as Dove, and garments all to torne,
Forladen with the Isycles that dangled up and downe
Uppon his gray and hoarie bearde and snowie frozen crowne.

(II. 36–9)

In the same passage the fine resonant line:

Sors tua mortalis, non est mortale quod optas. (II. 56)

loses all power when rendered:

Thy state is mortall, weake and frayle, the thing thou doest desire
Is such, whereto no mortall man is able to aspire. (II. 74–5)

His inversions, too, unexcused by compression, sometimes produce grotesque and unintelligible effects. Golding was not a great poet (though he influenced those who were) but he was a readable craftsman. His poem is vast but the flexible use of the metre prevents it from becoming monotonous. This he does by varying the caesura and employing enjambment. Thus Dis, spurring on his team, overruns the end of the line:

The Catcher drives his Chariot forth, and calling every horse
By name, to make away apace he doth them still enforce.

(V. 503–4)

The passage describing the devastation at Ceres' neglect illustrates this fluidity of style:

The plenteousnesse of that same Ile of which there went such brute
Through all the world, lay dead: the corne was killed in the blade:

Now too much drought, now too much wet did make it for to
    fade.
The starres and blasting windes did hurt, the hungry foules did
    eate
The corne in ground: The Tines and Briars did overgrow the
    Wheate . . .
Then *Arethuse*, floud *Alpheys* love, lifts from hir *Elean* waves
Hir head, and shedding to hir eares hir deawy haire that waves
About her foreheade sayde: O thou that art the mother deare
Both of the Maiden sought through all the worlde both far and
    neare,
And eke of all the earthly fruites, forbeare thine endlesse toyle.
(v. 598–609)

As a good readable source of narrative Golding was very
popular, and many scholars have rejoiced in finding direct
borrowing from Golding in the major poets, especially Shakespeare. Golding's poem was called *Shakespeare's Ovid* by W. H. D.
Rouse,[7] but there is plenty of evidence that Shakespeare read
Ovid in the original. If, however, translations such as Golding's
were used as an aid to study, it would be most likely that Shakespeare used, and remembered, Golding and Ovid together as a
composite source. Pound's sweeping statement that Golding's
Metamorphoses was 'the most beautiful book in the language . . . in
my opinion and I suspect it was Shakespeare's'[8] rather ignores the
fact that Shakespeare's most conscious borrowing from Golding
is of a rather scornful and mocking nature. *A Midsummer Night's
Dream* is a play fairly saturated with Ovid and, at times, Golding.
Though Titania is Ovid's not Golding's name for the Goddess
associated with 'triceps Hecate', 'triple Hecate'; and the dragon-
drawn chariot she sent for Medea is Golding's phraseology which
appears when Puck says:

Night's swift dragons cut the clouds full fast (III. ii. 379)

and:

we fairies, that do run
By the triple Hecate's team. (v. i. 373–4)

Titania's 'coronet of fresh and fragrant flowers' (IV. i. 51) for
Bottom is Golding's phrase. The passage on Sicily's desolation,
quoted above, as well as the description of the flood (*Met.*, I.

320ff.) is echoed in Titania's speech on the desolation caused by her and Oberon's displeasure (II. i. 81–117). In Theseus and Hippolyta's discussion of hounds, she says:

> I was with Hercules and Cadmus once,
> When in a wood of Crete they bayed the bear
> With hounds of Sparta. Never did I hear
> Such gallant chiding . . . (IV. i. 111–14)

Theseus replies:

> My hounds are bred out of the Spartan kind;
> So flewed, so sanded . . . (IV. i. 118–19)

The passage is a remarkable hotchpotch of anachronistic names and places. Theseus and Cadmus were generations apart in myth. (Cadmus founded Thebes, Theseus was associated with it when it was a great city); Cadmus, Hercules and Hippolyta are none of them associated with Crete. However, in Golding's poem the story of Cadmus and the founding of Thebes follows the story of Jupiter's abduction of his sister Europa to Crete and is followed by the description of the death of Actaeon (Cadmus' grandson) in which are the lines:

> This latter was a hound of *Crete*, the other was of *Spart* . . .
> . . . Rugge with other twaine that had a Syre of *Crete*
> And dam of *Sparta*: T'one of them callde Jollyboy, a great
> And large flewd hound: . . .   (*Met.*, III. 247, 267–9)

a juxtaposition which may have suggested details to Shakespeare. However, the most important borrowing in the play is Ovid's story of Pyramus and Thisbe which is acted by the 'rude mechanicals', and in this, Shakespeare, where he imitates Golding, does so in the spirit of parody. Golding's lines, which do not show him at his best, give Shakespeare plenty of scope and show a close affinity to Peter Quince's:

> The wall that parted house from house had riven therein a crany
> . . . To talk, togither secretly . . .
> O thou envious wall (they sayd,) why letst thou lovers thus . . .
> And yet thou shalt not finde us churles: we thinke ourselves in
>   det
> For the same piece of courtesie . . .
> They did agree at *Ninus* Tumb to meete without the towne,

... One night (he sayd) shall lovers two confounde,
Of which long life deserved she of all that live on ground.
... His sworde, the which among his guttes he thrust, and by
    and by
Did draw it from the bleeding wound beginning for to die. ...
Alas what chaunce my *Pyramus* hath parted thee and mee?
Make aunswere O my *Pyramus*: It is thy *Thisb*, even shee ...
This said, she tooke the sword yet warme with slaughter of hir
    love
And setting it beneath hir brest, did too hir heart it shove.
                                                    (IV. 83–197)

Quince's play often falls into the Golding rhythm and echoes him
closely:

By moonshine did these lovers think no scorn
To meet at Ninus' tomb, there, there to woo ...
... such a wall as I would have you think
That had in it a crannied hole or chink,
Through which the lovers, Pyramus and Thisbe,
Did whisper often, very secretly ...
Thanks, courteous wall: Jove shield thee well for this!
... like Limander, am I trusty still.   (Leander?)
And I like Helen till the Fates me kill.   (Hero?)
Not Shafalus to Procrus was so true.   (Cephalus, Procris?)
... Come tears confound/Out sword, and wound/The pap
    of Pyramus ...
Thus die I – thus, thus, thus.
Now am I dead ...
... O Pyramus arise!
Speak speak. Quite dumb? ...
O sisters three/Come, come to me/With hands as pale as milk;
Lay them in gore/Since you have shore/With shears his
    thread of silk.
Tongue, not a word:/Come, trusty sword,/Come blade, my
    breast imbrue.   (V. i. 136–336)

Such lines certainly imply a good knowledge of Golding but do
not betray unmixed admiration.

The myth most recurrent in *The Merchant of Venice* is the Jason–
Medea story and here too phrases of Golding recur. Bassanio,

referring to Portia's suitors as Jasons in quest of the fleece, describes Belmont as 'Colchos' strond' (I. i. 171) while Golding wrote 'and so with conquest and a wife he loosed from Colchos' strand'. Lorenzo and Jessica, 'outnighting' each other, allude to the moonlit night when 'Medea gathered *the enchanted herbs* That did *renew* old Aeson' (v. i. 13–14) and the italicized words are Golding's on the same subject (VII. 142, 381). This story in Golding's poem is the most notable example of Shakespeare's use of him, and of Ovid. In Golding, Medea's incantation to Hecate runs thus:

> Ye Ayres and windes, ye Elves of Hilles, of Brookes, of Woods alone,
> Of standing Lakes, and of the Night approche ye everychone.
> Through helpe of whom (the crooked bankes much wondring at the thing)
> I have compelled streames to run cleane backward to their spring.
> By charmes I make the calme Seas rough, and make the rough Seas plaine
> And cover all the Skie with Cloudes and chase them thence againe.
> By charmes I rayse and lay the windes and burst the Vipers jaw
> And from the bowels of the Earth both stones and trees doe drawe.
> Whole woods and Forestes I remove; I make the Mountaines shake
> And even the Earth it selfe to grone and fearfully to quake.
> I call up dead men from their graves; and thee O lightsome Moone
> I darken oft, though beaten brasse abate thy perill soone
> Our sorcerie dimmes the Morning faire, and darkes the Sun at Noone.
> . . . Among the Earthbred brothers you a mortall war did set . . .
>   (VII. 265–80)

Prospero's renunciation of his magic in *The Tempest* (v. i. 33–50) echoes this in many places:

> Ye elves of hills, brooks, standing lakes, and groves,
> . . . by whose aid –
> Weak masters though ye be – I have bedimmed

The noontide sun, called forth the mutinous winds,
And 'twixt the green sea and the azured vault
Set roaring war; to the dread rattling thunder
Have I given fire, and rifted Jove's stout oak
With his own bolt; the strong-based promontory
Have I made shake, and by the spurs plucked up
The pine and cedar; graves at my command
Have waked their sleepers, oped, and let 'em forth
By my so potent art.

The similarity is obvious, almost too obvious. Phrases such as
'standing lakes' and 'darkes the Sun at Noone', being expansions
of Ovid's words, can be shown to influence Shakespeare's choice,
but he selected the harmless elements, expanded the spirits of
night and water with attributes peculiar to English fairies, omitted
the serpents and lunar eclipse, and gathered all the other phenomena into one tremendous tempest. Sometimes, in fact, he is
closer to Ovid than Golding was, when he gives 'rifted Jove's
stout oak' for *sua convulsaque robora terra* where Golding only
has 'trees', and for *exire* Shakespeare's 'let 'em forth' is closer
than Golding's 'call up'. Another popular story from the *Metamorphoses* where Golding seems to have provided a phrase which
stuck in Shakespeare's mind is that of Philemon and Baucis in
Book VIII. Golding described the cottage which sheltered the
Gods as 'thatched all with straw and fennish reede'. In *Much Ado
About Nothing*, II. i. Don Pedro speaking to Hero refers to this
and the prose falls into the rhythm of the 'fourteener':

P. My visor is Philemon's roof; within the house is Jove.
H. Why, then, your visor should be thatched.
                    P. Speak low, if you speak love.

In *As You Like It* Shakespeare follows an Ovidian train of
thought when Touchstone says to Audrey:

I am here with thee and thy goats as the most capricious poet,
honest Ovid, was among the Goths . . . When a man's verses
cannot be understood nor a man's good wit seconded with
the forward child Understanding, it strikes a man more dead
than a great reckoning in a little room. (III. iii. 6.) (A passage
containing a Latin pun on goats, capricious and *caper*, and a
reference to the *Tristia*, especially III. 14.)

Jaques exclaims:

> O Knowledge ill-inhabited, worse than Jove
> in a thatched house!

Golding also contributes briefly to Shakespeare's poetry when, in *Venus and Adonis*, Venus' description of the boar recalls Golding's from the Calydonian boar hunt. Golding wrote:

> His eies did glister blud and fire: right dreadfull was to see
> His brawned necke, right dredfull was his haire which grew
>   as thicke
> With pricking points as one of them could well by other sticke.
> And like a front of armed Pikes set close in battell ray
> The sturdie bristles on his back stoode staring up alway.
>
> (VIII. 376–80)

Shakespeare, on the boar which killed Adonis, has the lines:

> On his bow-backe he hath a battell set,
> Of bristly pikes that ever threat his foes,
> His eyes like glow-wormes shine, when he doth fret . . .
> . . . His brawnie sides with hairie bristles armed
> Are better proofe than thy speares point can enter . . .
>
> (619–26)

Shakespeare's knowledge of and deep debt to Ovid are amply demonstrated throughout the plays and poems, and the particular nature of his debt I will consider later, but Golding's translation, while Shakespeare mocked its poetry, seems often to have furnished him with a quick reference and sometimes with a felicitous phrase. Many of the poets who imitated Ovid may have known the Latin original still better, but the undeniable popularity of Golding's work did a great deal to make Ovid's myths part of the general background of English thought.

If Golding's was, in matter, the most influential translation, Christopher Marlowe's translation of the *Amores* or *Elegies* was the most influential in style. His knowledge of Latin at times left something to be desired, but his great achievement was to reproduce Ovid line for line with all his balance and elegant precision. He reduced Ovid's eleven-footed elegiac couplet to the ten feet of two iambic pentameter lines and added the intricacy of rhyme. I suppose this pattern is, to us, the most apt and

natural manner of rendering Latin verse, especially elegiacs. The
poets of the eighteenth century confirmed its predominance but
it was Marlowe, in these translations and in his *Hero and Leander*
who established the tradition. The polish, lightness of touch, and
humour so excellently rendered in Marlowe's poems, as well as
the obviously Ovidian delight in sensual appreciation of beauty,
became the keynote of Ovid's influence. In the original *Heroides*
Ovid showed he had considerable understanding of deep and
serious love; his heroines take themselves and are taken very
seriously; the bewildered desolation of Briseis and Ariadne, the
sincere longing of Laodamia, the suffering of Hermione whose
life story seems one betrayal after another, are universal, timeless
and real, however elaborate the language of complaint; but this
Ovid only rarely penetrates into English poetry. The light-
hearted, even cynical insincerity of the *Amores* and *Ars Amatoria*,
their art, elegance and enjoyment, probably best transmitted by
Marlowe, became all important. The frank sensuality of the
famous *Amores*, I. 5 wherein Corinna comes to her lover's bed one
afternoon, gives a precedent to innumerable catalogues of feminine
beauty, while the throwaway wit of the final couplet:

> Judge you the rest: being tir'd she bade me kiss;
> Jove send me more such afternoons as this.

mocks the love it relishes, and found innumerable echoes in
poetry and drama thereafter. The prayer to Aurora to delay the
dawn has the lyricism of Romeo and Juliet's parting:

> The air is cold, and sleep is sweetest now,
> And birds send forth shrill notes from every bough:
>
> (I. 13. 7–8)

but the extravagant reproach and elaborate conceit which were to
become so characteristic of Ovidian poetry are both displayed.
Marlowe's rendering is melodious but light yet it was a line from
of his poem, *lente currite, noctis equi* which recurred so powerfully
in Marlowe's tragic work as Faustus cried out for delay in the
hour of damnation. The witty balance which Marlowe is the first
to capture is particularly evident in the cynically candid confession
of *Amores*, II. 4:

> If she be learn'd, then for her skill I crave her;
> If not, because she's simple I would have her. . .

And when one sweetly sings, then straight I long
To quaver on her lips even in her song.
Or if one touch the lute with art and cunning,
Who would not love those hands for their swift running?

and the comparison of Love and War in *Elegy* 1. 9:

What age fits Mars, with Venus doth agree,
'Tis shame for eld in war or love to be.

Both of them watch: each on the hard earth sleeps;
His mistress' doors this, that his captain's keeps.

Doubtful is war and love: the vanquish'd rise,
And who thou never think'st should fall, down lies.

Although the *Elegies* were not published until 1597 (and rapidly suppressed then) it is probable that Marlowe wrote them in his Cambridge days, before 1584, and that they circulated in manuscript, as such university poetry often did.

To move from the important field of translation to the most peculiarly sixteenth-century manifestation of Ovid's influence, the epyllion or minor epic, I shall consider certain important and influential treatments of the genre in some detail as, more clearly than in other forms, the assimilation and transformation of Ovid's work and the development of English poetry in consequence can here be seen. Here, too, Marlowe was all-important. His *Hero and Leander* (Sestiads 1 and 11) has been called 'the most shameless celebration of sensuality which we can find in English Literature. . . . We look out from it upon a world transformed by the hard, brittle splendour of erotic vision.'[9] Ostensibly it was based on Musaeus' poem, a Greek epyllion of the fourth or fifth century A.D. but from the letters exchanged between Hero and Leander in Ovid's *Heroides* Marlowe gained the art, hyperbole and passion of Ovid. Many descriptions echo the *Metamorphoses*, but it is probably the light, tongue-in-cheek eroticism which he acquired from the *Amores* – professing love as an uncontrollable fire, showing it as an art and affectation, switching from romantic declaration to shrewd calculation: the tone which he had caught so well in his translations of the *Amores* – which makes *Hero and Leander* so great and so Ovidian. Marlowe sacrifices consistent characterization for witty or erotic effect: thus Leander who, in

the first book, woos Hero 'like to a bold, sharp sophister' with all
the popular arguments against virginity, proves both an inexpert
suitor and a totally ignorant lover. Hero drops her fan 'thinking
to train Leander therewithal,/He being a novice, knew not what
she meant,/But stayed . . .' and when they first meet at the tower:

> . . . as a brother with his sister toyed,
> Supposing nothing else was to be done,
> Long dallying with Hero, nothing saw
> That might delight him more, yet he suspected
> Some amorous rites or other were neglected.
>
> (II. 52–64)

though, at their second meeting (which, incidentally, strongly
recalls Troilus and Criseyde's courtship in Chaucer's poem) he
shows no such diffidence. Hero, the more developed figure, in her
reactions to Leander often recalls Ovid's Helen with just the
slipping, equivocating tone of her letter in the *Heroides*. First
meeting Leander in the temple where she was priestess, she is
half-won at first sight:

> Chaste Hero to herself thus softly said:
> 'Were I the saint he worships, I would hear him.'
>
> (I. 178–9)

and to his railing against her vowed chastity she is very equivocal:

> Who taught thee rhetoric to deceive a maid?
> Aye me, such words as these should I abhor,
> And yet I like them for the orator.   (I. 338–40)

Most of all, the poet's ironic asides give the poem its ironic
piquancy which most resembles the cynical wit of Ovid's *Ars
Amatoria*, thus:

> These arguments he us'd and many more,
> Wherewith she yielded, that was won before.
> Hero's looks yielded, but her words made war;
> Women are won when they begin to jar.   (I. 329–32)

> Tis wisdom to give much, a gift prevails,
> When deep persuading oratory fails.   (II. 225–6)

Hero welcomes Leander after his swim and Marlowe remarks:

> Where seeing a naked man, she screech'd for fear,
> Such sights as this to tender maids are rare.   (II. 237–8)

and as she strives to defend herself:

> . . . Treason was in her thought,
> And cunningly to yield herself she sought.
> Seeming not won, yet won she was at length,
> In such wars women use but half their strength.
>
> (II. 293–6)

Marlowe demonstrates admirably in this poem most of the important features of Elizabethan minor epics. The myth of the lovers parted by the Hellespont is vastly expanded by his own imagination, and elaborate artificial settings are described in evocative detail. Thus his picture of Venus' temple, its carvings and figures, while it owes something to the tapestry of Arachne in the *Metamorphoses*, adds a very individual wit to the tone of the poem. Considering the lines:

> A lively vine of green sea agate spread;
> Where by one hand, light-headed Bacchus hung,
> And with the other, wine from grapes outwrung.
> Of crystal shining fair the pavement was.
>
> . . .
>
> There might you see the gods in sundry shapes,
> Committing heady riots, incest, rapes . . .
> Jove slyly stealing from his sister's bed
> To dally with Idalian Ganymede,
> Or for his love Europa bellowing loud,
> Or tumbling with the Rainbow in a cloud. (I. 138–50)

I might also suggest that Marlowe, a notorious anti-Christian was parodying a Christian cathedral, that Bacchus, hanging on the vine, wringing out wine, might be seen as a parody of Christ on a crucifix and that the statues of the gods parodied the common display of statues or bas-relief figures illustrating the lives of saints. The almost obligatory catalogue of charms with which the heroine is usually described, Marlowe supplies abundantly, if somewhat unusually, in that Hero is almost always described in terms of elaborate dress whilst Leander supplies the catalogue of physical charms. The usual joy in myth-making, within the original framework, is also very evident. This can take the form of casual hyperbole – Hero's beauty was so great that since her death half the world has been black; Leander was so beautiful that:

Fair Cynthia wish'd his arms might be her sphere;
Grief makes her pale because she moves not there.

(I. 59–60)

but it can also take the form of a long interpolated story within
the poem; thus Marlowe invents the story of Mercury and the
Fates to explain first why the Fates are hostile to love, and then
why they are hostile to scholars. Other myths are casually evoked
for the richness of association; Leander's hair is richer than the
Golden Fleece; Hero wears a picture of Venus and Adonis;
Neptune recalls the story of Narcissus. Marlowe's particular
talent for neatly balanced epigrams is also well displayed in *Hero
and Leander* as, for example, in the lines:

Where both deliberate, the love is slight:
Who ever lov'd, that lov'd not at first sight?

(I. 175–6)

Who builds a palace and rams up the gate,
Shall see it ruinous and desolate.   (I. 239–40)

Maids are not won by brutish force and might,
But speeches full of pleasure and delight. (I. 419–20)

Sweet are the kisses, the embracements sweet,
When like desires and affections meet.   (II. 29–30)

(She) ran into the dark herself to hide.
Rich jewels in the dark are soonest spied.

(II. 239–40)

It has been suggested that Marlowe wrote *Hero and Leander* as
well as translated the *Amores* while at university and that he
circulated the former long before the poem was printed; while
there is no evidence for this assumption, it is, I think, clear that
he translated the *Amores* and assimilated Ovid's style before
writing *Hero and Leander*. If it was indeed written in his Cambridge
days, before 1587, it would in fact precede the otherwise acknowledged beginner of the fashion by some years, as Lodge's *Scillaes
Metamorphosis* was published in 1589. If this were the case it
would appear that the first epyllion, *Hero and Leander*, was probably
the best of the genre and more likely to provoke widespread
imitation than the lachrymose and mediocre *Scillaes Metamorphosis*.

Thomas Lodge's poem depends on the basic myth only very

loosely; it is framed within the poet's own complaint, thus moving the classical glories of nymphs, gods and goddesses to the banks of the Isis and contemporary England. The longest part of the poem is devoted to Glaucus' complaint and this, in imitation of the complaints of the heroines, together with the catalogue of beauty, the subsidiary myth-making and strong visual element, gives us a typical sixteenth-century epyllion whose Ovidian ancestry is clearly interwoven with Arcadian pastoral and the lushness of Lyly. Ovid, especially in the *Metamorphoses*, is a very pictorial writer; the school of thought to whom 'poetry was a speaking picture and painting, silent poetry', found Ovid a prime example and he became the painter's bible. This aspect of his poetry Lodge captures when his poem gives us a succession of tableaux; his pictures are very static and Glaucus gives his grief expression simply by describing a setting where, in the 'pathetic fallacy', Nature sympathises with him:

> The flouds doo faile their course to see our crosse,
> The fields forsake their greene to hearc our griefe,
> The rockes will weepe whole springs to marke our losse,
> The hills relent to store our scant reliefe,
>   The aire repines, the pencive birds are heavie,
>   The trees to see us paind no more are leavie.   (Stanza 19)[10]

He also uses allegorical figures in a Spenserian rather than Ovidian way, but the exact proportion of influence and relation between mediaeval allegory and the personification of qualities such as Envy and Fame as demi-divinities in Ovid's work is very difficult to determine.

Another crucial feature of this genre which derived from the *Heroides*, certain stories in the *Metamorphoses*, and Ovid's preoccupation throughout his work with feminine psychology in general, is the character of the female wooer, appearing first in the repentant Scilla. Shakespeare's *Venus and Adonis* (1593), Heywood's *Oenone and Paris* (1594), Drayton's *Endimion and Phoebe* (1595), *Faunus and Melliflora* by John Weever (1600) and Beaumont's *Salmacis and Hermaphroditus* (1602) all depend on this for their narrative and include some of the finest examples of the genre. *Venus and Adonis*, however, presents us with a strange anomaly. Shakespeare was considered, even by his contemporaries, to be a particularly Ovidian poet; his debt to Ovid via Golding alone has already been seen to be considerable and a subsequent consideration of Ovidian elements in his finest and most original plays will bear this out. Francis Meres, writing in 1598 in *Palladis Tamia*, specifically associates Ovid with Shakespeare's *poems*: 'the sweet, witty soul of Ovid lives in mellifluous and honey-tongued Shakespeare, witness his *Venus and Adonis*, his *Lucrece*, his sugared sonnets.'[11] Yet *Venus and Adonis*, although it undoubtedly contains finely polished phrasing and highly wrought description, is somehow curiously un-Ovidian and very ambivalent. To Ovid (except perhaps in the *Remedia Amoris*) love-play is always graceful and attractive (or should be; the *Ars Amatoria* is almost as much about etiquette as it is about love) – at least to the poet. *Venus and Adonis* is apparently as sensuous a poem as *Hero and Leander* (on the principle of 'procrastinated rape' one might say it was more so), but there is something consciously grotesque, even repulsive about it. Ovid can describe almost any situation, however immoral, with a certain decorum, charm and elegance, the virtues which are so commended throughout the *Ars Amatoria*, and no one can doubt Shakespeare's ability to create eloquent and charming lovers; but in this poem all the standard techniques seem to be wilfully devoid of grace until the story has moved from passion to pathos. There is no indication that the poem was ever, in its time, taken as an anti-epyllion, *militating against* the values of the genre, but in comparison with other far less musical and poetically able works, this seems to be its effect. The beauty of Adonis is constantly alluded to but, except in generalities of brightness, red and white, is not realized. Venus gives a brief catalogue of her charms, but the only character whose beauty is described and praised at length, point by point, is Adonis' horse (Stanzas 49 and 50). Occasionally, when Venus is at her most timid, Shakespeare gives us an image of real beauty as when Venus takes Adonis' hand:

> Full gently now she takes him by the hand,
> A lillie prison'd in a gaile of snow,
> Or Ivorie in an allabaster band,
> So white a friend ingirts so white a foe:
>   This beautious combat wilfull and unwilling,
>   Showed like two silver doves that sit a-billing.
>
>   (361–6)[12]

The verse is full enough of Ovidian conceit, word-play and visual precision but rarely do such moments occur and the six-line stanza produces both static pictures and diffuse diction. Shakespeare was perhaps too realistic a poet, for the picture of the Goddess wooing the unwilling boy, which might have been a charming idyll, is spoilt by the blockish sullenness of Adonis and, much more, by the stifling, overblown lecherousness of Venus. Shakespeare makes her so overpowering in sheer weight and bulk; she is continually damp and moist, and almost the first thing she says to Adonis is that she will *smother* him with kisses. For all her saccharine effusions of highly wrought compliment, the lines of actual narration are anything but decorative. Her first action is to bundle him up like a load of washing:

> Being so enrag'd, desire doth lend her force
> Couragiously to plucke him from his horse , , ,
> Over one arme the lustie coursers raine,
> Under her other was the tender boy. (29–32)

> . . . Backward she pusht him, as she would be thrust
> And governed him in strength though not in lust. (41–2)

> Panting he lies, and breatheth on her face . . . (62)

> By this the love-sicke Queene began to sweate. (175)

The sort of love she is so eagerly urging is perfectly illustrated by the horses, an incident inserted where some corresponding myth might have been expected. Adonis, instead of matching eloquent lust with eloquent virtue, resists Venus dumbly, with childish sullen irritation, until late in the poem when he suddenly urges his youth, inexperience, and mistrust of love in words which would have been effective in the beginning but now appear only excuses to get away from her. Her love is seen constantly as gluttonous feeding, the gorging of a bird of prey. Kissing him she is described:

> With blindfold furie she begins to forrage,
> Her face doth reeke, and smoke, her blood doth boile,
> And careless lust stirs up a desperat courage. (554–6)

> Hot, faint, and wearie, with her hard imbracing. (559)

> . . . He now obayes, and now no more resisteth,
> While she takes all she can, not all she listeth. (563–4)

and when Venus recoils with fear at the thought of Adonis hunting the boar, the scene is pure farce, which if it has a parallel in Ovid at all, then it is in the tale of Priapus in the *Fasti*, not in his more romantic works:

> She sinketh downe, still hanging on his knecke,
> He on her belly falls, she on her backe.
> Now is she in the verie lists of love,
> Her champion mounted for the hot encounter,
> All is imaginarie she doth prove,
> He will not manage her, although he mount her.
>
> (593–8)

Only in the conclusion, where Adonis is changed into a flower, does the language regain Ovidian delicacy of touch, but, compared with the truly Ovidian polish of *Hero and Leander*, this poem seems almost a parody of the style.

Heywood's *Oenone and Paris* (1594) has been found to be very derivative from both Shakespeare and Marlowe, but Oenone is a much more sympathetic wooer than Venus and though her invitation to Paris is partly comic in its extreme ardour, it is closer to the Ovid who wrote *militat omnis amans* (*Amores*, I. 9) and *anule formosae digitum vincture puellae* (*Amores*, II. 15) than to the farcical comedy of *Venus and Adonis*. Based quite closely on *Heroides*, V and drawing also on XVI, the complaint and sophistical excuses are both strongly Ovidian and popular in subsequent epyllia. *Cephalus and Procris* by Thomas Edwards is an example of the genre's weaknesses; one of the least happy, the language, diffuse and obscure to the point of unintelligibility, makes the transition from Aurora's wooing to comment on contemporary poetry positively cryptic. Compared with the pathos of Ovid's narrative it shows all the dangers of a poor craftsman trying to 'gild the lily'. Drayton's *Endimion and Phoebe*, though probably less popular than his *Heroicall Epistles*, points one direction in which Ovidian verse developed, from the gay amorality of the original and such followers as Marlowe, to a different kind of moralizing, the Neo-platonic, almost mystical. Drayton's powers of description are of almost unparalleled richness and luxuriance and though the poem lapses into picture-making for its own sake it has a Spenserian dignity which transforms the tone. *Endimion and Phoebe* is a hymn to Chastity, culminating in the gorgeous tableau of Endimion on the ivory chariot, drawn by unicorns with ropes of pearl and Phoebe in a 'Chrystall Coach' drawn by 'milk-white Hinds' and wearing all the lights of heaven. Its celebration avoids the possibilities of lingering temptation and totally barren rejection by a glorification of heavenly love seen somehow as part of divine harmony expressed in numerology. The numerological passages may be little to our taste, but Drayton's expression is graceful without being obscure and provides the necessary apotheosis without undue confusion to the mythology.

The Ovidian epyllion, following this path, reaches its strangest expression where, overtly most concerned with Ovid, it is in fact least his issue, in Chapman's strange poem *Ovids Banquet of Sence*. In summary it might appear to follow Ovid at his most licentious, as the 'Argument' describes it.[18]

> Ovid, newly enamoured of Julia, (daughter to Octavius
> Augustus Caesar, after by him called Corynna,) secretly
> convaid himselfe into a Garden of the Emperors Court: in an
> Arbor whereof, Corynna, was bathing; playing upon her Lute
> and singing.

Ovid expatiates on the exquisite satisfaction of his senses, first of hearing, then of scent, then of sight. He betrays himself and woos Corynna for a kiss to satisfy taste and finally caresses her, satisfying his touch, but they are interrupted. In other hands, or indeed in Ovid's own, the poem might have far surpassed *Hero and Leander* for sheer sensuality; clues for the incidents can be found in the *Amores*, yet for all its tremendous testimony to physical beauty, the physical reality of the situation seems to dissolve totally into words and abstruse metaphysical thought. As an example, when Ovid first ventures to look at Corynna, one would expect the usual catalogue of feminine beauty; this, in a sense Chapman gives, in some phrases of striking beauty, but overall so refined and magnified to cosmic proportions that the physical woman seems to fade into a vision of Paradise:

> Shee lay, and seemd a flood of Diamant
> Bounded in flesh; as still as Vespers hayre,
> When not an Aspen leafe is styrrd with ayre.

Shee lay at length, like an immortall soule
At endlesse rest in blest Elisium:

Sweet fields of life which Deaths foote dare not presse,
Flowred with th'unbroken waves of my Loves brests.

Her body doth present those fields of peace
Where soules are feasted with the soule of ease.

To prove which Parradise that nurseth these,
See, see the golden Rivers that renowne it:
Rich Gehon, Tigris, Phison, Euphrates,
Two from her bright Pelopian shoulders crowne it,
And two out of her snowye Hills doe glide,
That with a Deluge of delights doe drowne it. (Stanzas 56-9)

The rivers of Paradise are in fact Corynna's arms and legs but it
takes a curious metaphysical imagination to draw the comparison.
To compare this with Ovid's actual description of Corinna naked
before him, I quote from *Amores*, I. 5:

> quos umeros, quales vidi tetigique lacertos!
>   forma papillarum quam fuit apta premi!
> quam castigato planus sub pectore venter!
>   quantum et quale latus! quam iuvenale femur!
> singula quid referam? nil non laudabile vidi
>   et nudam pressi corpus ad usque meum. (19-24)

(What shoulders, what arms did I see and touch!
How perfectly the form of her breasts was made to be caressed!
How smooth was her body beneath the firm bosom!
What a long and beautiful side! What a youthful thigh!
Why should I recount such detail? I saw nothing undeserving of
    praise
And I clasped her naked body to my own.)

To Ovid beauty is certainly not too rich for use. When Chapman's
Ovid has persuaded Corynna first to allow him to kiss and then to
caress her, he cries out not:

> proveniant medii sic mihi saepe dies.

(Jove send me more such afternoons as this.)

but:

> Alas why lent not heaven the soule a tongue?
> Nor language, nor peculier dialect,
> To make her high conceits as highly sung,
> But that a fleshlie engine must unfold
> A spirituall notion . . . (Stanza 111)

He vows to write the *Art of Love* in honour of his glorified senses and to write for Corynna poetry:

> . . . Where Angels shall appeare,
> The praise of vertue, love, and beauty singing.
> (Stanza 115)

Not, one would have thought, a common description of Ovid's poetry. Chapman's poem is a remarkable achievement, often of great beauty, and, with his conclusion of *Hero and Leander*, it shows the later development of English poetry away from pure honeyed description and towards the more intellectual mode of the metaphysicals. However far its high Platonic tone may seem from the love poetry of Ovid, seeds of the development might be found in the Pythagorean passage of the *Metamorphoses* rather than in the former moralizing Christian tradition.

Running the opposite way, Ovid's influence produced a more salacious and 'debunking' strain of poetry; perhaps unconsciously present in *Venus and Adonis*, it found clearer expression from the pen of that ever ambivalent poet, Marston; half satire, half exaltation of lust in his poem *The Metamorphosis of Pigmalions Image* (1598). Here is the physical catalogue *par excellence*, and, significantly, the woman only exists physically as the perfect body. Carved in ivory, gloated over point by point, she is made human only to satisfy her creator's desire and pleasure. She does not even have a name. Ovid's name is invoked and truly one must admit that Marston is near enough to the spirit of the *Ars Amatoria* if not of the *Metamorphoses* in his cynical asides such as:

> And therefore Ladies, thinke that they nere love you,
> Who doe not unto more then kissing move you.
> (Stanza 20)[14]

The actual metamorphosis is simply equated with the surrender of any living woman, thus:

Each part like Waxe before the sunne did melt,
And now, oh now, he finds how he is graced
By his owne worke. Tut, women will relent
When as they finde such moving blandishment.

(Stanza 29)

He hovers too long on the brink of titillation entirely to escape censure; without being as explicit as Ovid in the *Ars Amatoria* he dwells on details too long and with too much relish to justify his satirical claims. He protests too much and omission is made more obscene than Ovid's most simple statement:

And now me thinks some wanton itching eare
With lustfull thoughts, and ill attention,
Lists to my Muse, expecting for to heare
The amorous discription of that action
Which Venus seekes, and ever doth require.

Let him conceit but what himselfe would doe
When . . . arms, eyes, hands, tong, lips and wanton
thigh,
Were willing agents in Loves luxurie.

Could he abstaine midst such a wanton sporting
From doing that, which is not fit reporting?

(Stanzas 33–5, 37)

This line of development results in Ovid's sensuality becoming stripped of its elegance and grace; it passes through the mocking parodies such as Harrington's *The Metamorphosis of Ajax* (1599) and the anonymous *Metamorphosis of Tobacco* to culminate in the parodies and excesses of Rochester and the Restoration poets.

What one might call the mainstream of Ovidian epyllion, avoiding mystic Platonism on the one hand and obscene travesty on the other, following Marlowe, produced one of its finest examples just after the period covered by this essay, in 1602, when Francis Beaumont published *Salmacis and Hermaphroditus*, based on Ovid's story in *Metamorphoses*, IV. 285–388. Beaumont's swiftly moving narrative, though much longer than the original because of a great proliferation of original myth-making, keeps very close to Ovid in both word and spirit. The delight in mythical hyperbole common in *Hero and Leander* is obvious in the description of Hermaphroditus. Thus, roses were white till they saw his beauty and blushed, Cupid had eyes till Venus stole them from him. Beaumont displays Ovid's skill and generosity in story-telling as he interpolates extended myths about the gods (as Marlowe had added the story of Hermes and the Fates). He tells how Jupiter fell in love with Salmacis, travelled to the tower of Astraea and provoked Venus' jealousy of the nymph; another story tells of Bacchus' passion for her and his revenge on Phoebus for thwarting him. His tales are elaborate, lively and very much in the spirit of the *Metamorphoses*, while his description of Salmacis closely follows Ovid's description of Corinna quoted above (*Amores*, I. 5. 19–24); and when Salmacis and Hermaphroditus meet, the poem follows Ovid very closely indeed, which, with the well-balanced couplets, gives the same effect as Marlowe's in conveying Ovid's tone and intention. A favourite motif such as the Narcissus theme, which finds its way into almost all the epyllia, is here expanded into the conceit that Salmacis must shut her eyes to woo Hermaphroditus or he will fall in love with his image in her eyes. Beaumont even keeps Ovid's similes, as when Hermaphroditus in the water is compared to a 'white lilly in a cristall glasse' (864) (in Ovid 'vel candida lilia vitro' [*Met.*, IV. 355]) and the nymph embracing him is likened to 'The flattering Ivy . . . Inclaspe the huge trunke of an aged tree' (869–70), and by Ovid *utve solent hederae longos intexere truncos* (*Met.*, IV. 365). The poetry has all the vigour, invention and enjoyment which so distinguished Ovid's own.

The particular flowering of Ovid's influence through the epyllion in the sixteenth century is significant; he was the young man's poet in whom the Elizabethans found a kindred spirit, assisting them to express the ebullient vivacity and richness of their new-found freedom and confidence in language. The elements with which Ovid's spirit combined caused it to change and develop in certain surprising directions, but it left an indelible print on English poetry of polish, balance, wit and luxuriance without which its nature would have been incalculably different.

Ovid's influence on the work of the major poets has been shown to be widespread in translation and imitation. Spenser offers an interesting example: his serious and religious intentions are greatly at variance with the spirit of Ovid's poetry and his Neo-platonism may have done much to suggest the mystical strain which, in later writers, so transformed Ovidian subjects. Yet he used Ovid as a source of allegorical description, as in the passages on the Wood of Error (*Met.*, x. 86f. *Faerie] Queene*, 1, i. 7–9), the Cave of Sleep (*Faerie Queene*, 1. i. 39–41) from the Cave of Envy (*Met.*, 11. 760–82) and the Cave of Sleep (*Met.*, xi. 592–615) and Chaos in the Garden of Adonis (cf. *Met.*, xv. 252ff. and *Faerie Queene*, 111. iv). The seduction of Hellenore by Paridell (*Faerie Queene*, 111. ix–x) is based on the letters between Paris and Helen in the *Heroides*. Hellenore's exploits with the satyrs (*Faerie Queene*, 111. x. 43–60) may also reflect rather more enjoyment of the scurrilous side of Ovid than Spenser would be expected to display. One of the most telling examples, however, is in Book 111. xi, when Britomart sees the tapestry of Busirane. It is a prologue to the Masque of Cupid and the horrors of Amoret's torture, and the scene is associated with 'fowle Idolatree', but the whole description, a catalogue of the loves of the Gods, straight from the *Metamorphoses*, is far from unattractive – the lines on Jove and Leda have both great beauty and a wry, sophisticated humour:

> Then was he turn'd into a snowy Swan,
> To win faire *Leda* to his louely trade:
> O wondrous skill, and sweet wit of the man,
> That her in daffadillies sleeping made,
> From scorching heat her daintie limbes to shade:
> Whiles the proud Bird ruffing his fethers wyde,
> And brushing his faire brest, did her inuade:
> She slept, yet twixt her eyelids closely spyde,
> How towards her he rusht, and smiled at his pryde.
>
> (*Faerie Queene*, 111. xi. 32)[15]

This is much nearer Ovid's tone, at least in the *Metamorphoses*, than anything in the *Amoretti* where the love poems strike an uneasy compromise between the ideality of Platonic love and the practicalities of marriage.

Much has been written on William Shakespeare's debt to Ovid. I have already referred to T. W. Baldwin's extensive study. S. G. Owen's essay on *Ovid and Romance*[16] and several of Douglas Bush's works[17] have also contributed to the field, so I will not dwell upon it extensively. However, it seems worth noting that Shakespeare made the most direct and frequent use of Ovid in his particularly original, virtually sourceless, plays: *Love's Labour's Lost*, *A Midsummer Night's Dream* and *The Tempest*. All are plays greatly concerned with art itself, especially the art of words, and the relationship of imagination and reality; here, where, unfettered by the design of another's invention, Shakespeare wrote most clearly of his own preoccupations, he seems to bear out at least part of Meres' remark that he and Ovid were kindred souls, for his most original works are, verbally, his most Ovidian. I have already referred to Holofernes' commendation of Ovid. Along with all the technicalities of grammatical and stylistic analysis which make *Love's Labour's Lost* his most scholastic comedy, the constant word-play and, above all, the sophistry of Berowne, who undertakes to justify any course he happens to take, are very reminiscent of Ovid's excuses for love and infidelity. The lovers are more moved by their own conceits than by reality, as they are shown when, wooing the wearers of their favours, they court the wrong women. 'Style not sincerity' is all and love is the game of skill taught in the *Ars Amatoria*. I have already examined (pp. 217-19), the many Ovidian references in *A Midsummer Night's Dream*; apart from those which show a resemblance to Golding's translation, the situation of the lovers constantly recalls Ovid's work in general. Hermia and Lysander swear by '[Cupid's] best arrow with the golden head' (i. i. 170) and 'that fire which burned the Carthage queen/When the false Trojan under sail was seen' (i. i. 173-4); Helena's position complaining of and wooing her faithless Demetrius is in the tradition of the *Heroides* and her recriminations often echo those of Ovid's heroines. Oberon's 'mermaid on a dolphin's back/Uttering such dulcet and harmonious breath/That the rude sea grew civil at her song' (ii. i. 150-2) recalls Arion in the *Fasti* and indeed his fantasy of Titania doting on a beast 'lion, bear or wolf or bull' may owe something to Ovid's stories in the *Metamorphoses* and his references in the *Amores* and *Ars Amatoria* to women's desire for beasts, and especially to Pasiphae. The magical mixture of the midsummer night when any wonder may happen, men and demi-gods mingle, men turn into the shape of beasts, and back again, love turn to hate and hate to love, and all in polished, highly wrought poetry, is famous as one of Shakespeare's most individual creations, but could it have existed at all without the *Metamorphoses*? *The Tempest* contains one of Shakespeare's more extensive borrowings from Ovid, Prospero's renunciation, which has already been quoted. It also creates a world of strange visions and unnatural happenings, while the masque of the three Goddesses, Iris, Juno and Ceres, plays on the stories of the Olympians. All these plays have pageants of some sort, based on mythological characters from Ovid's work, as well as lovers courting with the aid of the romantic art of his poems; furthermore the latter two spring from the world of magic and miracle he so infused with life.

The most classical of the Elizabethan playwrights, Ben Jonson, provides a surprising exception to the rule of all-pervading Ovidian influence. He had little time for Ovid, making Horace his hero and even adopting his persona. In his plays of contemporary low life such as *The Alchymist* Jonson comments on the popularity of Ovid, remarking, for example, that young courtiers and gentlemen courted their mistresses 'out of Ovid', using his works as a textbook of love. He did, however, produce one work of interest for the study of Ovid's influence, though a little after the period covered here. *The Poetaster*, acted in 1601, is a satire set in Augustan Rome in which all the major poets of the period appear. Its prologue is spoken by Envy, very much after Ovid's description of her, and one of the plots is the story of Ovid's love for Julia, Augustus' discovery of them and several other characters in a blasphemous orgy, and Ovid's banishment. The opening scenes, showing Ovid arguing with his father, who preferred him to study law and neglect his natural gift of poetry, follow Ovid's own references to the subject very closely and contain several close translations from the *Amores* and *Tristia*, but the character never seems to have much life and only in the lovers' parting does it reach any poetic, though not very Ovidian, height.

Ovid's influence on English literature, from the pure translation to the greatest literary artist's best work, is demonstrably powerful and widespread. It not only created a new genre but also contributed much to the development of others. On the popular, non-literary level it is less demonstrable but at times no less pervasive. Pictorial art seems, in England, to be a remarkable exception. In Italy throughout the fifteenth century, in the first great flowering of the Renaissance, the artists' subjects became increasingly mythological. Illustrations in the major editions of the *Metamorphoses* were a considerable influence. The tapestry industry in France and the Low Countries began to produce principally mythological works. Ovid penetrated even to the throne of Christendom itself when, in 1445, Filarete's bronze doors for St Peter's displayed many stories from the *Metamorphoses*. The works of Raphael and Sebastiano del Piombo in the Villa Farnesina, Piero di Cosimo and later Titian, Bernini and Rubens furnish many examples of masterpieces of the highest quality inspired by Ovid's works. An indication of how far he had become the artists' 'bible' is the inclusion in Dutch and German technical works of a complete translation of the *Metamorphoses*. In England the pictorial arts were not well financed during the sixteenth century and no notable native school developed; there was on the continent a profusion of genres, but in England one genre only, that of the portrait. The innumerable portraits of major and minor aristocracy and citizenry were dynastic investments; new men and women, proud of their real dignity and material prosperity, were portrayed in an unparalleled luxuriance of dress – but not in mythological representation. The royal portraits were an exception in that they were concerned with the propagation of a myth, an image, but it was the Tudor myth not the Ovidian. Elizabeth may, to her poets, have appeared as Oriana, Gloriana, Diana, Minerva or any other virgin goddess they could find or invent but to her artists she was Elizabeth, sovereign of England, first and last. The exceptions to this rule are slight, few, and of doubtful attribution (possibly by the Dutch painter, Hans Eworth) but the only notable one is a picture of Elizabeth confounding the contending goddesses, Juno, Pallas and Venus, by bearing off the golden apple herself. The only picture of the period where Ovid's influence is manifest, significantly demonstrates only the Tudor myth's supremacy over the Ovidian.

Popular art, however, gives an interesting indication of how far Ovid's stories penetrated into the common currency of thought. The very popular art form of the Emblem book, a series of pictures with a verse and sometimes a quotation attached illustrative of some moral maxim, show the extent of his popularity. To take the example of a very influential English Emblem book by Geoffrey Whitney, published at Leyden in 1586 and called *A Choice of Emblemes*, in the first volume alone there are thirteen full plates illustrating morals purely from Ovidian mythology including Niobe, Actaeon, Icarus, Tantalus, Medea, the judgment of Paris, and Envy (following Ovid's description).

There is also a very Ovidian illustration of the power of Love, and a very high proportion of the Latin quotations and references attached to the Emblems are taken from his works.

Whatever one's assessment of Ovid as a poet or as a moral influence, as an artist he gave a language to the imagination, a set of images to the thought of Western civilization. In England his poetry, through the story-tellers, teachers and translators, formed fashion and taste in the sixteenth century and acted as a source and a catalyst to the major writers of the age. In him they found a fertility of invention with a refinement of expression which profoundly influenced the subsequent development of English literature. To Ovid, Britain would probably have been as barren and uncomprehending as Pontus, but it was here, 1,500 years after his expulsion in disgrace to the edge of barbarism, that his spirit became again the centre of a lively, talented society just discovering its full potentialities.

Notes

1 L. P. Wilkinson, *Ovid Recalled* (Cambridge, 1955), chs XI–XII.
2 *Metamorphoses* (Venice, 1492), ed. with commentary by Raphael Regius.
3 Madeleine Doran, 'Some Renaissance "Ovids" ', *Literature and Society*, ed. Bernice Slote (Lincoln, Nebraska, 1964), 44–62.
4 *Love's Labour's Lost*, ed. G. B. Harrison (London, 1953), IV, ii. All references to Shakespeare's plays are to the New Penguin (where available) and Penguin editions.
5 *Harrison's Description of England in Shakspere's Youth*, New Shakespeare Society Series 6, no. 1, part 1, ed. Frederick J. Furnivall (London, 1877), 83.
6 John Brinsley, *Ludus Literarius* (London, 1627), 195.
7 *Shakespeare's Ovid. Being Arthur Golding's Translation of the Metamorphoses*, ed. W. H. D. Rouse (London, 1961).
8 Quoted in *Ovid's Metamorphoses. The Arthur Golding Translation*, 1567, ed. John Frederick Nims (New York, 1965), p. xiii.
9 C. S. Lewis, 'Hero and Leander', *Elizabethan Poetry: Modern Essays in Criticism*, ed. Paul J. Alpers (London, 1967), 236–7. References to Marlowe's poems are to the edition of Millar Maclure (London, 1968).
10 References to *Scillaes Metamorphosis* are to the edition of Elizabeth Story Donno, in *Elizabethan Minor Epics* (London, 1963).
11 Francis Meres, *Palladis Tamia* (London, 1598), 282.
12 *Venus and Adonis, Complete Works of Shakespeare*, ed. Herbert Farjeon (London, 1953). References to this poem are taken from this edition.
13 George Chapman, *Ovid's Banquet of Sence* (London, 1595). All my quotations are taken from the edition of Elizabeth Story Donno in *Elizabethan Minor Epics* (London, 1963).

14 I refer to the edition of E. S. Donno, *op. cit.* (n. 13).

15 References to the works of Edmund Spenser are to the ed. of Edwin Greenlaw, C. G. Osgood and F. M. Padelford, 11 vols (Baltimore, 1932–45).

16 S. G. Owen, 'Ovid and Romance', *English Literature and the Classics*, ed. G. S. Gordon (Oxford, 1912), 167–95.

17 E.g. Douglas Bush, *Mythology and the Renaissance Tradition in English Poetry* (New York, 1932).

Subject Index

adultery, 2, 40–1, 78–9, 112, 173
Aeneid, 52–5, 59–65, 118, 120–2, 125, 138, 205
Aetia, 74, 116
Alchymist, The, 239
Alexandreis, 194
Alexandrian poetry, 137
allegory, 145, 198, 203, 228
 theological, 210–11
alliteration, 37–8, 51, 58, 137, 144
allusion, 29, 33–6, 39–40, 64, 120
Amores, 1–42, 65–6, 89, 94–7, 112, 192, 196–7, 200, 204–5, 212, 214, 222–4, 227, 231–3, 238–9
 Propertius as model for, 4, 6–7, 21, 23–4, 26, 34–6, 39–40
Amoretti, 237
Amorosa Fiammetta, L', 204
anachronism, 64
anaphora, 15
anti-climax, 51, 58
antidotes, 110, 112
antithesis, 14–15, 19, 37–8, 119, 144
archaisms, 120–2
Ars Amatoria, 3–4, 68, 70, 77, 84–102, 110, 113, 155, 171–4, 192–3, 196–7, 199–200, 223, 225, 229, 234–5, 238
Ars Lectoria, 193
Ars Versificatoria, 194
Astronomica, 91
As You Like It, 66, 221
Augustan régime, 40–2, 55, 86–7, 105
Augustans, 41, 78, 101, 126
autobiography, 3, 158, 162–9, 175, 180–1

balanced structure, 37
Bellum Civile, 118
Book of the Duchess, The, 205, 211

Cambridge Songs, 195
Canterbury Tales, 205, 211
career, Ovid's, 3, 41, 43, 87–8
caricature, 7, 22, 38, 39, 41
Carmina Burana, 195
Carolingian period, 192, 207
Carthaginians, 60–1
Cephalus and Procris, 231
character, Ovid's, 156
Choice of Emblemes, A, 240
Christianity, 191–2, 198, 202, 210–11, 226
Claris Mulieribus, De, 204
comedy, 7, 21, 28, 66, 93, 120, 196
Confessio Amantis, 206, 211
Contra Symmachum, 191
couplet, 9–10, 14–16
 balanced, 16
 final, 31
 heroic, 205
 see also elegiac
creation, 108–9, 210
critics, 56–60, 116–17, 128–9, 138, 143, 145, 156, 186–7, 194
Culice, De, 201
Cynegetica, 91
Cypassis poems, 3, 6, 18

dactyls, 116, 118, 122, 126–7, 129, 134
death, 8, 22
descriptive technique, 140–5, 182
didactic poetry, 89–99, 110, 176
diptych poems, 4, 6, 30
Divina Commedia, 203

Eclogues, 138
 Messianic, 210
economy of means, 105, 127
education, 212

243

elegiac comedies, 196
  couplet, 15, 65, 104, 116, 130, 222
Elegies, 214, 222, 224
elegy, 29, 68
  autobiographical, 3, 158, 162–9,
    175, 180–1
  descriptive, 164, 181–2
  epic and, 25–7, 65
  love, 1, 6, 8, 65–6, 85, 94
  Roman, 93–4
ellipse, 130
Emblem book, 240
enallage, double, 131
Endimion and Phoebe, 228, 231–2
enjambment, 15, 116, 124–5, 134,
    137–8, 140, 144, 152
epic, 5, 25, 27, 61–2, 64, 88, 116–17,
    120–2, 125
  elegy and, 25–7, 65
  minor, *see* epyllion
epigram, Hellenistic, 7, 85
  introductory, 7
Epillia, 215
Epistles (Horace), 28
Epistulae ex Ponto, 49–68, 158, 159,
    160–1, 186, 192–3, 206
epyllion, 224, 226, 232, 235–6
exile, 68, 81, 84, 154–9, 164, 167, 170,
    174–6, 179–80, 186–7, 192, 239;
    see also Tomis

Faerie Queene, 237
Fasti, 67–8, 105, 168, 191, 193, 198,
    200, 205–6, 211–12, 214, 231,
    238
Faunus and Melliflora, 228
flattery, 169, 172, 183
Flores Poetarum, 212
Florilegia, 201, 207
Flos Amorum, 194

Gauls, Rome's defeat by, 100
Genealogia Deorum, De, 204
Georgics, 85, 90–2, 99, 100, 104, 125
Glastonbury, 192
Goliardic poets, 195
graffiti, 191
grammar, 128–31

Halieutica, 201
Hero and Leander, 223–7, 229, 231–2,
    234–5
Heroycall Epistles, 213–15; *England's
    Heroicall Epistles*, 215, 231
Heroides, 27, 49–81, 159, 186, 193–4,
    197, 204–6, 211–12, 214–15,
    223–5, 228, 231, 237–8
heroine as elegiac figure, 49–68
hexameter, 14–16, 31, 33, 37, 104,
    116–17, 132, 138
  dactylic, 118
House of Fame, The, 205, 211
humanity, Ovid's, 113
humour, 7–10, 15, 17–18, 32, 102,
    104, 113
hyperbaton, 129
hyperbole, 9, 224, 235

Ibis, 201, 213
Iliad, 64–5, 173
illustrations, 239
imagery, 123, 133, 162, 164, 166–9,
    186
imitation, 19, 23, 29, 35, 201–2
immorality, 171–3
impotence, 22–3
incongruity, 7, 9, 13, 18, 28, 38,
    40
irony, 10, 23, 25, 31, 37, 53, 74, 113,
    225

Judaism, 100
juxtaposition, 6, 96, 164, 218

Laboribus Herculis, De, 205
Legend of Good Women, The, 205,
    211
letters, *see* Epistles; Epistulae ex
    Ponto; love letters
Libro de Buen Amor, El, 197, 203
Lombardo et Lumaca, De, 202
love, 72–3, 75, 81, 94–5, 229–31, 241
  epic, 117
  letters, 30–40, 49–81
  as occupation, 89
  poetry, 88–9, 100–1, 173, 198
  see also elegy

lover, comic, 8, 11, 18-19
  elegiac, 7, 20, 22, 29, 33, 41, 66-7, 96
Love's Labour's Lost, 238
Ludus Literarius, 213
lyric poetry, 88

marriage, 85, 97
martial prowess, 40
Medea, 3, 27
Medicamina Faciei Femineae, 68, 93, 202
Medicamine Aurium, De, 202
medicine, 201-2
Merchant of Venice, The, 219-20
Metamorphoses, 67-9, 81, 104-5, 116-45, 191, 193-4, 197-207, 210-13, 215-18, 221, 224, 226, 228, 234-40
Metamorphosis of Ajax, 235
Metamorphosis of Pigmalion's Image, 234
Metamorphosis of Tobacco, 235
Metamorphosoes Volgare, 210
metaphor, 17, 31, 100, 169
metre, 23, 123, 126-7, 129-30, 137, 222; *see also* hexameter; pentameter
Midsummer Night's Dream, A, 217, 238
Minnesängers, 195
Mirabilibus Mundi, De, 202
monologues, 69
monotony, 186-7
Monte Cassino, 193
Moralia super Ovidii Metamorphoses, 200
moralizing, 20, 199, 204, 215, 231, 234
mortality, 177; *see also* death
Much Ado About Nothing, 221
Mythologiae, 191

naïvety, 18-19
natural simplicity, 57, 59
New Comedy, Greek, 93
Nugis Curialium, De, 194
Nuncio Sagaci, De, 197

obscenity, 84-5
Odes, 64
Odyssey, 173
Oenone and Paris, 228, 231
originality, 158-9
Ovids Banquet of Sence, 232-5
Ovidius Christianus, 202
Ovidius Ethicus, 202
Ovidius Maior, 198-200, 203
Ovidius Moralizatus, 199, 202, 210
Ovidius Puellarum, 197

Paelignians, 41
Pamphilus de Amore, 196-7, 203
paradox, 134
parallelism, 14, 31
parenthesis, 137, 144, 151
Paris University, 195, 197
Parlement of Foules, The, 205
parody, 7, 9, 12, 29, 33, 35, 39, 40, 42, 91, 198, 226
pathos, 67, 117, 186
pedantry, 144
pentameter, 14-16, 31, 33, 37, 222
permissiveness, 171, 173
Phaenomena, 90
Philomena, 199
pictorial art, 239-40
plaintiveness, 69-71, 74
Poetaster, The, 239
poeticisms, 120, 122, 128
Pompeii, 191
portraits, 240
prayer motif, 50-1, 58
promiscuity, 21
prostitutes, 73
Pulchris Puellis Clero Traditis, De, 202

Rape of the Sabine Women, 86, 105-7
realism, 19
recusatio, 3
Reductium Morale, 199
Registrum Multorum Auctorum, 197
religion, 40
religious orders, 198, 202
Remedia Amoris, 68, 101-13, 193, 197, 200-1, 205, 214, 229
Renaissance, 191, 197, 203-5, 239

repetition, 50, 132
Rerum Natura, De, 90–1, 110, 200
Rescue of Ariadne, 107
Restoration poets, 235
rhetoric, 53–4, 63, 131–5, 140, 143, 162, 165, 212
  schools of, 191
Roman d'Eneas, 199
Roman de la Rose, 200, 205
Romanticism, 56, 64
Rome, 41, 96–7, 156–7, 163, 171, 181–2

St Gall, 193
St Peter's (Rome), 240
Salmacis and Hermaphroditus, 228, 235
Satires (Horace), 29, 97
Saturnalia, 99
schools, 212
science, 200–1
Scillaes Metamorphosis, 227–8
seduction, 155, 197
Shakespeare's Ovid, 217
Sigillaria, 99
simplicity, natural, 57, 59
social life, Roman, 97–9, 105, 173
sophistication, 55, 57, 65, 67, 105
Speculum Stultorum, 198
Stoics, 89
style, 17–19, 23, 30–3, 37–9, 53, 57–8, 101, 116–19, 123–45, 210–11
Sulmona, 206
swan, dying, 49–50, 53–4
Sygambri, 3–4, 20, 43

syllepsis, 125
syntax, 128–9, 131

Tempest, The, 220–1, 238–9
theatre, Roman, 105
Tomis, exile at, 154, 157, 159, 161, 174–5, 178, 183
  journey to, 161–3
topoi, elegiac, 18, 69
tragedy, 3, 6, 64, 88, 120
translations, 57–9, 62, 199, 213
Tribus Puellis, De, 197
Trionfi d'Amore, 204
Tristia, 84–5, 93, 154–87, 192–3, 205–6, 211–12, 214, 221, 239
Troilus and Criseyde, 205, 225
Trojans, 52, 54, 77–81, 194, 206
Troubadours, 195

Venus and Adonis, 212, 222, 228–31, 234
Versus Ovidii de piscibus et feris, 201
Vetula, De, 202
Victorian prejudice, 57
visual brilliance, 105
vocabulary, 16–17, 37–8, 50, 58, 120–8

wife, Ovid's, 164, 170, 175, 180, 183–4
wit, vii, 3, 8, 13, 22, 24, 33, 36, 40, 42, 58–9, 62, 65, 67, 76, 102, 105, 119, 186–7, 223, 225
word-order, 128–30, 133–5
Works and Days, 89–93, 98, 100

Name Index

Achelous, 135
Acontius, 70–1, 74–7
Actaeon, 210, 218
Addison, Joseph, 56–7, 59, 143
Adonis, 229–31
Aegisthus, 112
Aeneas, 49, 51–2, 54, 58–64
Aimeric, 193
Albrecht, M. von, 116–17, 151
Albrecht von Halberstadt, 194
Alcmaeon, 134
Alcuin, 192
Alcyone, 123, 205, 211, 213
Alexander of Villa Dei, 193
Amphiaraus, 134
Andrew 'the Chaplain', 194
Andromache, 60
Apollo, 124–5, 140
Apollonius, 64, 137, 139
Arachne, 226
Aratus, 90–1, 100, 104
Archpoet of Cologne, 195
Arctophylax, 168
Arethusa, 67
Ariadne, 64, 66, 69, 107, 223
Aristaenetus, 83
Aristotle, 197
Arnold of Villa Nova, 201
Arnolph of Orléans, 193
Augustine, 195
Augustus, Emperor, 40–1, 52, 55, 81,
    84–7, 110, 154–5, 169, 171–3,
    183–4, 186, 232, 239

Bacchus, 183–5
Bacon, Roger, 203
Bagoas, 9
Baldwin, T. W., 212–13, 237
Bandello, 214
Baucis, 221

Baudry, Bishop, 193
Beaumont, Francis, 228, 235–6
Bell, A. J., 150
Bernbeck, E. J., 146
Bersuire, Pierre, 199
Boccaccio, 203–4, 214
Bömer, F., 118–19, 131, 133, 141
Bonsignori, 210
Bosch, Hieronymus, 145
Brinsley, J., 213
Briseis, 64–5, 223
Brown, 214
Bush, Douglas, 237
Byblis, 81, 139, 144

Cadmus, 218
Callimachus, 74, 90, 143, 201
Calypso, 108
Cameron, A., 44
Canace, 82
Cato, 87, 97
Catullus, vii, viii, 7, 42n., 59, 64, 85,
    97
Ceos, 83
Cephalus, 104
Ceres, 8, 24–5, 216
Ceyx, 123, 211, 213
Chapman, G., 232–5
Chaucer, Geoffrey, 55–6, 200, 205,
    211, 225
Chrétien de Troyes, 199
Chrétien of Legouais, 199
Churchyard, Thomas, 213–14
Cicero, 85, 88, 100, 122, 156, 213
Conrad von Wurzburg, 194
Cordier, A., 120–1
Corinna, 1–9, 11–13, 18, 20, 22, 30,
    33, 40–1, 43, 223, 232, 236
Coronis of Larissa, 124
Cotta Maximus, Aurelius, 154

Cupid, 62
Cyane, 143-4
Cydippe, 70-1, 74-8, 80
Cynthia, 7, 9, 20-1, 35, 94, 97, 227

Daedalus, 104, 108
Dante, 203
Daphne, 132, 140-1
Davies, Sir John, 214
Deianira, 64, 66
Delia, 22, 24
Demophoon, 21
Diana, 75-6
Dido (Ovid), 49-68, 81; (Virgil), 52-7, 59-63, 65
Diomedes, 12
Dipsas, 17
Dorrie, H., 83
Drayton, M., 215, 228, 231
Dryden, John, 56-9, 62, 116
Dürer, A., 145

Edwards, Thomas, 231
Elizabeth, Queen, 240
Elyot, Sir Thomas, 212
Empedocles, 90
Ennius, 91, 122
Erasmus, 212
Eriphyle, 134
Euripides, 64, 66-7, 139
Europa, 141, 218
Eworth, Hans, 240

Faustus, 223
Filarete, 240
Fortunatus, Venantius, 191
Fränkel, H., 189
Fulgentius, 191

Gallus, Cornelius, 1, 42n., 66, 94, 159
Giovanni del Virgilio, 203
Glaucus, 228
Glover, T. R., 116
Golding, Arthur, 213, 215-22, 238
Gower, John, 206, 211, 214
Graecinus, 21
Grattius, 91

Green, P., 116
Grosseteste, Robert, 201
Guillaume de Blois, 196
Guillaume de Lorris, 200, 205

Halaesus, 28
Harrington, Sir John, 235
Heinsius, N., 81n.
Helen, 70-1, 77-81, 205, 225
Hellenore, 237
Hercules, 66, 135, 218
Hermaphroditus, 213, 235-6
Hermione, 214, 223
Hero, 70-4, 80, 215, 224-7
Herr, Margaret W., 150
Herter, H., 116
Hesiod, 89-93, 98, 100
Heywood, T., 228, 231
Hildebert of Lavardin, 193
Hippolyta, 218
Holkot, Robert, 200
Holleman, A. W. J., 113n.
Holofernes, 211-12, 238
Homer, 60-1, 64-5, 67, 107-8, 152, 203
Horace, 9, 28, 33-4, 40, 64, 69, 97, 121-2, 126, 169, 198, 203, 212, 239
Howell, Thomas, 213
Hubbard, William, 213
Hugo of Trimberg, 197
Hypermnestra, 64, 82
Hypsipyle, 64

Icarus, 104, 108
Isidore of Seville, 200

Jacques d'Amiens, 199
Jason, 136-7, 219
Jean de Meun, 200, 205
John of Garland, 193, 199
John of Salisbury, 200
Jonson, Ben, 239
Joseph of Exeter, 194
Julia, 155, 232, 239
Juno, 62
Juvenal, 88-9, 135

Kenney, E. J., 42n., 114n., 158–9, 169–70
Kraus, W., 82

Laodamia, 64, 223
Lavinia, 200
Leander, 70–4, 215, 224–7
Lee, A. G., 158–9, 196
Lesbia, 42n., 97
Levy, H. L., 43
Little, D., 146
Livia, Empress, 169–70
Livy, 121–2, 204
Lodge, Thomas, 227
Lucan, 118, 128–9, 135–6, 191, 203, 206
Luck, G., 44
Lucretius, 85, 90–1, 104, 109–10, 121–2, 127–8, 200
Lycoris, 42n.
Lyly, J., 228

Macaulay, Lord, 174
Mackail, J. W., 116
Maecenas, 8, 25
Magnus, Albertus, 200
Manilius, 91
Mantuan, 214
Map, Walter, 194
Marlowe, Christopher, 214, 222–7, 231, 236
Marston, J., 234
Martial, 85, 169–70, 187, 191
Matthew of Vendôme, 193–4, 196
Maurus, Rabanus, 200
Maximianus, 191
Medea, 64, 134, 138, 217, 219–20
Menelaus, 77, 79
Meres, Francis, 229, 238
Merklin, H., 82
Messalla, 8
Mettus, 166
Miller, F. J., 130
Mirandula, O., 212
Modoin, Bishop, 192
Moschus, 141
Munari, F., 44

Musaeus, 224
Myrrha, 138–40

Nape, 30–3, 35–6
Narcissus, 213, 227, 236
Neckam, Alexander, 200
Nemesis, 24
Nicander, 90–1, 104, 110
Nigellus, Ermoldus, 192–3
Nims, J. F., 132
Niobe, 191

Otis, Brooks, 188
Owen, S. G., 173–4, 237

Pacuvius, 120
Palmer, Arthur, 81n.
Paris, 70–1, 77–81
Peend, Thomas, 213
Pelias, 134
Penelope, 60, 64–6, 169–70
Perilla, 174–8
Petrarch, 199, 203–4, 207
Phaedra, 64–5, 67, 82
Phaethon, 141–2, 144
Philemon, 221
Philodemus, 85
Phyllis, 67
Piso, L., 85
Planudes, 195
Plautus, 121, 196
Pliny, 200–1
Ponticus, 25–6
Postgate, J. P., 128
Pound, Ezra, 217
Priapus, 93, 230
Procris, 104
Propertius, vii, viii, 4, 6–9, 20–1, 23–7, 34–6, 39–41, 65, 67, 69, 93–5, 97, 110, 121–2, 128, 159–60
Proserpine, 133
Prudentius, 191
Pyramus, 210, 218

Quince, Peter, 218–19
Quintilian, 3, 117, 121

Rahn, H., 83
Regius, Raphael, 210
Rhesus, 108
Richard de Fournival, 202
Rochester, Earl of, 235
Romulus, 86, 105–7
Rouse, W. H. D., 217
Ruiz, Juan, 197, 203

Sabinus, Georgius, 211
Sallust, 88
Salmacis, 213, 236
Salutati, Coluccio, 205
Scot, Michael, 200
Segal, C. P., 146
Seneca, 66, 191, 206
Shakespeare, William, 56, 66, 207, 212, 217–22, 228–31, 237–9
Smith, Adam, 143
Sophocles, 64
Spenser, Edmund, 236–7
Statius, 191, 203
Stoessl, F., 47
Stroh, W., 146
Sychaeus, 61

Tacitus, 87
Taylor, L. R., 43
Terence, 95, 196
Themis, 134
Theodolph of Orléans, 192–3
Theophrastus, 95
Theseus, 69, 218
Thibault, J. C., 113n.

Thomas, Thomas, 211
Tibullus, viii, 1, 3, 6–7, 9, 22–5, 41, 93–4, 112, 122, 159
Titania, 217–18, 238
Torquatus, 28
Tränkle, H., 44, 152
Traube, L., 191
Trivet, Nicholas, 205–6
Turberville, 213–15
Turner, Paul, 92

Ulysses, 66, 107–8
Underdown, T., 213

Varro, 122, 200
Venus, 62, 77–8, 229–31
Viarre, Mlle, 141
Vincent of Beauvais, 201
Virgil, 28, 52–7, 59–63, 65, 67, 85, 90–2, 99, 100, 104, 116–22, 125–8, 131, 138–40, 169, 191–2, 197–9, 201, 203–6, 210, 213
Vital de Blois, 196

Walter of Châtillon, 194–5
Weever, John, 228
Whitney, Geoffrey, 240
Wilkinson, L. P., 113n., 116, 140, 156, 160, 162, 164, 174, 186–7
Williams, Gordon, 97
Wireker, Nigel, 198
Wolsey, Thomas, 212
Worstbrock, F., 119, 145n.